Woodbourne Lib
Washington-Centerville P
Centerville, Oh

DISCARD

D1209795

Sparky and Me

ALSO BY DAN EWALD

Bless You Boys (with Sparky Anderson)

Sparky (with Sparky Anderson)

They Call Me Sparky (with Sparky Anderson)

On a Handshake (with John E. Fetzer)

The Detroit Tigers Encyclopedia

Michigan Memories (with Bo Schembechler)

Tradition (with Bo Schembechler)

Hello Everybody, I'm George Kell (with George Kell)

That's Just Kramer (with Ron Kramer)

Who Could Ask for Anything More? (with Bob Browne)

Six (with Al Kaline)

If These Walls Could Talk (with Jon Falk)

Sparky and Me

★

My Friendship with Sparky Anderson and the Lessons He Shared About Baseball and Life

DAN EWALD

Thomas Dunne Books
St. Martin's Press ⚏ New York

THOMAS DUNNE BOOKS.
An imprint of St. Martin's Press.

SPARKY AND ME. Copyright © 2012 by Dan Ewald. All rights reserved.
Printed in the United States of America. For information, address
St. Martin's Press, 175 Fifth Avenue, New York, N.Y. 10010.

www.thomasdunnebooks.com
www.stmartins.com

ISBN 978-1-250-00026-2

First Edition: May 2012

10 9 8 7 6 5 4 3 2 1

To Carol—
For sharing our best friend with me
for so many years

CONTENTS

TUESDAY: SOME SERIOUS STUFF

NINE DAYS LATER

TWO WEEKS LATER

TODAY

ACKNOWLEDGMENTS

I owe so much for the inspiration from Dan Jr. and the loving loyalty of Kathy throughout this project. The unwavering support of Amy, Andrea, Marc, Isabel, Audrey, Kevin, Mykell, Todd, Alex, Brian, Susan, Lee, Albert, and Shirlee is cherished forever.

I particularly appreciate the uncompromising toughness of editor Peter Wolverton and generous assistance of Anne Bensson. And thanks to all the St. Martin's Press staff who help to make the words sparkle.

PREFACE

Sparky and I drove back to my home in Detroit after an appearance he made in Marion, Ohio. We managed only a few hours of sleep before hustling through a cup of coffee and doughnuts, and then I drove him to the airport for an early-morning flight back home to Los Angeles.

In midafternoon, he called to say he had made it home safely. Only one thing was wrong. His teeth were missing.

Sparky wore a partial bridge at the time but couldn't find it in his travel bag or his toiletry bag, or anywhere in his home. Of less concern to him was one missing black sock.

I told him I would carefully search the bathroom and the guest room he always used.

I scoured each room and stripped the bed down to the mattress, but nothing unexpected turned up. Then I stuck my head under the bed and saw a single black sock. And almost like a magic trick, the bridge fell to the floor when I shook the sock.

I immediately wondered how his teeth could possibly have found their way into a sock. But I'd come to understand that anything was possible with Sparky.

I called him to say he owed me for my professional detective services. He told me to bring the teeth on my trip to his home five days later.

I wrapped the teeth in a plastic bag and put them in my jacket pocket. But a funny thing happened on my way to the airport departing gate, something that only Sparky's teeth could have triggered.

"Yours?" a security agent asked in a matter-of-fact tone. A strange question, I thought, because to whom else did he think they would belong?

"Not really," I answered. "They belong to my friend."

He eyed me curiously. "What're you doing with your friend's teeth in your pocket?" he asked.

"It's a long story, sir," I answered. "Totally harmless, but not really interesting."

"What's your friend's name?" he asked.

"George Anderson," I answered.

Another curious look. "That's Sparky Anderson's real name," said the guard, obviously a rabid baseball fan.

"And those are his real teeth," I said. "Sort of real teeth, I mean."

The guard smiled and wished me a good day.

Walking to the gate, the man who had been standing in line behind me tapped me on the shoulder. "How much you want for the teeth?" he asked.

We both just smiled and went our separate ways.

When I told the story to Sparky, he joked that I should have sold them. "Maybe I coulda got me a whole new set," he laughed.

I had spent 32 years working for Sparky, or only a few months shy of half my life, when he died in 2010. During that time I had lived a dream. I had negotiated countless handsome commercial contracts for Sparky. I'd made travel arrangements and accompanied him to major and smaller cities around the country for various events. We'd even written three books together. There was nothing we didn't share.

But transporting teeth from Michigan to California marked a first among our mutual favors and gave us both a smile.

With Sparky, of course, life always bordered on the bizarre. He lived for the moment, making each day special. There was no way to predict how each day might unfold.

Maybe that's why we enjoyed each day together as if it were our last.

Besides being a Baseball Hall of Fame legend, Sparky was a genuine colorful character, a throwback to a time when the game just seemed to be more fun.

He was a teacher and patiently taught me baseball from the viewpoint of a master. More important, he taught me that treating people properly is even bigger than the game.

Sparky taught by example and with stories that he loved to tell. He may have fractured the English language into more pieces than the number of dollars in the national debt. But each story that he spun included at least a little lesson on how to live a more meaningful life.

Sparky was a showman. He loved the spotlight of the stage. He loved to laugh and truly enjoyed making people feel good.

Above all else, we were friends: best friends without conditions who shared a sacred trust.

Friends are remembered more for life's little things than for all the records contained in a library of books. Those little things are captured in memory and bring a smile when it's needed most.

With Sparky, there are many little stories that bring to life the true character he was. Some bring a smile. Some bring a tear. Some are inspiring. And some are just old-fashioned, feel-good baseball yarns that affirm his conviction that baseball is the greatest game on earth.

The following stories reflect the spirit of Sparky. They're the kind of stories that touch us all. I hope you hear his crackly, mischievous voice in those that I share.

SUNDAY

★

A Time to Share

Three days in October of 2010.

That's all the time we had left to share. Neither one of us talked about it. But both of us knew.

My best friend was dying.

Neither held any secrets from the other. In fact, we had become so close during our lifetime together that each of us could tell without asking if the other had changed his brand of deodorant.

Now we were down to our last three days together. Each moment became more precious than all the others. We had to embrace each one.

My best friend was George Lee Anderson. Still is. But anyone who knows that a baseball is round and a real bat is made out of wood still refers to him as "Sparky."

There are a whole lot of people in America unfamiliar with all of the spectacular Baseball Hall of Fame accomplishments of his colorful career. But somehow the mischievous sound of the name "Sparky" rings at least a distant bell in the minds of most Americans. On more than one occasion, for instance, the catchy name was used as an answer on the popular TV game show *Jeopardy*. And who knows how many times the name has been used as a part of the *New York Times* crossword puzzle.

"You never read the *New York Times* in your whole life and here you are again in the middle of the crossword puzzle," I used to tease him all the time.

"I think it's for my ruggedly handsome looks," he would shoot back.

It's one of those names that fit the character as snugly as the tights on Robin Hood's legs. With his snow-white hair, a smile engaging enough to make a hangman drop the rope before pulling it, a language filled with words he created as he went along, and an optimism bubbly enough to make Ebenezer Scrooge want to go to a Christmas party, Sparky was a come-to-life cartoon figure.

He just happened to pop up as a baseball manager.

Sparky was refreshingly approachable for any adult or child anywhere who wanted to talk about baseball or just say hi. He could make a frightened child feel like he was talking to his grandpa. He was tough enough to challenge any bully fool enough to take advantage of an innocent underdog in front of his eyes.

And, man, he knew baseball and how to make the game fun for everyone. He also knew how to treat people with the tender respect that every human being deserves. He had a gift for making each individual he met feel as if they had been best friends for life.

Sparky was one of those rare personalities that are becoming extinct in baseball and, in fact, in all professional sports. He was a true colorful character who still enjoys single-name recognition not only by hard-core sports fans, but even by the most casual observer, who probably isn't aware that there once was a time when gloves were used only by fielders, not batters, that a "pitch count" referred only to the number of balls and strikes, and that radar guns were only used by state troopers to snatch unsuspecting highway speeders.

Throughout history there have been only a handful of single-name notables. Babe. Yogi. Mickey. Reggie. Casey. There have been others, but not enough to field a full team. Beyond all their baseball talent, they brought an enchanting kind of magic to the game that transcended all their records.

They not only influenced the history of the game, but actually made at least a minor impact on society. Along with their obvious superior baseball talent, they were born showmen who used the diamond as their stage. Sparky was certainly one of them. In fact, center stage was his best position.

The game now stands somewhat naked without those larger-than-life figures. They had the power to make people laugh or get angry. They had a gift for touching nerves and pulling the strings of the heart.

Somehow no one thought Sparky could ever die. He truly was bigger than life. So why not death? But on November 4, 2010, Sparky joined the majority.

We had become lifetime traveling partners throughout the United States, Canada, Mexico, even the Caribbean. Big cities. Small cities. Some towns so tiny on a map that I had to use a magnifying glass to make sure I was looking at the right one. Kathy and I were fortunate to have been guests of Sparky and his family on seven straight Caribbean cruises.

Because of Sparky, I was privileged to meet many influential people who make the news, not report it: captains of industry, governors of many states, actors, authors, entertainers, even a president of the United States.

There were also many average working-class people who merely wished to shake Sparky's hand and maybe catch a dash of the magic that twinkled in his eye. Those were the ones he treasured most. So did I.

The impact of those three days in October will forever remain indelibly etched into my memory and my heart. And neither Sparky nor I ever could have imagined that they would be spent almost entirely sitting at the kitchen table in his home in Thousand Oaks, California.

Sparky was failing quickly that autumn. So quickly, in fact, that each welcome of another morning sun became an unexpected bonus.

Carol knew her husband of 57 years was dying. His children—Lee, Shirlee, and Albert—knew he was dying. I knew he was dying.

And all too hauntingly, Sparky knew it too.

I had been planning another trip to Sparky's home for early in November. We enjoyed watching a full slate of Saturday college football games together at least once each fall. He fired the TV remote control like a pistol, jumping from one game to another.

I hastily adjusted my plans and arrived in Thousand Oaks two days after Carol suggested that I had better move the timetable up. Sparky was suffering from dementia, a hideously unforgiving disease of the brain that eventually causes physical maladies. And time was running short.

On the flight to Los Angeles I tried once more to determine exactly how life had unfolded whereby Sparky and I wound up being such inseparable friends. In my mind—for at least the 10,011th time in my life—I laid all the factual material on the table.

- Growing up in Los Angeles, Sparky developed a lifelong incurable love affair with baseball and played from morning till night.
- Growing up in Detroit, I did the same.
- Sparky was raised in a section of the city within walking distance of Watts, site of the 1965 race riot.
- I was raised in rugged southwest Detroit, within walking distance of the site of the 1967 race riot, and of old Briggs Stadium just north of the Detroit River.
- After graduating from high school, Sparky achieved the first step of his dream by signing a professional contract with the Brooklyn Dodgers.
- After graduating from college, I wound up as the baseball beat writer for the *Detroit News*.
- Working tirelessly through old-fashioned baseball's hierarchy, Sparky got his shot at managing in the big leagues.
- Working tirelessly through old-fashioned journalism, I got my shot at serving as public relations director for the Detroit Tigers.

But all of those similarities could be mere factual coincidences. There had to be something more. Something serendipitous. Something inexplicably magical.

Whatever that may be, neither of us—not even for a day—took

his good fortune for granted. We always remembered where we had come from.

Sparky was eleven years older than I. He was not old enough to be a father figure, and both of us were too bullheaded for him to be a big brother.

So we became friends. Such close friends, in fact, that I handled all of Sparky's personal business affairs. Neither Sparky nor I liked the sound of the word "agent." We tried "manager" for a while. And then "adviser." Finally, when telling people about our relationship, we settled on the word "friend." The truth is always simple.

Throughout the decades, the only symbol of our business relationship was a handshake we had shared to confirm our agreement shortly after we met. Carol eloquently explained our unique relationship in the simplest of terms.

"He trusted you," she said. "And you both loved each other."

That trust and love provided the freedom to share our deepest secrets and the confidence to draw upon the strength of the other during our most trying moments. There was nothing we didn't share. We shared our families. We shared our homes. We shared problems and anxieties. We even shared a suite on the road.

Sparky never tried to analyze the roots of our friendship. He had the wisdom simply to live it. We talked about it often, but only to the point of being grateful for realizing that a friendship such as ours is likely never to happen again in baseball.

The game has changed too much. It's too corporate, with too many gimmicks. Society has changed also. There's not enough trust.

It's hard to consider any baseball franchise a "club" when all more closely resemble a mere extension of the parent holding company. The exorbitant amount of money in the game, and the demands on time to earn a slice of it, stifle a friendship like the one Sparky and I shared.

Together, all those changes affect managers, players, and even the game on the field itself.

That doesn't make it bad. It just makes it different. So much of the innocent simplicity now is gone forever.

"They're all makin' so much more money than we ever did," Sparky often said. "And that ain't no bad thing. But nobody will ever have the kind of friendship that we had. We were the lucky ones. It'll never happen again."

I arrived at the airport just before noon on Sunday. Upon reaching the front door of the Anderson home, I was blessed by a spontaneously magical moment, the kind that's better to simply enjoy than to try to understand.

Because of his rapidly failing condition, Carol did not tell Sparky about my surprise visit until after he arose that morning. She didn't want to run the risk of any transportation delays. After deplaning, I called Carol to let her know I had arrived in Los Angeles.

"If you could have one wish today, what would it be?" she asked him after hanging up the phone.

Sparky wasn't sure what she meant.

"If you could see one person today, who would it be?" she clarified.

"I'd like to see Dan," he answered.

"Well, maybe it's your lucky day," she said with a smile she knew he would understand.

She then told him that Marty Sliwak, a family friend and baseball coach at California Lutheran University, was on his way to the airport to pick me up.

Sparky greeted me at the door, and we embraced. We smiled. Not one word was spoken. A tear trickled down both of our cheeks as we both stood unashamed to look the other straight in the eye.

That's what best friends do.

I didn't even have the opportunity to take my travel bag to the first-floor bedroom that, over the years, had become as familiar to me as my own at home in Detroit. He told me to sit down at the kitchen table.

"We got some talkin' to do," he said.

And except for when he could manage to get a few hours of fitful sleep, the kitchen is where we spent the rest of Sunday and the next two days.

The kitchen eating area in Sparky's house opens onto a one-step-down family room that features a giant HDTV screen that can easily be watched during any meal of the day. It sits in the corner; above it an almost room-length mantel is mounted to the wall. The mantel is filled with an assortment of awards and honors that Sparky accumulated throughout his colorful managerial career.

A Cincinnati Reds–commissioned portrait of Sparky in a Reds uniform anchors one side. On the other is an inscribed replica of Sparky's plaque that hangs on one of the walls of the Baseball Hall of Fame in Cooperstown, New York.

Next to the plaque stands a picture of Sparky and me together at one of the countless functions we attended.

"That's the closest I'll ever get to making it into the Hall of Fame," I joked with him on each of my visits.

The back wall of the family room features a pair of doors to the patio. The rest of the wall is completely covered by volcanic rock from ceiling to floor. It was designed and installed by his son Lee. The ambience of the family room is comfortably enticing.

It's the kitchen, though, where all the action occurs.

This is the room where all big decisions are made. This is the room where bills are paid. This is the room where arguments are instigated and resolved. And this is the room where all political and world problems are solved. Or at least reshaped the way we wanted them to be.

Subjects during these discussions over the years flashed freely around like the blurred, blinking images on the TV screen with Sparky's hand in control of the remote. No one knew exactly which show he was watching at any given moment. He had a curious mind and an eclectic appetite for knowledge. He never wanted to miss a thing.

Even a serious discussion with Sparky wound up with at least a small slice of humor. That's the way he was. There was always room for a smile.

"It don't hurt to feel good," he explained. "More people oughta try it once in a while."

Regardless of the subject matter, Sparky always spoke in superlatives. The economy, for instance, was never steady. It was either booming or getting ready to bust. No politician was either pretty good or pretty bad. Like ballplayers, they were either the best or the worst. Fortunately for all of our sakes, there were far more of the former.

That was Sparky's world. He liked to keep things simple.

Over the years, Sparky, Carol, and I spent countless hours at that maple-wood kitchen table, which I remember from my first visit decades ago. The table and chairs are sturdy, handsome, well preserved, and functional. Neither Sparky nor Carol ever entertained the thought of a replacement. So it always felt like being at home.

Those three days in October, however, were different. Eerily different.

What do you say to a dying person who's been your best friend for half of your life? How do you thank him for all the knowledge, wisdom, and goodwill that he generously shared with you? How do you show that through him you have learned so much?

By that time Sparky was too weak to play golf at his beloved Sunset Hills Golf Club. He didn't feel like taking a ride to Albertsons supermarket, where he so much enjoyed kibitzing with all of the cashiers and stock clerks. He had even lost interest in making his almost daily drive to the post office to pick up the voluminous amount of fan mail that he personally answered. We couldn't even take the daily morning walks with a dedicated and lovable group of neighbors whom I had come to appreciate so much over the years.

He simply wanted to swap some stories and peacefully reminisce about the good times we had shared.

Of course, we talked about baseball. We had spent 17 seasons together. There had been more than 2,500 games, not including nine in the playoffs, five in the World Series, and who knows how many hundreds more in spring training.

But it wasn't just baseball stories that kept us so busy in the kitchen for those three days in October. We resurrected a kaleidoscope of memories from all of our experiences together that we once innocently thought would go on forever.

Strung together, they made a fairy tale neither of us could ever have imagined.

We talked about all the trips we had taken during our baseball careers and the career we forged afterward. We talked about all the people we had been privileged to meet—not necessarily the celebrities or the so-called beautiful people, but the blue-collar real people with whom we both felt more comfortable.

We laughed at some of the hilarious situations we had gotten ourselves into. It was amazing how soon after one of us started a story, the other almost instantly began to laugh. Of course, we knew how each story would end. But that didn't steal a moment of the good feeling the story stirred.

It didn't matter how many times we had told those stories before. For those three days, those stories lifted themselves from our memories and became so alive that we thought we could reach out and touch them.

Baseball stories resemble wartime tales. Some are told as they actually happened. Others are told as we think they did. Regardless of the specifics, all of them are true.

Sparky never wasted a story. For him, a story was composed of more than mere words. There was something to be taken from it, something special that transcended the words. There was something to be learned, and something to be practiced.

Some stories gave more meaning to baseball. Others put more meaning into life. Baseball was always Sparky's passion. Treating people kindly and with respect was the very principle upon which his life was founded. Sparky certainly practiced what he preached.

To return the loyalty that Detroiters gave him for 17 seasons, he established Caring Athletes Team for Children's and Henry Ford Hospitals (CATCH), a charity to enrich the quality of life for needy Detroit children. CATCH now enjoys an endowment of more than $5 million.

Few celebrities in any sport in any city have initiated such generosity.

Sparky and I spent the better portion of our lives living those stories. Then he was wise enough to make sure I knew how critical it was to keep them alive.

Looking back, I realize that those three days in October spent in Sparky's kitchen were something of a seminar to discover how much I had learned over the years. It was important to him that I preserve their value forever.

Throughout the years, he took time to teach me much about baseball, and gave me insights into all of the game's nuances. He took even more time to demonstrate that life was bigger than baseball.

The stories that we shared were totally unscripted. Sparky loved spontaneity more than he did banana cream pie. Stories flowed as freely as an e. e. cummings stream of consciousness poem. Most brought smiles; some, a few tears. All carried a message he wanted me to keep alive.

No one has been privileged to have a better teacher than Sparky. No one has been blessed to have a better best friend.

Three days in October at a kitchen table in Thousand Oaks, California. A lifetime gift from a friend for a lifetime. A gift whose memory will never die.

1

"Daniel, My Boy"

Although I didn't realize it at the time, the first lesson I learned from Sparky occurred during our initial meeting more than 40 years ago. I, of course, was well aware of his reputation. He, in turn, had no idea who I was.

But as our brief encounter progressed, that didn't matter to him.

No one forgets the thrill of his first meeting with Sparky. No player. No manager. No celebrity. No member of the media. And certainly no wide-eyed, tongue-tied fan.

While memories of countless subsequent events with Sparky have blurred through the passing of so many years, our first meeting remains incredibly fresh. I can still recall it quicker than retrieving a filed computer document.

At the time of our first acquaintance, I was a bottom-of-the-totem-pole *Detroit News* sportswriter primarily covering high school sports. Any pipe dream of working for Sparky eight years later was as remote as the chance of watching one of my golf drives trickle into the cup.

It was early Sunday evening, July 11, 1971, with a hot summer sun still hanging over the city. Only four short years had passed since Detroit was stained by the hideous, historic race riot that shamed the nation. It took lives, leveled large pockets of the city, and planted the seeds of disintegration that Detroit still struggles to overcome today.

Once more the nation's eyes were squarely focused on Detroit. Rather than watching destruction, however, this time the country watched a celebration of success.

Baseball's All-Star Game was scheduled for two nights later at historic Tiger Stadium, a few short blocks up from the newspaper on Michigan Avenue, on the western edge of the heart of downtown.

This was the site where a century earlier Tigers legend Ty Cobb flashed his spikes and compiled the highest lifetime batting average in history. This was the site where Babe Ruth hit a gargantuan home run that left the park and didn't stop rolling until it was 612 feet from home plate. And this was the site where Yankees immortal Lou Gehrig ended his record-setting streak of 2,130 consecutive games played.

This was also the site to which I often walked when I was a kid. I lived in the old neighborhood just west of the park, which was known at the time as Briggs Stadium. I learned to love the Tigers there. It also was the site where I learned to hate the New York Yankees.

I loved to watch the majesty of Mickey Mantle and that quirky batting stroke of Yogi Berra. But nobody could love any other American League team without hating the Yankees. Except for when they represented the American League in the World Series. And that was almost every year.

Now the best of both leagues convened in Detroit to make more history at the park that lay almost down the street from where I had been raised. History certainly was written with one monstrous swing of the bat by the then young Reggie Jackson, whose now-famous home run crashed into the light tower above right-center field a nanosecond after his bat crunched the ball.

Had the light tower not interfered with the flight of the ball, it might have landed in Windsor, Ontario, Canada, on the opposite bank of the Detroit River. The sight was majestic. The sound of bat on ball was furiously frightening.

"I thought someone had shot off a rifle when that ball was popped,"

Sparky told me several years later. "I was standing in the dugout and ducked my head a little. I thought the American Leaguers were takin' the game real serious and started to shoot at me."

As manager of the 1970 National League champion Cincinnati Reds, Sparky was honored to serve as his league's manager. Unlike some players and even managers who prefer to use the All-Star break as a three-day vacation away from the park, throughout his career Sparky relished any opportunity to participate in the game.

"That's a privilege no man should try to duck," he always maintained. "There's plenty of time for vacations once the career is over."

I was assigned to write a feature story on Sparky, the hottest young manager in either league, who had led the Reds to the pennant in his rookie year when he was only 36 years old.

The meeting occurred on fashionable Washington Boulevard just outside of the old Book-Cadillac Hotel, where the All-Star players and league representatives were housed.

The high-rent stores of downtown lined both sides of Washington Boulevard. With theaters, restaurants, hotels, shopping, taxis, buses, streetcars, and an endless stream of locally made automobiles congesting almost every street, Detroit was a vibrant antithesis to the image it bears today.

Despite its creeping demise, the blue-collar city was proud of its rich sports tradition, and the All-Star Game couldn't have enjoyed a finer setting.

My fondest memories of growing up in the shadow of the ballpark still center on baseball. Detroit was a scrappy newspaper town, and I devoured each word written about each game in all of the three dailies operating at the time.

Then, the Tigers had such memorable players as Jim Bunning, Harvey Kuenn, Norm Cash, and Ray Boone. Of course, Al Kaline was the centerpiece of all those teams. He became the youngest American League player in history to win a batting title with a .340 average in 1955 at the age of 20. He played forever and wound up in baseball's Hall of Fame. Working for the Tigers at the time of his 1979 induction, I was privileged to write his induction speech.

Although at the time I had never met any of those players, I had once caddied for long-ago Tigers manager Jimmie Dykes when I was a kid. Never did I dare to imagine, however, that one day I would be assigned to interview Sparky Anderson before an All-Star Game.

And get paid for the privilege!

Even before all of his hair turned toothpaste white, Sparky had the jagged facial features that made it impossible for him to blend into a crowd. Upon seeing him step out of the cab he had taken from the airport, a swarm of kids and a few adults surrounded Sparky, begging for his autograph. I decided to slip inside of the lobby and wait until he was finished.

I watched him closely and noticed that despite the hassle, a smile never left his face. Suddenly, the circle of autograph hounds bolted toward a cab that stopped slightly up the street. Out of a back door emerged Hank Aaron, leaving Sparky free to enter the hotel.

"I gotta use that trick more often," Sparky joked to the bellman. "Kinda funny how small someone gets when Henry comes around."

As Sparky was walking toward the front desk, I worked up the nerve to introduce myself to ask if he would be willing to answer a few quick questions before retiring to his room.

My stomach was doing double-time jumping jacks, and he must have sensed the apprehension bubbling in my gut. Over the years I discovered how compassionate Sparky always was to every member of the media. Representatives from dailies, weeklies, or battery-assisted radio stations were all treated the same.

Gently he led the conversation just enough to allow me to recover some semblance of control.

The interview was brief, and I've forgotten almost all we talked about. One significant memory of the occasion, however, remains forever fresh in my mind. Throughout the interview, he repeatedly referred to me by name, almost as if he had known me for several years instead of from the moment when I introduced myself.

"Daniel, my boy," he started. He enjoyed using my full first name throughout our years together. "You gotta know somethin' before we even start. You got the most beautiful ballpark right up the street from here. This is what a big-league ballpark is supposed to look like. And don't you ever forget it. It's the best one around."

I already knew that. It didn't matter at the time that the only other major-league park I had ever personally seen was Cleveland's Municipal Stadium. In retrospect, however, I now realize what he had done.

With just a smile and a few kind words about the park I had loved since being a kid, he had taken control of the situation. As always with the media, he was the man in charge.

He then told the story about when he was 18 years old and his Los Angeles American Legion baseball team won the 1953 national championship at the park when it was called Briggs Stadium. "We got the chance to meet Joe Louis," he said proudly. The heavyweight champion who captured America's heart with his knockout of German Max Schmeling had been raised in Detroit. "I never was the kind to idolize any particular athlete," Sparky continued. "But Joe Louis was special. Besides my father, Joe Louis was probably the only man I ever idolized. That made Detroit very special to me."

I remember no other specifics of the meeting other than the fact that Sparky was the closest thing to Ozzie Nelson I had ever met. He was reassuring without any hint of presumption. He thanked me for the interview for which I still remain grateful.

Our next meeting occurred in March 1973. Sparky was still busy putting together all the parts of what came to be known as the Big Red Machine. I was a rookie baseball writer covering my first spring training.

The Tigers were playing Cincinnati in Tampa, and we met in the Reds' clubhouse before the game. Once more I introduced myself, and again he was the gracious diplomat. He spent as much time answering questions for me as he did for a longtime veteran from the *New York Times,* or even for a writer from one of the two Cincinnati dailies.

I thought about how fortunate those two beat writers were to cover a manager as graciously cooperative as Sparky day after day. The manager of the Tigers was Billy Martin. Billy was a fiery and competent manager. But his personality was never mistaken for Sparky's . . . and certainly not Ozzie Nelson's.

"Who cares about what a paper's circulation is?" Sparky often asked. "Shouldn't the guy from a small paper be treated with the same respect as somebody from one of the high rollers? Do the so-called big guys know more words? They both got the same job. Sometimes the little guys know more about the game than those big-city hotshots. I listen to what they ask and what they say. Ain't nobody foolin' me when it comes to somethin' like that."

And that's the way he operated throughout his entire career.

Sparky was close to obsessive about attaching the right name to the right face. He had a gift for remembering names and worked hard never to slip.

"Sometimes people are crazy," he used to say. "They're afraid to call someone by his name. What are they afraid of? Do they think they're better than the other guy? Do they think that using his name is some silly sign of weakness? Don't the other guy deserve the same respect that he gives to me?"

Sparky's courtesy stretched far beyond the media, the politicians, and all the captains of industry he felt privileged to meet. He took just as much pleasure spending time with the guy working the midnight shift in one of the auto factories. He loved to share his optimism and peppy zest for life with everyone he met.

While managing in Detroit, Sparky started his daily ballpark rounds with a visit to general manager Jim Campbell's office. Once in a while they talked about club matters. Once in a while they merely swapped stories that only two baseball lifers could fully appreciate.

Next he stuck his head into the office of everyone else on the third floor. It was just a quick hello, but everyone waited to see his smile each day. From there he made his second-floor route, with his final stop at my office.

"I trust you're gonna give me some of your precious time in my office before the game," he would say sarcastically, and then he'd wink as he walked out the door.

Finally, he was ready to make his tour through the concourse of the stadium on the way to his clubhouse office. That was a show itself.

Along the way, he waved to and chatted with all of the concessionaires, who were busy preparing hot dogs, popcorn, and the regular menu of baseball staples for another game in the stadium Sparky loved more than any he had ever seen. And he greeted each worker by first name.

All the workers smiled and waved. Some who lived in the neighborhood had worked at the park for more than 40 years. They thanked him for being the first manager to extend so much courtesy.

"We love you, Sparky," some of the older ladies would say. "Thanks for all you do for us. Please don't ever leave. Please stay here forever."

Some of the early-arriving players who happened to witness Sparky's regular routine asked him how he got to know all the names of so many workers.

"It's really hard to do," he said with obvious sarcasm. "I asked them. And then I wasn't afraid to use those names. They're all mothers and fathers and grandparents, too, you know. They got families just like us. They gotta work to feed their kids. Why don't you try askin' 'em sometime? It might make you feel good."

Sparky accidentally discovered that another baseball legend who just may have been history's purest hitter shared his proclivity for using first names.

That discovery occurred before a Tigers exhibition game against the Boston Red Sox in Winter Haven, Florida. Sparky was standing near the batting cage watching the Tigers take batting practice. He was holding court with the media when a uniformed visitor sneaked up from behind him. The captivating figure put both hands on Sparky's shoulders to spin him around.

"Ted Williams," the visitor said as he extended his right hand. "How ya doin', Sparky?"

Pontificating to the writers about any subject they threw at him screeched to a stop. And maybe for the first time in his life, Sparky stood mute as a mime.

"My God," Sparky finally said in awe. "You don't have to tell me who you are. The pope all the way over in that place where he lives knows who you are."

Williams smiled and wrapped his long arms around Sparky's shoulders. "Just makin' sure, Sparky," Williams said. "You never know how a person is gonna react. Better to get it over with so nobody gets embarrassed."

The only other trait the two legends shared was that each had a pair of arms and legs. Obviously, as a player, Williams made more out of his two pair than did Sparky.

Williams, of course, started to talk about hitting. Sparky listened like an honor roll schoolboy. No one ever said a word when Williams talked about hitting. On that particular matter, he enjoyed papal infallibility.

"Just tell me one thing, Ted," Sparky joked. "If I understand everything you're sayin', how come I couldn't hit like you?"

Williams broke into one of his bottom-of-the-gut laughs that made everyone within hearing distance feel part of the conversation.

"'Cause you're just a little sawed-off twig that probably chased the first pitch you thought you could hit," Williams cracked back. "You didn't know how to wait for the pitch you knew you could hit. I told you so many times that pitchers are dumb. Just wait. . . . They'll give you something to hit."

The two legends jabbered until it was time for the grounds crew to haul the batting cage away. The writers scribbled notes as fast as their fingers could move. Sparky and Williams together was the opportunity for a spring-training holiday. With a story like this, nobody cared what happened in a meaningless game.

"I'm gonna see you in the Hall of Fame when you finally take off that uniform, you little squirt," Williams said before heading to the Boston clubhouse.

Sparky smiled and probably was blushing behind those chiseled lines on his face. "Not because I hit like you," he managed to spit out.

"Well, goddamn it," Williams countered. "Check out my managerial record. How in the hell do you keep doing it year after year after year?"

Sparky had a gift for making every visitor feel special, from Ted Williams to the rawest rookie on the roster, from the president of the Ford Motor Company to the grease-stained hourly worker on the line. For just that moment, Sparky made a visitor feel as if he were the most important person in the world. Chances are, they would never meet again. For that one precious moment, though, Sparky was that person's best friend.

"It all goes back to the greatest lesson my daddy ever taught me," Sparky explained. "He never had much money, so he couldn't give me much. But he gave me the most valuable lesson any father could give a son.

"He taught me that it don't cost a dime to be nice to people. In fact, it's easier to be nice than thinking up a new way to be a jackass. What's wrong with making another person smile? Maybe that's the only one he'll get the whole day."

Sparky smiled often. He loved to share his warmth with others. And he always started by calling someone by his name.

Is anything more precious to anyone than a name? Sparky made the lesson easy to understand.

As I grow older, it's becoming more difficult to remember the names of all the good people I am fortunate to have met. But I still try. Sparky made sure of that.

2

★

Armed with Words

We were two best friends simply sharing three days together. Sitting at the kitchen table, we had no schedule, no script to follow. We were just swapping the same precious stories we had laughed about for so many years.

Maybe it was the mention of Ted Williams that triggered a memory from Boston. No one tugged both ways on New England hearts more than "Teddy Ballgame."

Not even Boston-born poet Edgar Allan Poe.

Williams was apotheosized and booed mercilessly by the Red Sox faithful. The memory actually had nothing to do with Williams, but was my initial opportunity to watch Sparky play classic puppeteer with the worldwide media.

It was just a flash, a perhaps meaningless incident that, though funny at the time, probably was forgotten by most who packed the closet-size manager's office in peculiarly charming Fenway Park.

And though quite incidental, the image still remains vivid in my memory as symbolic of the way Sparky's spontaneity and goodwill established a mutually appreciated compromise between himself and the media throughout his 26 seasons in the big leagues.

I was covering that historic 1975 World Series between the Cincinnati Reds and the Boston Red Sox, seven dramatic games that many baseball historians remain convinced are the most memorable in World Series history.

The incident occurred the day before Game 1, at a Cincinnati workout at venerable Fenway Park.

Media members from around the world stood flesh to flesh in the visiting manager's office, which was no larger than a boxing ring and as aesthetically appealing as an unfinished concrete basement. The manager's desk and chair looked as if they had been there since Babe Ruth pitched for the Red Sox. Each member of the media felt like a single fresh shrimp squeezed into the middle of a bowl of those famous Boston delicacies. I know. I was one of those shrimps.

The visitors' clubhouse in Fenway was as compact, rickety, and spartan. Even today it looks like it did when the Babe used it after his celebrated trade to the New York Yankees. For players who use it and the media who must visit, it's sarcastically referred to as "New England chic."

The aesthetically bankrupt surroundings, however, didn't matter. The opportunity to hear Sparky philosophize was worth any spatial inconvenience. Everyone wanted at least a little piece of the fastest tongue in the National League. And with his feet propped on the desk and smoke puffing from his mouth, Sparky savored every moment.

As dean of the notoriously caustic Boston press corps, Cliff Keane was accorded a chair at the desk directly across from Sparky. Keane was a crusty *Boston Globe* veteran. He was Boston's answer to Don Rickles and could fire a litany of stinging one-liners at the Red Sox as easily as at their opponents. Beneath all the sarcastic jabs, however, the longtime Bostonian was as much a Red Sox diehard as the young fans who filled what was left of the cheap seats in deep right-center field.

The rest of the room laughed loudly while Keane fired daggers at Sparky. Sparky laughed too. In a good-humored way, Keane referred to Sparky as "Busher," the classic baseball term for someone just called up from the minor leagues.

Keane predicted a quick and bloody exit for what had come to be known as the Big Red Machine. Sparky sat quietly entertained as the Keane show played on.

Suddenly, Sparky jumped from his chair and managed to squirm through the throng. Upon reaching Keane, and without saying a word, he bent down and kissed the startled writer on the top of his balding head.

"That's how we do it in the National League," Sparky said with a smile and a wink.

A thunder of laughter shook the tiny room. Writers from around the world had their sidebar for the next day's edition. Sparky had grabbed control of the media by choosing to "kill the Red Sox with kindness" instead of the firepower of the Cincinnati bats.

After I had finished retelling the story, Sparky laughed once more about the incident, which he said he remembered. "Ain't that what baseball stories are supposed to be about?" he asked. "The game ain't life and death. Give the boys what they want."

Sparky's babbling sometimes sounded like an obtuse Chinese proverb written backward.

But it was a show he never tired of playing.

Instead of the tense, suspicious, and somewhat combative relationship with the media that many baseball managers seem to bring to the job, Sparky whipped them with jokes and kindness.

"They got a job to do and I got a job to do," he always told me. "If you're slick enough, you can lead them guys into makin' your job a whole lot easier. And besides, sometimes those guys do a better job than me."

Usually, though, he came out on top.

Sparky needed the press to keep the Sparky character vibrant. He never ran into a camera he disliked or an audience he couldn't charm. And the writers certainly needed Sparky to keep their stories bouncy and fresh.

Need a story on a slow news day? Go to Sparky.

Need a punchy one-liner to spice a routine story? Go to Sparky.

"No page left unfilled" was Sparky's policy for all writers interviewing him. If he noticed a notebook with even one blank page, he quickly cooked up a few more quotes before anyone could leave. He believed the proximity to the press was one of baseball's inherent charms. No other sport enjoys such daily intimacy.

Sparky had an innate feel for what a writer was searching for. He also made it a point to learn how each sector of the media worked. He knew the difference between morning and evening deadlines and shaped his stories accordingly. Those were the days before cell phones, blogs, tweets, and the 24-hour-a-day news cycle.

Today the press never sleeps. It can only be imagined how large Sparky's legend would be if his career were to start today.

"All you gotta do is be nice and tell 'em a few stories," he used to say. "Then they'll come back for more and you got 'em in your back pocket."

Sparky spoke in parables. He loved using little stories to make his point, which almost always had something to do with living a better life. During our 32 years, I probably heard him use more parables than are found in the Bible.

"I guess that makes me the chief 'parabler,'" he said after I told him.

Before each stop in a city during a road trip, Sparky asked me to brief him on the names of all media members that might approach him. He called each by his first name to establish a more relaxed rapport. It also sent a quiet message that he would be watching every word they wrote.

As public relations director for the Tigers, I escorted him to numerous media functions, which often included politicians and influential civic leaders. We developed a routine that made each individual at the affair feel like the most important person in the room.

Walking slowly into the room, Sparky would nod at a certain person. Sometimes he would discreetly point at a person standing across the room. With equal discretion I whispered the person's first name. That was all Sparky needed.

"Hey, Tom," he'd say, approaching an individual. "I'm Sparky Anderson. Glad to see you."

The room now belonged to him.

Often I received a phone call from a writer in another city asking if it would be appropriate to use a quote that he had seen attributed to Sparky.

"If he didn't say it, he will at some point," I would reply. "Go ahead and use it."

Sparky laughed each time I told him of such an occurrence. "Yeah," he said. "But how about tellin' me once in a while exactly what I was supposed to have said."

At times during a grueling baseball season, as one day crawls slowly into the next, story ideas for writers get stale and often are difficult even to concoct. A visit to Sparky's office often carried a writer for the next couple of days. And, without a doubt, Sparky could have given the writer more.

No time passes as painfully slowly, however, as the last couple of weeks of spring training. The games are meaningless because the roster is usually set. Managers don't want to risk injuries to players facing the grind of another 162-game season.

Sparky got anxious each spring at that time. He felt the lull in the clubhouse more than any player. He often looked for ways to break the monotony, not only for the media, but also for himself.

"Let's come up with something new for the boys tomorrow," he once told me. "Let's at least give 'em a laugh before everyone falls asleep."

At breakfast early the next morning, I told him to talk about the "zifferrod."

He looked at me as if those final two weeks had already made me crack. "What the hell is the zifferrod?" he asked.

"I have no idea, and neither will anyone else," I said.

Sparky got the point. He dropped the word into the middle of his meeting with the press as if he had rehearsed it for weeks. He reviewed the hitting, pitching, and defensive strengths of the club. He then moved to the zifferrod, which had the roomful of writers looking at each other and scratching their heads.

Had Sparky really cracked?

"I think we'll be all right if we can get one more reliever and the zifferrod stays solid," he said. "It really gets down to the zifferrod."

Finally, someone broke the silence: "What the hell is a zifferrod?"

"How the hell do I know?" Sparky replied. "But it sure beats the hell out of talking about the same old stuff all the time."

A few years after convincing Sparky to come to Detroit as manager of the Tigers in June 1979, longtime general manager Jim Campbell was asked what was the most significant change he'd seen in the club with Sparky there.

Campbell smiled and shook his head in mock disbelief. "Well, for me"—he took a long pause—"I don't sleep as well as I used to. I wake up a lot earlier now. I get both newspapers and scour every story written about the Tigers. I want to know what kind of outrageous statement the little manager made to the press this time before leaving the park the night before."

Campbell laughed. Members of the media attending the gathering laughed. Even Sparky broke into a wide smile.

"Once in a while, I can't get my tongue to stop wagging," Sparky added, and another round of laughter filled the room.

Because of Sparky's gift for jousting with the media, he was always compared to New York Yankees legend Casey Stengel.

That's where Sparky drew the line. Besides Joe Louis, Casey was the closest Sparky had to an idol. "I'm honored," he often said. "But there's only one Casey."

The same has been said of Sparky, who joked about any such suggestion. "Thank God for that," he said. "Could you imagine another one of me?"

Only if the fans had their way.

Once in a while, when I'm dealing with a problem, I still think of how Sparky always used to say: "It don't hurt to laugh."

I think about how he taught me that a kind word is far more persuasive than any threatening remark. Sparky may have fractured the English language, but he understood that a kind word is far more persuasive than a whip.

That's a lesson that the "great parabler" always practiced.

3

★

The Old Man

As much as Sparky had a knack for charming the media, he also had a proclivity for picking peculiar friends. They were all genuinely good people, or he wouldn't have kept them around. They were just a mismatched pair of socks that happened to be the most comfortable pair in the drawer. Or maybe a 53rd card in a regular playing deck.

Sparky knew everybody in baseball. And most felt Sparky was their best friend. But those he kept closest were carefully selected. And they were decidedly few.

"How do you keep finding a fresh slice of bread in the middle of a moldy loaf?" I once asked him.

"Don't worry about it," Sparky cracked. "I found you, didn't I?"

Major-league baseball has always been the Hotel California for quirky characters that often appear to be only visiting this planet. Their attraction to those in the game—or maybe the game's attraction to them—has been woven into baseball's fabric since Ty Cobb was busy sharpening his spikes and stealing bases as if they all belonged to him.

Few people in baseball knew a character named George McCarthy.

He brought his magic only to a fortunate few like us. What he left, though, is a treasure trove of warm memories and a spirit of kindness that still lives in me today. They're poignant reminders that not all baseball stories worth remembering are created by the guys who wear a uniform.

Never could one of our storytelling sessions go very long without at least a chuckle about the elfin figure we lovingly called "the Old Man." Over the years, he had spent many hours in Sparky's kitchen. He would have kicked his heels and planted a kiss on both of our foreheads for even being mentioned during these three days in October.

The Old Man was an aging street-smart roustabout who tickled Sparky's imagination before capturing his heart.

Whether Sparky found him or it was the other way around really doesn't matter. Serendipity is less concerned with details than with results. And the spontaneously formed bond between the two was as serendipitous as a rainbow following a stubborn summer storm.

Had Damon Runyon discovered him before Sparky did, the Old Man would certainly have been turned into an iconic literary character. Runyon was the master at creating colorful, lovable misfits for his stories, which were transformed into the plays that changed the face of Broadway.

Imagine if Runyon had happened to come upon Sparky and McCarthy at the same time. Even Broadway might not have been ready for something like *Sparky and the Old Man*.

The Old Man died around ten years ago. No one knew his age for sure, but everyone asked him if he had ever met Babe Ruth . . . when the Babe was still growing up in Baltimore's St. Mary's Orphanage. And by the way, some teased, did he actually see Betsy Ross sew the first American flag?

The Old Man loved the teasing. He was just as good at taking the jabs as he was at shooting them back.

Shorter than Sparky—if anyone can believe it—the Old Man was so skinny that we all asked if he had to run around in the shower each morning just to get himself wet. Always neatly groomed and dressed in a baseball cap, a golf shirt, slacks, and gym shoes, he bore a striking resemblance to the late George Burns.

With his glasses perched tightly on the bridge of his nose and a sense of humor drier than a new sponge, he looked like God in the movie *Oh God* made famous by Burns. He spoke with a gravelly voice that a deaf man could have distinguished.

"What do you do?" Sparky once asked the Old Man. "Gargle with a glass of sand every morning?"

Sparky first met the Old Man playing golf at the Sunset Hills Golf Club in Thousand Oaks. The Old Man knew who Sparky was but never acted overly impressed by his celebrity. It took a lot to impress the Old Man.

"So he wore knickers and a baseball cap to work every day," the Old Man joked about Sparky. "I'm still wearing a baseball cap, but I quit wearing knickers when I was a kid. My mother told me they had gone out of style."

He was more concerned with Sparky's drives, which resembled a metronome landing left to right, right to left on either side of the fairway on almost every hole he played. "I've got an uncle who hits 'em straighter than you," the Old Man cracked. "And he's gettin' ready to croak before the week is over. I'll try to get you his driver. He won't need it where he's headed."

The Old Man had a sense of humor that would have turned Don Rickles's face green with envy. He fired one-liners more furiously than Nolan Ryan fired fastballs. They came just as fast and were just as penetrating. Foursomes playing adjacent holes knew the Old Man was there just by seeing his three playing partners bent over in laughter next to their golf carts.

Sparky was captured by the Old Man's quick, stinging wit and by the stories he spun from sunup till sundown.

George McCarthy was a Harvard Man. Maybe not in the traditional sense of the term, but he did spend a large portion of his working career at the elite university and was proud of every minute.

McCarthy was the caretaker of many of the scientific experimental labs. His responsibilities included maintaining the animals used for experimentation in medicine and psychology. He was proud of the small part he played in the advancement of science. "Harvard is such a wonderful institution," he said. "I had the opportunity to meet so many beautiful minds. But it just goes to show you . . . even a place like Harvard is filled with mice. And somebody's gotta take care of 'em."

After hearing countless stories about the Old Man, I finally was privileged to meet him on one of my visits to Thousand Oaks. Needless to say, the performance exceeded even Sparky's advance hype.

Sparky, the Old Man, and I were trying to squeeze in a round at Sunset Hills late one afternoon. We were moving briskly and were confident we could easily finish 18 holes before dusk—until we ran into a foursome of ladies ahead of us, for whom each hole took longer to play than the one they had just finished. Careful not to drive into them from behind, we finally caught them on the tee of a par-3 hole.

Ever the diplomat, the Old Man approached them with a smile and the natural twinkle in his eye. "How are you beautiful young ladies doing today?" he asked.

The ladies were charmed by his courtly demeanor and smiled when they recognized Sparky sitting in the cart.

"Ladies," the Old Man said, "we're pretty quick players, and we wonder if perhaps you might allow us to play through."

One of the ladies—at least a full head taller than the Old Man—asked what his handicap was.

The Old Man stood motionless. He was frustrated at the failure of his courteous proposal. "My handicap is that I can't fuck anymore," he answered bluntly, honestly, and without any malicious intent. "Now do you think we might be able to play through? My bedtime is coming up real soon."

Sparky's face turned a deeper shade of red than the color in the Cincinnati hat he used to wear. I felt an unnatural sense of suspension. I was floating over the set of a George Burns movie.

Only the Old Man could get away with such bawdy comedy. And, indeed, all four of the ladies were laughing.

They looked young enough to be the Old Man's granddaughters. They appeared to be more amused than offended by the bluntness of the encounter. They smiled and told us they would be "honored to follow us."

"Hope you can take care of that handicap problem of yours," one of them shouted as we drove down the fairway after our drives. Even the Old Man cracked a slight smile.

"Yeah . . . and maybe you can help," he snapped once out of hearing range.

Sparky's attachment to the Old Man was a tribute to McCarthy's honesty and sincerity. He appreciated the pride that the Old Man felt for doing an honest job in an environment that normally rewards those holding the most prestigious academic degrees. Even an institution like Harvard knows to appreciate the honest menial work of those behind the scenes.

At the beginning of one February, Sparky turned the street-smart old-timer into a boy getting his first bicycle with the surprise of his life.

"I want you to start packing," Sparky said.

"Why?" the Old Man asked. "Did I do something wrong and I'm going to jail?"

"You're goin' to spring training with me," Sparky said.

For the first time in his life, perhaps, the Old Man's tongue got tangled in the gravel at the back of his throat. But he quickly accepted the shockingly unexpected invitation. He didn't want to take a chance at having to be asked twice.

"There's one condition before we go," Sparky told him. "Don't you go dyin' on me down there. I don't wanna have to put you in a box and ship you back home. Do you have any idea how much that would cost?"

The Old Man promised he'd make every effort to stay alive, and Sparky bought him a round-trip airline ticket from Los Angeles to Tampa, Florida. When the two arrived in Tampa, I picked them up at the airport for the short trip to Lakeland, where the Tigers have held spring training since 1934.

"You were an old man when the Tigers first started training here," Sparky jabbed him with a smile. "Do you know if there were any Indians runnin' around here back then?"

As soon as we passed the city limits sign, the Old Man's eyes sparkled, and the town belonged to him. Sparky's order for a room with twin beds was waiting when the odd couple arrived.

"Now don't go wanderin' out on me once I go to sleep," Sparky told him. "I don't wanna hear about you dancin' in some honky-tonk. And if you get thrown into jail, don't call till the morning. You might run into some old friends of yours in there anyway."

Through general manager Jim Campbell, Sparky arranged for the Old Man to share in the free breakfasts and lunches in the cafeteria available to all Tigers executives and players throughout the entire minor-league system. "If you show us you can behave, we'll even take you to dinner," Sparky said.

Sparky never talked about it, but he was proud to give this impossible dream to someone who appreciated it so much more than even the Old Man could put into words.

Quirky as he was, the Old Man did, in fact, behave. I issued him a press credential that allowed him into any press box where we played a game. Once he entered a press box, he became so rigidly quiet that I had to pinch him once in a while to make sure he hadn't gone comatose.

"Don't forget what Sparky said," I reminded him. "You're not allowed to die down here."

"My father taught me a long time ago," he told me. "Never go into another man's house and start rearranging the furniture."

The Old Man knew the unwritten rules. That was always one of Sparky's tests for those he wished to trust. Players on the team also took a quick liking to the Old Man. So did a lot of kids in the stands before the games, when the Old Man slipped a generous number of baseballs from the ball bag to hand to them when he thought no one was looking.

"We're gonna run out of balls before camp is over at the rate you're givin' 'em away," Sparky said when he caught him.

"Don't worry about it," the Old Man said. "I'm makin' you look good. I tell every kid that you told me to give him a ball."

Sparky made the same arrangements for the Old Man the following spring training. He even paid for a trip to Detroit one season so the Old Man could see Sparky in action in a real big-league game.

When he got too old to travel, the Old Man moved from Los Angeles to the Palm Springs home of one of his sons. During one of my visits, Sparky and I made the three-hour drive just to let him know he had not been forgotten.

"You guys made an old man feel like a boy," he said emotionally before we left. "I can never thank you enough. I'll cherish the footprints you left on my heart for the rest of my life."

The tears in his eyes and the quiver in his voice certainly were more than either of us had expected. Within a few months, the Old Man died.

After we finished the story, I noticed that tears had also gathered in the corners of Sparky's eyes. Keeping them focused on the floor, he rose from his chair and walked into the garage for the bag of bird feed he distributed daily. He kept at least a couple of 20-pound bags of feed at all times. He never missed a day of feeding.

Sparky studied the birds and marveled at how they knew when to gather at their feeding bowl. He always had a smile for when his birds returned.

"The Old Man would want us to smile about him," Sparky said. "Let's make sure to do the right thing."

Sparky had a compulsion for sharing the good fortune that somehow fell his way. No one will ever know how many family members and friends fell under his umbrella.

"Some families never get a break," he often told me. "Once in a while a pot of gold falls into one guy's lap. That guy didn't get there all by himself. He had a lot of help from everyone around him. You can't forget those people if you happen to be that lucky guy."

One of those people who played an integral part in Sparky's life was Billy Consolo. He was a childhood friend who made it to the big leagues quicker than Sparky. Sparky played shortstop and Billy played third base for the Dorsey High School team that won 42 straight games, still the record for the most consecutive victories in Los Angeles high school history.

They also played together on the Crenshaw Post American Legion team that won the 1953 national championship. The final series was played in Detroit's old Briggs Stadium, which later became Tiger Stadium.

Sparky was good enough to sign a modest contract with the Brooklyn Dodgers and was immediately shipped to the minor leagues. Billy signed with the Boston Red Sox as what was then called a "Bonus

Baby." Baseball rules at the time dictated that any player signed to a contract equal to or above a specified monetary figure had to spend the first two years with the major-league club. Billy's signing bonus was $80,000—an incredible amount at the time.

Growing up, Consolo was the proverbial "man among boys." He could hit a ball farther, throw a ball harder, and beat the fastest kid in the city by at least a couple of steps—even without wearing shoes. He made everything look easy.

Sparky was mesmerized by all the talent Consolo could summon at will. If ever Sparky looked up to a player, Billy Consolo was the man.

Billy wound up as a 10-year major-league journeyman bouncing from one team to another. He finished with a .221 average. Sparky, of course, only made it through one major-league season as a player. For the 1959 Philadelphia Phillies he batted .218 with no home runs. But he did hit the ball to the warning track a couple of times . . . during batting practice.

Billy never reaped the benefits of the Major League Baseball Players Association's lucrative pension. He wound up as a barber in the shop the Red Sox purchased for his father as part of Billy's signing bonus.

While managing the Reds, Sparky inherited a strong coaching staff, which he kept. One of the conditions for signing with Detroit was that Consolo be hired as an infield coach. He served in that role throughout Sparky's 17 years with the Tigers. The pension he accrued under Sparky was worth far more than anything he had earned during his playing career.

Billy had a peculiar personality that ingratiated him with players and the rest of the coaching staff. He was a throwback to what is called baseball's "golden years" of the 1950s, when players had to scrap for one-year contracts and work during the off-seasons with almost any job they could find.

Today, practical jokes and a looseness in the clubhouse have been replaced by a more corporate atmosphere. Average players now draw CEO-type salaries, making the clubhouse feel completely different from those of the colorful '50s and '60s.

Billy had a droll sense of humor and a knack for spiking a laugh even in the middle of a six-game losing streak. He was the master at mixing a little bit of history with a splash of absurd hyperbole to make a team bus ride back to the hotel or the airport rock from the roar of laughter.

No Tigers player who served with Billy will forget the man with the whistle.

Billy strutted around the field and the clubhouse with a whistle strung on a chain around his neck. The players were too young to recognize the character, but he was Harpo Marx with a whistle instead of a horn. Billy used the whistle to draw the players' attention as well as to instigate some good old-fashioned baseball bitching.

During batting practice before a game, some of the more aggressive players would wrestle Billy to the ground and snatch away his whistle. Others watched for Billy to leave his whistle unattended in the locker and stole it before he returned.

They snatched whistles. They stomped them. They hid them. And once in a while they threw them into a urinal and told him where to find it. Billy must have bought whistles by the boxful. The next day he had a new one, and he tweeted it more than the day before.

"He was always that way," Sparky recalled. "Even as kids. That was just his way of getting everyone to calm down. He was loyal to a fault and I trusted him with my life."

Sparky knew Billy would be good for the team. He had big-league experience. He could give tips to the infielders. And his bizarre sense of humor was impossible to ignore.

Never married, Billy got a bonus by living rent-free in the basement of both homes Sparky and Carol owned during their stay in Detroit.

When my daughter, Andrea, was compiling invitations to celebrate her high school graduation, she put Sparky and Carol on the list. Then she asked, "What about the man who lives in the basement? Should I invite him?"

At first I was confused about whom she meant. Then I realized she had forgotten Billy's name . . . or maybe she had never known it.

"If you want to make sure that everybody gets a laugh, I'd suggest you invite Billy," I replied.

Sparky was always particular about those he kept closest. Those chosen were not wealthy. None was even a blip on the meter measuring social status. But their honesty and loyalty were as unshakable as Sparky's.

Because of his baseball accomplishments, his engaging personality, and his home in Southern California, Sparky was often invited to a variety of social events that involved many of the area's "beautiful people" in the movie and entertainment industry. While many people would pay for the opportunity to attend, Sparky remained unimpressed. Except for certain charity golf tournaments, Sparky chose never to attend such events.

"That other stuff ain't me, Daniel, my boy," he used to say. "If you gotta be seen with certain people to feel better about yourself, then you got yourself a big problem. I know who I am."

Through Sparky's selection of those closest to him, I learned to appreciate the real meaning of friendship. Friendship is measured from the inside, not by the outside package.

And the yardstick Sparky graciously gave me is one I'll treasure for life.

4

★

"Got Ya"

Even when we didn't see each other for a month to six weeks, our daily telephone conversations kept us current with all business affairs and personal matters. There were never any secrets.

It was always easy to slip into any story we wished to share.

Sitting in that so-familiar kitchen spawned one funny story after another. All had been told countless times before. But on that particular Sunday each tale carried a dash of magic impossible to explain.

I'd spin one yarn and Sparky would spin another. Then Sparky would follow each with a specific lesson that he wanted me to understand.

Stories about spring training carry their own particular charm. It's a magical time of year, filled with hope and humor that defy all logic. It's a season of hope for the good, the bad, and the mostly in-between. All sins of the past are forgiven, and the slates of all teams and players are wiped clean.

But seven weeks of baseball before a grueling 162-game regular season is considered, by most, to be as painfully unnecessary as a 10-month pregnancy.

Players don't need that much time. With year-round weight training and player salaries large enough for them to purchase a personal workout facility of their own, most are baseball ready by the end of the third week.

Managers don't need as much time as before. With the technology of computers that spit out excruciatingly detailed information on every player in every professional league, they need only a few good looks to determine if a young player is ready for the big time.

Members of the media are quick either to raise the expectations of readers back in the snow or to confirm their dismal off-season fears that no pennant will be flying come October. Usually by the end of the third week, writers are searching for fresh stories that only the regular season promises to bring.

Like Christmas stirs at least a seasonal spirit of goodwill, however, spring training still revives the anticipation of sun and better times to come.

Sparky, like everyone else, rejoiced in the spirit that the "wait till next year" gloom of the previous season was over. Spring training always comes with promises to keep.

As much as Sparky reveled in anticipation of a new season, there was always a speck inside of him that wasn't quite ready to leave his family and golfing buddies at home. Until that period of daily workouts was finished and the exhibition season started, Sparky remained uneasy. He needed some games to measure the amount of talent he had on the team each year.

Well before the end of spring training, he had a good idea about what to expect from each team. But whether it was good, bad, or simply mediocre, he got antsy for the regular season to start.

Almost predictably, by the end of the fourth week, time began to drag, and he searched for ways to make it move faster. Those last couple of weeks were like waiting for the six o'clock bus when it's already seven.

"Think of something we can pull off," he once told me. "We gotta liven things up around here."

Sparky's sense of humor was always sharper than the slider any of his pitchers could throw. Once in a while, he even liked a practical joke. The more he loved someone, the more mischievous he could be.

With Cincinnati coming to Lakeland for a night game, we decided to play a practical joke on Bernie Stowe, the Reds' crusty longtime equipment manager. He and Sparky had developed a lifetime friendship during Sparky's nine years with the Reds. Sparky told me to come up with a plan and have it ready before the Cincinnati bus showed up at the park. "And this one better be good," he added.

I called on Bill Tinsley, Lakeland's director of parks and recreation, who was responsible for stadium operations. I asked him to arrange for a couple of uniformed Lakeland police officers to orchestrate the plot I had devised.

The officers stood on either side of the gate that led to the home and visiting clubhouses down the right-field line. Sparky and I stood hidden behind the wall and to the sides of the officers. We struggled to keep our laughter silent as the plot began to unfold.

When the Cincinnati bus arrived, players hustled toward the clubhouse. As equipment was unloaded from beneath the bus, Stowe finally descended the steps. I quietly nudged the officer standing in front of me to let him know our "suspect" had arrived.

Just before Stowe stepped through the gate, both officers shifted to the center. There was no place for Stowe to move.

"Excuse me, sir," one of the officers said. "Are you Mr. Bernie Stowe?"

Stowe looked puzzled, but not nearly as bewildered as when the officer informed him about what they were going to do.

"I'm sorry, Mr. Stowe," he said. "You can't proceed any further."

With a ball game only an hour away from starting, Stowe was becoming more agitated than confused.

"What do ya mean I can't go in there?" he said. "I'm the equipment manager for the Cincinnati Reds. I got a game to take care of. This is my job. If you don't let me get that equipment set up it could be the end of my job."

Remaining somberly straight-faced, both officers completed the plan as if they had rehearsed it for a week.

"We know who you are, sir," one officer said. "That's why we're here. We recognize your face from the pictures we have on file."

By then Stowe was beginning to fume.

"What the hell kind of pictures are you talkin' about?" he shouted. "You don't have any pictures of me."

The officers didn't flinch. They were prepared to run the routine for as long as we let them.

"I'm sorry, sir," one said. "We're gonna have to take you downtown to headquarters. You've been positively identified in an armed robbery of a 7-Eleven store."

By that time, Sparky and I were bursting from laughter. We slipped from behind the wall, to the shock and relief of Stowe. He probably didn't know if he should smile or grab one of his bats and beat both of us over the head. But then he would have been run into jail for sure.

"You got one comin', buddy," he said with a smile, and hugged Sparky. "But when that time comes I'm gonna really have 'em put you behind bars. Don't you have a game to manage tonight?"

During another lull in spring training's dog days, we devised a skit to unleash on another unsuspecting friend of Sparky's who happened to be about 2,100 miles away at the time.

A half dozen of Sparky's friends from Thousand Oaks decided to visit him in spring training. They spent a week watching games in as many camps as possible. Of course, I got to know them and arranged for tickets at the various parks. Charlie Fieweger was the unofficial tour leader, and he never let me forget the incident during my trips to California.

About a week after they had gone home, Sparky decided it was time to spring the joke.

I called Fieweger with a greeting guaranteed to strike fear in every man's heart.

"Mr. Fieweger," I said seriously into the phone. "I'm Special Agent Joe Scoboni of the Internal Revenue Service. I don't want to alarm you, but we have some serious concerns about the tax claim you filed for your business."

The silence on the other end of the line was creepy. Then I actually thought I could hear sweat dripping down Charlie's forehead. Sparky began to laugh so hard, he briefly stepped out of his office so his friend at the other end of the line couldn't hear him.

"Please don't be alarmed, Mr. Fieweger," I continued. "Perhaps we can clear this matter up with as few penalties as possible. Please, get your material in order and I'll call you at the beginning of next week."

Still silence at the other end.

"Do you know who this is, Mr. Fieweger?" I asked while just about ready to end the charade.

"Yes sir," he replied. "You're Special Agent Joe Scoboni from the IRS."

I finished the conversation by telling him I would call at 10 a.m. on Monday.

Tears of laughter started to run down Sparky's cheeks. He took the receiver from my hand and placed it in its cradle.

Upon reflection, this was one joke we may have carried one step too far. It was a Friday afternoon when we placed the call. Charlie spent the whole weekend poring over the business records he had used for filing his return. When Carol heard of the escapade, Sparky and I received a long-distance admonishment that both of us deserved.

Nevertheless, the joke produced the best laugh we had for the day. And now even Charlie likes to smile about the incident.

Even a member of the coaching staff wasn't exempt from Sparky's mischief. A practical joker himself, Consolo targeted young players on the team. He designed a different scheme for each long bus ride to spring training games.

Sparky and I eventually decided it was time to play a joke on him.

I doctored a white sheet of paper to make it look like it had been mailed from the United States Selective Service System. The envelope looked alarmingly official. I even ran the envelope through a postage meter in the office. I then slipped it under the door of his hotel room so he couldn't miss it when he returned from the park.

The letter, of course, began with "Greetings." In typical, brisk military style, it stated that Billy was to report to the Long Beach, California, naval station for a preinduction physical to determine his readiness to serve in one of the branches of the United States armed services.

Upon opening the letter after returning from a road exhibition game, Billy frantically took the letter straight to Sparky's room. Sparky would know how to handle this situation, he thought. After entering the room, he handed the letter to his friend and manager. In the five minutes between reading the letter and reaching Sparky's room, Billy had lost the tan he had acquired during a month under the Florida sun.

"You're not gonna believe this one," he said, dumbfounded. "I'm gettin' drafted."

Sparky fought harder not to laugh than he did to coax a long drive down the left-field foul line to stay in fair territory as it sailed over the fence. He came close to blowing it, but managed to keep it inside.

Sparky told him that was ridiculous. Coaches couldn't be drafted by another baseball team.

"Baseball team, hell!" Billy screamed. "This ain't just any other team. It's the U.S. Army! Now how's that for some other team? How the hell can they draft a 56-year-old man? I got bad knees. A bad stomach. And now I'm flat-footed as a duck. I got enough trouble hitting fungoes straight at a guy, let alone shooting a rifle."

Sparky kept struggling hard not to laugh. He reminded Billy that the draft had been abolished several years ago.

"Maybe I fall under some retroactive rule," Billy said. "The government's full of red tape. Whatever the hell the deal is, you gotta write a letter for me. You gotta tell 'em the season's gonna start in another couple of weeks. Tell 'em you need me here. Tell 'em they really wouldn't want me anyway. They'll pay attention to a letter written by Sparky Anderson."

Sparky said he wasn't sure about that. It wasn't like trying to argue a point with an umpire. He told Billy he was going to call me. "Let Dan read the letter," he said. "He understands these things. See if it makes any sense to him."

By the time I reached the room, Sparky was rolling on the bed howling like a hyena who had just captured his meal for the day. Billy was standing outside the room with the door wide open. He was counting every second till I arrived. He shoved the letter into my hand.

"What are you two guys tryin' to do to me?" he asked. "I'm 56 years old. I coulda had a heart attack. I'm closer to drawin' Social Security than a check from the army. You two guys are losin' it!"

After Billy settled down, Sparky invited both of us to dinner. "You earned this one, Billy," he said. "At least you ain't goin' off to fight in no war."

At dinner Sparky said it was best to keep this incident strictly to ourselves. We'd had our laughs. It had got us through one more day. Billy wasn't going off to war. What more could we ask?

These are baseball stories. As much as a three-run home run with two out in the ninth, they are part of the fabric of the game.

Few in history recognized the import of such stories as much as Sparky. And perhaps only a handful shared them with such grace. They were good for the individual. They were good for the team.

Besides, no sane person would ever put a rifle into Billy's hands.

The magic of a hearty laugh is worth far more than a couple of aspirins for a headache.

"That's something everyone should remember," Sparky said. "More people oughta try it."

5

★

"I'm Wayne Gretzky"

Sparky was color-blind when it came to assessing people. From black to white to all shades in between, color never mattered to Sparky.

Neither did a person's occupation. He had met his share of so-called celebrities from all walks of life, and he waited to see how they treated people before becoming impressed. There were, however, certain situations that made his stomach twist and turn like a yoga master.

Sparky was nervous at breakfast the morning after I arrived at his home in 2007. First he dropped a cup of coffee. Then he mistakenly poured milk into a glass half filled with orange juice.

I had no clue about what was bothering him but was sure something serious was running through his mind. I knew it was better just to wait. He could never hold anything inside for long.

"We ain't playin' at Sunset today," he finally blurted.

Less than a five-minute drive from his home, Sunset Hills was the golf club where he had been an honorary member since long before his retirement from baseball. Except for Los Angeles area celebrity charity tournaments to which he was a popular invitee, he played almost exclusively at Sunset.

When I happened to be in town and he was scheduled to play in a celebrity event, he was always able to convince a tournament director to let me join his foursome. Because of his persuasive power, I am fortunate to have played the prestigious Riviera and Bel Air Country Clubs. But I always preferred Sunset Hills.

Though only a guest, I had played more rounds at Sunset than at all the courses combined around metropolitan Detroit. I knew the course well. I knew many of the members. And I knew we always had fun.

"So what?" I told him. "We'll get some errands run and mess around at the house. I'll take your money tomorrow."

Then I discovered the real nature of his concern.

"We're playin' all right," he said. "But not at Sunset. We're playin' Lake Sherwood out in Westlake."

Now his problem suddenly became mine.

I told him I wanted no part of Lake Sherwood. That was the course for the "beautiful people" and was way out of my league. I told him I would feel perfectly content relaxing at home and reading a book on the back patio until he returned.

"Just zip it," he said. "You ain't readin' no book. I'm nervous enough. Don't make it worse. I don't wanna go either. But if you don't go, I don't go, and I already promised both of us would be there. There ain't no way of gettin' outta this one. We're goin' in together and we'll get outta there together as soon as we're done."

Through charity events and special invitations, Sparky had already played some of the nation's most celebrated courses, including Augusta National, Oakland Hills, and most of the breathtaking courses that hug the Pacific Ocean up and down the coast of California.

He always felt like a rhinestone in a display of dazzling diamonds on such courses, which thrive on conspicuous opulence. He enjoyed being the rhinestone.

He also enjoyed regular courses where mere mortals came to play. Now he had to deal with Lake Sherwood, that small slice of heaven with its lush green hills speckled with $25 million mansions surrounding the gorgeous course.

The community was developed by multibillionaire David H. Murdock. Sparky felt it was out of his league as much as I did that it was out of mine.

Though neither of us had ever been to the course, we had seen it several times on television when Tiger Woods and the rest of the professional tour players strutted proudly down the lush green fairways.

Though only a 30-minute drive from Sparky's house, it was anything but a workingman's course!

Over the years, Sparky had courteously declined several invitations from former major-league player Lenny Dykstra to play there. I immediately wondered how Dykstra had even become a member. Reluctantly, this time Sparky finally had to accept. A golfing buddy of Dykstra's wanted very much to meet Sparky.

Although neither Sparky nor I had ever met Dykstra's buddy, he certainly was no stranger. He just happened to own one of those $25 million mansions, along with almost every scoring record in National Hockey League history.

The mansion and records belonged to Wayne Gretzky, the one they call "the Great One." He was a longtime Sparky fan and wanted the opportunity to meet him.

The summer temperature was rising quickly even before we left home. We debated whether shorts were allowed on such a prestigious course as Lake Sherwood. Just before leaving, Carol suggested we throw our shorts into the trunk just in case they were permitted.

At a guard shack at the tip of a driveway that must have wound a par-5 yardage distance from the clubhouse, we stopped the car.

"Good morning, Sparky," the smiling attendant greeted us. "Your party is waiting for you. We hope you enjoy your experience at Lake Sherwood."

We looked at each other knowing the same thought was running through each of our minds: We'll enjoy it more on our trip out of the driveway.

We thanked the young man and asked: "By the way, are shorts allowed on this course?"

Again he smiled and said: "Of course."

He offered to park the car, but Sparky assured him we could handle it ourselves.

"An honor to meet you, Sparky," the attendant said.

Sparky smiled and shook his hand. With the course officially closed for the day, there was a sea of available spaces next to the shack. Sparky gunned the engine and drove so far down the lane that it would have taken a drive and a 4-iron to reach us.

I knew what he was doing. We were going to change into our shorts behind the far end of the car. Just as we were zipping up, a caddy drove up in a golf cart and said we were welcome to change in the locker room. Like a couple of boys caught with their hands in the cookie jar, we told him everything was all right.

"At least allow me to take your clubs and give you a ride to the driving range," the young man offered.

Sparky glanced at me before making a decision. He wanted no part of becoming a show.

"Take the clubs," he said. "We'll walk. Gotta loosen up."

We placed our bags on the cart, and each of us handed him $5 for his courtesy.

"There goes our dinner at Burger King tonight," I joked.

When we arrived at the range, our clubs were standing next to two adjacent tees. The head cover of each driver had already been removed. If they offered any more courtesies, they'd have someone hitting our shots for us. That was one courtesy I would have readily accepted.

"So this is how they do it in the big time," I joked with Sparky. "Here's another fine mess you've gotten us into."

He laughed and then spotted Dykstra on the putting green. He went to tell him we were ready to go whenever they were.

I was busy spraying practice drives all over the range when I heard someone from behind calling my name. Whom could I possibly know here? I quickly tried to recall if perhaps I had given my name to the caddy on the cart.

"Good morning, Dan," the unfamiliar voice said. "I'm Wayne Gretzky."

As we shook hands I told him there was no need to tell me who he was. I just wondered how he knew my name.

Gretzky wouldn't have known me from Joe Palooka without having taken the time to find out before we arrived whom Sparky had brought to play in the group. Immediately I was impressed by the courtesy and professionalism of the celebrated figure. I don't know much about hockey, but every sports fan at least knows Gretzky's name.

I escorted Gretzky to introduce him to Sparky, who greeted him the same way Gretzky had greeted me.

"I know who you are, Sparky," Gretzky said. "I used to watch you when I was growing up. It's such an honor to meet you. I hope you like the course. I've been looking forward to this day for a long time."

Along with Dykstra was former Gretzky teammate and longtime friend Rick Tocchet. With the course closed except for us, we played a fivesome and drove three carts. Even if the course had been open, was there any starter in America that would refuse an extra player in a group that featured Sparky and Gretzky? Dykstra rode alone while Gretzky and Tocchet shared a cart.

"You guys hit first," Sparky said as we arrived on the first tee. "You guys'll be a shopping mall ahead of us when your drives finally land. We got your backside covered. We promise not to hit you with our second shots. Matter of fact, we might be hackin' two or three more times before we say hello again."

Throughout the round, Dykstra and Tocchet challenged each other with drives halfway up to Santa Barbara. Gretzky didn't hit quite that far, but he was able to stand patiently in the fairway while the two big hitters searched for their balls in woods, water, and mountain brush.

Sparky and I delivered as promised. We covered their backs even though we tested plenty of woods and a fair share of water ourselves before returning to their sight lines.

Once in a while we switched riders between carts. The smile on Gretzky's face while riding with Sparky was worth all of the apprehension we had endured earlier in the day.

Born and raised in Brantford, Ontario, Canada, Gretzky loved baseball and was a Tigers fan while growing up. Detroit's southern border is the Detroit River. On the opposite side of the river is Windsor,

Ontario, Canada, accessible by bridge or tunnel. It's the only spot in America where one travels south to enter Canada.

Sparky regaled him with stories about his minor-league days playing in Montreal and from when he was the player-manager for Toronto when the team played in the International League. "I had nothing but good times when I played in Canada," Sparky said. "Minor league or major league, I loved going to those cities. Especially Toronto. The people there are always so nice and polite."

Sparky told him he had met Gordie Howe several times. Howe is the hockey legend who held all of the scoring records till Gretzky passed him.

"The thing I like about you hockey guys is that you ain't no sissies," Sparky said. "You guys get clobbered into the boards, get a puck to the teeth or a skate across the face, and you're ready to go back on the ice on your line's next turn."

Gretzky accepted the compliment and simply said that's the way the game was meant to be played.

"The boys in my game are a little bit different," Sparky continued. "Some of 'em get a hangnail and wanna go on the disabled list for a couple of weeks. I used to ask some if they ever saw a hockey game in their whole lives. I wondered if they knew what toughing it out really means."

The yarns rolled on and on and on. Sparky knew that was why he'd been invited. And he delivered. It was impossible for Sparky to let even the smallest audience down.

I rode with Gretzky for a couple of holes, and he peppered me with questions about Sparky. Gretzky wondered how he maintained his reputation for being so nice even in retirement. "Doesn't he ever get tired of all the commotion wherever he goes?" he asked. "He's been out of the game for a while and he's just as popular now as he was when he managed."

I smiled at Gretzky and told him that was easy to answer. I was impressed by his sincerity and admiration for Sparky.

"Just watch him," I said. "You'll see. Watch how he treats all the workers here at your club. He won't treat them any differently than the way he treats you guys. The stock boy at the market where he shops gets the same treatment as the president of the United States. And he's met four of them. And one pope."

On the 14th tee, with the sun now scorching, four Mexican American grounds crew workers backed to the side while we teed off. Gretzky went to the cooler in the back of his cart and pulled out four bottles of soda for the workers to share. They smiled and nodded profusely, obviously in appreciation for the cold drinks and in recognition of two legitimate sports legends.

"Lemme tell you something, Daniel," Sparky told me as we drove down the fairway for a change. "This guy is for real. What he did for those workers was the real deal. He didn't do that for no show. That's why he is who he is. He ain't no different than you or me. He remembers where he came from."

It was of no particular interest to anyone in the group but me, but on the next tee my shoulders, arms, hips, and legs accidentally assumed a totally unfamiliar position. I somehow managed to clothesline a drive dead center down the fairway. It didn't stop rolling till it slid past Gretzky's drive. Not by more than the length of a wedge but, nonetheless, legitimately past. Gretzky complimented the drive and urged me not to forget how well I had used my body.

My memory, obviously, didn't do me any favors. During my second shot, my shoulders, arms, hips, and legs returned to their familiar disjointed position. I followed my dream drive with a customary slice into the woods. Riding the cart toward the green, I ordered Sparky to make me a promise: "I want a line on my tombstone that says I outdrove Wayne Gretzky on one hole."

"Do you want me to say anything about the other 17 holes?" he cracked.

When we finally finished the round, Gretzky invited us to join him in the dining room to share cold drinks and sandwiches while we swapped lies about our game.

Now it didn't matter that Sparky couldn't stay within 20 shots of Gretzky, Dykstra, and Tocchet. It was his turn to shine by telling one story after another that had all three laughing too hard to finish their sandwiches.

Walking back to the car, we agreed that our apprehension had been needlessly overexaggerated. So what if the golf course was one of the world's most prestigious? And who cared if for the day it featured two of sports' most legitimate legends?

We'd just been five guys playing a round in the sun and sharing some laughs along the way. That's what made it special.

"It's so easy when you're treated right by people," Sparky said. "Don't ever forget that, Daniel, my boy."

Of course, Sparky earned that treatment by practicing it himself.

We didn't worry about having to change back into our long pants for the ride home. It had been a good day. The next day we'd be back at Sunset. Sparky could tell the boys about how well we had been treated. And I could tell them about one particular drive.

6

★

Who's He?

As we continued to fire up one story after another, Sparky smiled as he recalled one that served as a reminder that everyone—once in a while—needs a reality check.

Even himself.

Sparky was restlessly pacing his room in the Minneapolis Hyatt Regency Hotel that Wednesday morning before the Tigers played the Minnesota Twins in the first game of the 1987 American League Championship Series.

We had arrived in Minneapolis the day before, and Sparky was still euphoric about his overachieving team, which now stood only four victories away from playing in another World Series.

The Tigers had capped a historic final week of the regular season by shutting out the Toronto Blue Jays, 1–0, on the last day of the regular season. The Tigers, in fact, had swept the last three games with Toronto in overcoming a $3^{1}/2$-game deficit in that last week.

The game that evening was scheduled for seven o'clock, and Sparky couldn't bear to be trapped in a hotel room all day. We had coffee and doughnuts in his room at sunrise. Then he started pacing while I completed the rest of my public relations preparations in the adjoining room.

This was a special team for Sparky. It didn't possess the talent that a lot of his former teams had enjoyed. It wasn't the best team in the American League, perhaps not even in its division.

But it did possess the one quality that Sparky admired most about a team. Even when down, it simply refused to quit. "I respect that 1987 team as much as any team I ever managed," he always said. "Even the three that won a World Series."

A little before noon he walked into my room and asked why I couldn't do my work at the ballpark. I said I could.

"Then let's get the hell out of here," he said. "Better to be at the ballpark than locked up here in a hotel room."

Sparky didn't like the Metrodome. No baseball purist did. The infield and outfield carpet was as hard as ice. Strips of steel that supported the roof occasionally got in the way of pop-ups and fly balls. The stadium was built more for football. Or maybe a county fair. Too many unpredictable things that didn't bear any semblance of real baseball regularly occurred during almost every game.

But he did enjoy Minneapolis. He liked the neatness of the downtown area and a friendliness in the people that suggested a strong work ethic. Until he was nine, Sparky lived in Bridgewater, South Dakota. Minneapolis was the city that made him think most about home.

More often than not over the years, we had walked from the hotel to the Metrodome. This time he suggested we take a cab. He was anxious to get there. He always felt more at home wearing his baseball undershirt and knickers and making small talk in a clubhouse than he did being trapped inside of a hotel room.

We jumped into the first cab in line outside the hotel lobby. It was far too early for any rush of traffic, and the park was almost visible from where we began. A few minutes later, we were at the service entrance to the park, ready to go to work.

Neither Sparky nor I liked taking a cab for this short distance. We didn't like pulling a cabbie out of line and perhaps forcing him to miss a far more profitable trip to the airport or maybe to St. Paul.

I handed the driver three $5 bills, which amounted to a tip more than three times the fare. He looked at me and tried to hand one of the fives back before I told him it belonged to him.

"Big-time spender," Sparky teased.

"You should talk," I said. "It's the playoffs. The driver deserves a little something extra out of this too."

Sparky smiled at the thought of one of his recurring lessons taking seed. Besides, that's what making it to the playoffs meant . . . even to a PR guy.

Sparky went to the clubhouse, and I walked up to the press box to finish my work. By the time I returned to the field, he was already holding court with a herd of media members, who could never quite get their fill of colorful Sparky quotes.

The game wasn't as much fun as his pregame sideshow. After the Tigers took a 5–4 lead with two runs in the top of the eighth, the Twins rallied for four in the bottom half of the inning and held on for an 8–5 victory.

The following morning we followed pretty much the same routine as we had the day before. This time Sparky was even more restless, so we left even earlier for the cab to the park. The maintenance crew would still be cleaning some of the sections from the previous night's game. Once we were seated in the back of the cab, I nudged Sparky and whispered: "This is the same driver we had yesterday."

We both winked and read each other's mind.

We began to speak boldly, and loudly, about how the Tigers were going to manhandle the Twins that night.

"Gibby's gonna hit a ball straight through that roof of the dome," Sparky started.

"All the way to St. Paul," I replied.

"They'll be dancin' in the streets of Detroit," Sparky said.

"And you'll be playin' the music," I added.

The driver said nothing. He kept his eyes straight ahead.

"The Twins will run through so many pitchers, they'll have to sign a couple of fans from the stands to finish the ninth inning," Sparky said.

"Those guys from the stands are probably better than the whole

Minnesota staff," I answered. "I hope they don't forget to bring them all to Detroit."

We kept spewing such nonsensical bravado all the way till arriving at the service gate of the park. By now, we thought, the driver should be fuming. A few blocks back, we had expected him to stop the cab and order us to leave for having hurled so many insults at the home-town team.

Before stepping out of the cab, I tapped the driver on the shoulder, smiled, and told him to look at the face of my friend. "Do you know who this is?" I asked, expecting him to recognize Sparky and appreci-ate the humor of our obviously inflated boasting.

He stared straight at Sparky's face and then looked squarely at me. "I don't know who he is, but you're the guy who gave me the big tip yesterday," he said.

Sparky and I broke into laughter that must have made the driver hope we would keep coming back to him every day for the rest of the week. It made the long afternoon a little bit lighter. We thanked him for his honesty and again I handed him three $5 bills. We told him we wished the Twins good luck . . . and the Tigers even more.

As soon as the media started to arrive later in the afternoon, Sparky began to spread the story of the doubleheader cab ride with the most serious driver in Minneapolis. Each time he told it, the tip I had given the driver rose by a couple of bucks.

That's what good baseball stories are about. Just like mustard on a hot dog. Each extra dab makes it taste just a little bit better.

Of course, history proves that no amount of luck would have helped us that night. The Twins jumped to a 3–2 lead in the second inning and nursed the lead all the way to a 6–3 victory. The Tigers held on for a 7–6 victory in Game 3 back in Detroit. But the Twins bounced back with a 5–3 victory in Game 4 and sealed the American League pennant with a 9–5 win in Game 5.

After the game, Sparky walked across the infield toward the rau-cous Minnesota clubhouse. It's the loneliest walk any manager makes. Sparky couldn't let the Twins leave town without congratulating manager Tom Kelly. He shook his hand, wished him good luck in the World Series, and slapped a few Twins players on the back for playing such a good series. "Make the American League proud in the World Series," he told them. "You guys sure made believers out of us."

Sparky never took any loss easily. He always found something he thought he should have done differently. That's a bitter trip across the diamond for any manager to make. But Sparky always knew the right thing to do.

Despite the loss, Sparky was ebullient over the guts and determination his team had displayed throughout the entire season. He had managed two Cincinnati teams and one Detroit team to World Championships. Yet he was as proud of this particular team as he was of any of his winners.

"In all honesty, this club had no business going as far as it did," he said. "That's why I'm so proud of them. They were so low early in the season, they had to look up just to tie their shoes. But they never gave up."

Sparky always downplayed his role in the resurrection. It was not mere coincidence, though, that it started on his cue.

On May 11, the team was in sixth place, 9½ games out of first with an 11-19 record. Before the game against the California Angels, he stopped in my office and told me to come down to the field to watch his appearance on the TV pregame show.

"The town's gonna love me or think I really flew the coop," he said, "but I'm gonna shake things up. We gotta do somethin' to get this thing going."

When asked by the show's host to explain what was wrong with the team, Sparky responded "not to worry."

"By the end of the year, you guys are gonna love this team," he promised. "We're goin' all the way to the playoffs."

There may have been a collective gasp by everybody watching the show. It didn't matter what anyone thought. The players certainly responded to their manager's confidence and rolled to an improbable finish no one could have imagined.

The Tigers won six straight and 13 of their next 15 games to roar back into contention.

"That last week of the regular season was as good as anybody in the game has ever seen," Sparky said.

It wasn't merely good. It was miraculous.

The Tigers dropped three straight games in Toronto the next-to-last weekend to fall $3^1/_2$ games behind the first-place Blue Jays. They won the final game of that series in the 13th inning after Kirk Gibson homered in the ninth to tie the score. With seven games left they were $2^1/_2$ games behind. Despite only splitting four games with Baltimore, they still trailed Toronto by only one game when the Blue Jays visited Detroit for the last three games of the season.

The Tigers took the first game, 4–3, to tie for the lead. They needed 12 innings for a 3–2 victory in the second to go one game up. The final-game masterpiece was by Frank Tanana, a 1–0 complete-game shutout over Jimmy Key, who also fired a complete game.

All seven games of those season-ending series with the Blue Jays were determined by one run. The late-season surge by the Tigers lifted them to a 98-64 won-lost record, best in the game.

Sparky always maintained that players—not the manager—win games. But no manager simply stumbles into three straight one-run victories to clinch a division title without making all the right decisions to put his players in a position to win.

Not Mack. Not McGraw. Not Stengel. Not even Harry Houdini.

Without a doubt, that season stands as the most magnificent performance of determination I have ever seen.

Each spring training, Sparky lectured the team about playing every game as if it would be the last. "I promise all of you," he said, "that if you put every ounce of talent into every game you play, once you retire you'll never want to go to another ball game again. You won't have anything left because you gave everything you had."

The 1987 team certainly packed their bags after the season with every ounce of energy expended.

And an unsuspecting Minneapolis cabdriver did fairly well himself in two quick rides to the ballpark in October.

"Always remember, Daniel, my boy, you and I were blessed," he said. "There'd be a line a mile and a half long for either one of our jobs. The other guys in life need a break once in a while too. You ain't never gonna see that cabdriver's face again. But you'll always remember how happy you made him feel even for one simple moment. That's worth a helluva lot more than any amount of money you could've given him."

As we talked about that story for the final time, I was struck by the prophetic accuracy of what Sparky had told me almost 25 years ago.

I have forgotten that cabdriver's face. But I remember his surprised expression of gratitude. Not simply for the money. It certainly wasn't enough to change his life.

But he did appreciate the kindness of two strangers.

That's what Sparky wanted me to remember. That's how he made each lesson so easy to learn.

7

★

Maybe One Kid

I used to tease Sparky a lot about all the autographs he signed. And I did it again at the kitchen table on that Sunday afternoon, simply to make everything seem normal. "If anyone anywhere in the United States doesn't have one of your signatures, then that person must be living in a cave somewhere in Montana," I joked.

Sparky smiled and gently nodded his head. "It's all part of the program, Daniel, my boy," he said. "It's all part of it."

Sparky had a problem refusing almost any autograph request in almost any situation. He understood that autograph collecting and the memorabilia industry had exploded into what now may be a billion-dollar-a-year bonanza.

He just couldn't say no.

"What if it's for a kid or for a real fan who wants to keep it forever?" he would ask. "Sometimes the smallest thing done by a stranger turns out to be the biggest part of someone else's life."

And that was where the argument would always end.

Because of Sparky's unmistakable physical features and genuinely gracious personality, he was a magnet for autograph collectors of all degrees. It didn't matter which city or the time of day. It was impossible to travel anywhere without him being approached by any number of people seeking signatures on all kinds of objects.

New York, unsurprisingly, provided some of the more comical situations.

It started at the corner where the lower lobby of the Grand Hyatt Hotel turned dramatically into the Grand Central train station with its maze of subway lines radiating out to the far reaches of New York City.

A designated scout, somewhere between 13 and 16 years old, was usually stationed at the tip of the turn and charged with alerting the rest of his crew at the first sighting of their prime target.

This crew knew every visiting baseball team that stayed at the Grand Hyatt. They also knew the monetary values attached to the signatures of each player on all the teams.

"Here he comes . . . here he comes," the streetwise urchin blurted to his experienced and relentless gang hidden just out of sight. "Here comes Sparky. Here comes the Man." As if peeling themselves from the walls of the magnificent building, they surrounded Sparky, and the pleading began.

"Sign my card, Sparky . . . can ya please sign my card?" the first one almost whined. "I love you, Sparky. I love you."

"Sparky, how 'bout this ball . . . can ya sign this ball?" said the next. "On the sweet spot, Sparky . . . on the sweet spot."

There were about a dozen urchins that looked like they had just stepped out of a Bowery Boys movie. They carried photos, baseball cards, baseballs, snapshots, caps, batting helmets, and gloves. A couple had sparkling white 3-by-5-inch index cards that they carefully protected from dirt and damage.

I felt like a pulling guard walking in front of Sparky, trying to keep our route to the token machine as clear as possible. Once inside the terminal, we moved quickly to the platform for the D train and our underground adventure to Yankee Stadium.

Sparky used to spend slightly more time with the relentless autograph hounds before the first game of a normal three-game series. He made a quick mental snapshot of the face attached to each youngster clamoring for his signature. If he happened to recognize a face from the day before, he selected a request from one he didn't remember.

That didn't stop the more persistent of the bunch, but Sparky tried to accommodate as many fresh faces as possible first. Sparky knew the city. He knew the routine. Those supposedly loyal Sparky fans were selling their wares even before leaving the building.

It was comical, in fact, to spot an older figure standing in the shadows just outside the turnstiles. He was collecting all of the signed items and depositing them carefully in a burlap sack. He paid a couple of bucks for each signed item that his young, ragtag crew could collect. Quite a bargain for the faceless figure who could easily sell each of his purchases for anywhere between $20 and $50, depending on the item.

Sparky was wise to the system and certainly didn't enjoy the hassle.

"You can't con a con man," he liked to remind me. "And you know better than anyone, I put the *c* in con."

He was always concerned, though, about the possibility of one sincerely innocent kid not getting an autograph he was sure to cherish.

When we made it onto a train, he had cleared the first hurdle. The subway ride to Yankee Stadium was always filled with the promise of myriad possibilities, though. On one occasion, after Sparky had been recognized by a handful of passengers, the entire crowded car erupted into a seated and standing ovation.

"When's George [Steinbrenner] gonna bring you here, Sparky?" one shouted. "We want you here."

Sparky would smile and then compliment the Yankee manager of the moment as if that manager were a reincarnation of Casey Stengel himself. Sparky would have to sign a couple of tabloids, and then he'd kick me as a signal to tell the people he couldn't sign anymore.

It was the kind of reception any New York politician only dreams about.

Riding the subway in New York with Sparky was always one step away from chaos or comedy.

Early on one sun-filled Sunday summer morning, the train was sparsely filled and each of us had a bench to himself. The trip was hauntingly peaceful and would have gotten us to the Stadium in record time except for one unexpected situation. The train broke down.

At the 110th Street exit!

In the early morning, only a handful of people were walking the sidewalks. For blocks the streets looked naked. No car horns were blaring. There was barely a sound. This was not the city we had come to know.

Standing there in broad daylight felt a little spooky. After all, how many times does someone like Sparky pop out of a stalled subway car in the middle of Harlem?

I quickly scoured the streets for a taxi I knew wouldn't magically appear from around the corner. With his white hair a lightning rod for any unexpected visitor, I told Sparky to remain under the awning of a closed store. I planned to walk a few blocks up 110th Street to search for any misplaced taxi.

By the time I returned, Sparky had wandered to the corner. I asked if he intended to walk the next 51 blocks to Yankee Stadium.

"No," he said. "But I had to move around somewhere. You know I just can't stand in one place."

Approaching quickly from a block away, a young African American gentleman, dressed as if he was going to a church service, calmly greeted us. He probably wondered what we were doing in the neighborhood and surmised that we were looking for the quickest way out.

He said we would be waiting till tomorrow for any regular cab to drive by. He told us to remain where we were standing. He would hail an unmarked livery cab to take us to the park.

"Regular cabs don't roam the streets in this neighborhood," he said. "Just give me a minute and we'll get you a ride."

A few moments later he had an unmarked vehicle waiting at the curb. Sparky pulled out a $10 bill and offered it to the young man for his courtesy.

"Sorry, sir," he said. "I just can't accept it. You've already given me so much pleasure over the years. Thank you, Sparky."

Sparky had tucked the $10 bill tightly into the palm of his right hand. When he shook the young man's hand to thank him, he removed his own hand quickly to leave the bill in our rescuer's hand. He told the driver to take off immediately. As we resumed the most humorously calamitous ride to the ballpark either of us had ever made, I looked through the rear window to see the man waving with the $10 bill in hand.

Even on those stuffed streets of New York, it was impossible for Sparky to hide. He shook a lot of hands. Once in a while, he took time to pick up a child in his arms to make a memory for mama and papa they would never forget.

It's also impossible to total the amount of money Sparky pulled from his pocket to help a street person get through the day.

We were searching for a coffee shop early one morning on 42nd Street near Broadway. A blind man was sitting with his back propped against the wall of a building whose tip seemed to stretch into a cloud.

The man was playing disjointed chords on a harmonica that looked like it had belonged to Gabby Hayes in one of the old-time Roy Rogers Westerns. Behind his large, dark horn-rimmed sunglasses, his eyes were fixed straight ahead. His jacket was torn at the shoulders and all the buttons were missing. There were holes in the soles of each shoe, and his pants stretched only to the middle of his shins. A hat containing a handful of coins was surrounded by his curled legs.

Sparky reached into his pocket and dropped two $1 bills onto the change. Obviously, there was no noise from the paper money, but as we continued to walk, the harmonica stopped playing.

"Thank you, Mr. Sparky," we heard the man's voice for the first time.

Turning around, Sparky asked how he knew it was him.

"I gots my feelings, Mr. Sparky," he said. "I gots my feelings."

We looked at each other for a moment and then Sparky smiled.

"It don't matter if he can see or not," Sparky said. "The man does have feelings. And he's only doing what he has to do."

On the way back to the hotel, Sparky dropped a dollar bill into another beggar's cup. This time the contribution drew only a nod of the head.

"Don't you think that's enough for today?" I asked him.

Sparky laughed. He was feeling good.

"I wish I could put a little something into every beggar's hat in the city," he said.

"Then you better get that big contract from Steinbrenner because that line's gonna run from the Bronx to the Bowery," I said.

He nodded and winked. "We're lucky, Daniel, my boy," he said. "We certainly are lucky."

I winked back. "And don't you ever forget it," I said.

Once in a while I think about all those strangers we met on the streets of so many cities across the United States. Do they still remember the funny man with white hair who looked like someone everybody knew? Do they remember that playful smile and the bounce in his step? Do they remember the sparkle in his eye that could light up a cloudy afternoon?

I won't forget the lesson Sparky taught me. There's no greater gift than a smile straight from the heart. Sometimes just a nod of the head or the wink of an eye can make even a stranger feel that he belongs. It was always so easy for Sparky. And it always came straight from the heart.

8

A Piano?

Sparky rose from his chair in the kitchen and walked into the family room to stretch his legs. Neither of us was ready to stop telling stories. There were still too many to share, too many laughs to enjoy.

After a short break, I asked a simple four-word question: "What about the piano?"

That was all we needed to start us laughing and shaking our heads in disbelief.

Over our major-league careers, we had spent countless nights in some of the nation's finest hotels. None, however, compared to the one on our one-night stay in Washington, D.C.

On our way north from spring training in 1994, we played a day exhibition game in Richmond, Virginia. We then bused to Washington for a scheduled two-game series with Milwaukee before returning to Detroit for the start of the regular season.

It was still dusk when the bus pulled into the heart of the capital, and we watched night falling upon all the monuments and buildings that we normally see only on TV or in the newspapers. Just a couple of blocks after having passed the White House, the bus driver turned left onto a street and stopped in front of the lobby of the Marriott Hotel, where we were scheduled to stay.

Even the veteran players were impressed by the neighborhood.

After getting our keys from the traveling secretary, we discovered that the elevator to Sparky's room was different from those for the rest of the team. The key featured a button to only one floor.

When we reached the room, we understood why.

After flipping a light switch we were convinced a mistake had been made. A big mistake. The room resembled a condo more than a hotel suite. Not a regular condo, but rather a princely one quite suitable to host royalty.

To either side of the foyer was a living area large enough to host a substantial New Year's Eve party. Both rooms, of course, featured wet bars. One of the rooms offered a breakfast facility complete with a full set of silverware and handsomely painted glassware that included plates, bowls, cups, and an assortment of drinking glasses.

A bedroom was situated on the far side of either living area. But the biggest surprise came when Sparky thought he was opening the door to his bedroom.

"What the hell is this piano doing in my bedroom?" I heard him scream from what seemed to be a city block away.

I quickly scurried across all the rooms to discover that there was, indeed, a baby grand sitting in the corner of the room.

"That's definitely a piano," I assured him. "But you haven't even reached your bedroom yet. I think it's one more door down."

He moved to the next door and peeked inside. It was a bedroom, complete with a canopy bed.

"I can't play no piano," he said. "And how am I supposed to sleep with an umbrella over my head?"

We both laughed at the conspicuous ostentation and wondered how a pair of blue collars wound up in a place like this.

"The opulence of this place is suffocating," I said.

"I don't know nothin' about no opulence, but if it means stickin' tuxedos on a couple of pigs then we got a whole lotta opulence here," he said.

Sparky insisted that I call the coaches. They had to see our modest accommodations for the night.

"Tell 'em we gotta have a meeting," he said. "Don't say nothin' about the room, but get 'em up here as soon as you can."

One by one they arrived at the room, and one by one jaws dropped. As soon as the coaches left for dinner, Sparky said it was dinnertime for us, too.

"Did you get a peek at any of our regular places on the bus ride?" he asked.

I knew what he meant and told him I had spotted one just down the block. Fifteen minutes later I returned with a couple of Whoppers and two small bags of fries from the Burger King. We ate in the dining area, but didn't dirty any plates or silverware.

"If we can finish the season as high as the rent is for this room, we're gonna have a helluva year," I said.

We finished the season in fifth place, 18 games out of first. But no one in either league had a room like ours for a night. And the Whoppers and fries were delicious.

Sparky was a connoisseur of simplicity. He preferred basics without any frills. Hamburgers over steaks. Sneakers over dress shoes. A reliable 15-year-old scratched and dented Ford over a sparkling new luxury car—especially any foreign brand.

Saturday nights after day games were the only times we left our rooms on the road to have dinner with the coaches.

These were special times. One of the best managers in the history of the game with three coaches who had also played in the major leagues. And then there was me. Suffice it to say I rarely spoke until spoken to.

We were usually seated by seven o'clock and back in our rooms by nine. Dinners after a victory, obviously, were considerably more enjoyable than those after a loss.

It's a futile flight of fancy to think we had become familiar with all the finer restaurants of New York, Boston, Chicago, San Francisco, and the rest of the big-league cities. Once in a while, almost by accident, we did drop in on one. But our visits to the inflated "other side" of town were far more rare than a 10-game winning streak.

We preferred, instead, more inconspicuous places where a roomy table tucked into a corner could handle a handful of regular guys who chose anonymity over celebrity. We all had reached that age where any excitement was best left at the ballpark.

As often as possible we walked to and from the restaurant. When savoring victory, it felt good to walk on a warm summer night with the expectation of the next day's game. Walking also slightly soothed the sting of defeat.

Although Sparky and I actually preferred eating dinner in his room, he realized the importance of sharing a meal with the coaches, who did most of their work anonymously. Some opinions are more easily shared in offbeat privacy than in a clubhouse.

"Don't ever forget the guys who get you to where you got," Sparky told me. "Coaches don't get the headlines. They just do the work."

Operating from a club expense account, Sparky always picked up the bill and humorously reminded us about his supposed generosity. "Keep your meal money in your pockets, boys," he would always tease. "You can only say nice things about the old white-haired guy who's diggin' into the wallet tonight."

Of course, he always enjoyed it when the owner of an establishment picked up the tab after recognizing him. "The old guy's still got it," he would say kiddingly. He'd then sign a stack of napkins, which the owner would give to his preferred customers.

Dining with the coaches featured an established menu of meal conversation. How come the front office doesn't get us another pitcher? When are they gonna send us the left-handed hitter we need? Can any pitcher in our whole system throw the ball over the plate?

Even though the game has changed with its gallop into the corporate world, some parts of it always remain the same.

The best part about those dinners was listening to the baseball yarns that only the old-timers could spin. By the time they finished with the rerun stories about their playing careers, each one wound up with a batting average at least 30 points higher than what is recorded in the books. That's what old baseball yarns do. They're designed to make you feel good.

Sparky rarely contributed to those stories. This was a time for the coaches to enjoy. He was always content to listen and laugh.

I never tired of listening to Dick Tracewski. Known by everyone in baseball simply as "Trixie," he spent 30 years in the Tigers' organization as a player, minor-league manager, and major-league coach. He broke into professional baseball with the Brooklyn Dodgers organization and played for the Dodgers after their move to Los Angeles, from 1962 through 1965.

The Dodgers were a novelty to the movie stars and entertainers of Hollywood after their historic move to Los Angeles in 1959. After his promotion to the big-league club, Trixie befriended Roy Rogers and once spent five days at his ranch in Apple Valley, California.

He met entertainment luminaries such as Frank Sinatra, Dean Martin, Sammy Davis Jr., Doris Day, and Angie Dickinson. He never tired of repeating the same stories, and we never tired of smiling at his enthusiasm.

Alex Grammas was a former big-league player and manager. He got close to Sparky while a coach for him with the Cincinnati Reds. Grammas always conceded that the current players were physically stronger than those when he played. He could never quite understand, though, why they couldn't seem to master the fundamentals of the game.

Billy Consolo was the only one to have played with, arguably, the best hitter in the history of the game. Having signed an eye-popping bonus contract with the Boston Red Sox after graduating from high school in 1953, he woke up one morning as a teammate of the immortal Ted Williams.

We always loved to hear stories about Williams that only Consolo could tell. Any kind of story and as many times as Consolo wanted to tell it. Accordingly, Consolo loved to tell them night after night.

It never mattered if some were embellished after the first few times around the dinner table. If something was humanly possible to do with hitting, Williams had probably done it . . . or at least could have, given the opportunity.

I, of course, just listened and learned at those dinners. Sparky chattered more when we were losing than when we happened to be on a winning streak.

In the spring and summer we talked about golf. We turned to football in the fall. An upcoming championship fight always made for a heated dinner conversation. Mostly, though, we talked about baseball, comparing opposing personnel to the players on our roster.

After most night games, when players scattered for a couple of beers and a sandwich before going to bed, Sparky and I returned to our rooms for a late-night session with the TV.

Any glamorous nightlife belonged to the young. We were well past the age of strutting through any vibrant downtown, acting like big leaguers regardless of where we stood in the standings.

Sparky and I shared the manager's suite he was always given. A bedroom on either side of a comfortable living room made for memorable conversations that often carried past midnight.

These were precious times of learning for me. I discovered many nuances of the game that I hadn't even known existed. After a win or a loss, Sparky tested me about certain subtle situations that had occurred in the game just played.

It may have had something to do with a stolen base attempt and the count on a batter. It may have been something about an outfield shift. It may have been anything that the opposing manager did or didn't do. Or it may have been a seemingly meaningless piece of minutiae that only a manager like Sparky was wise enough to detect.

Sparky knew all of the baseball rules better than he knew the Bible. Except for the baseball rule book, the Bible was the only book he had read cover to cover. He never claimed to be a biblical expert, but he disciplined himself to finish it in one calendar year.

He never tested me on the Bible, but he did expect me to know the rules of the game. I was always tested after a game in which a controversial call was made.

At first I felt intimidated trying to match wits with a master such as Sparky. He was a patient teacher, though, and I appreciated having an opportunity that no one else in the game enjoyed.

Once in a while when particularly frustrated with a game, he would flip on the TV to watch anything but another game. He wasn't a fan of full-length feature movies. He favored shows such as *Law & Order*, where outcomes came quicker and plots were based on real-life cases.

More than anything, he was hooked on political talk shows. He fed himself with enough news and opinion to qualify as a certified armchair politician. Depending upon the political climate of the moment, he became mesmerized by the ranting and raving of the so-called experts.

Coming off a victory, he might be inclined to watch a few innings of another game. After a loss, he would generally search for scores during commercials of the show he was watching.

During our last few years with the Tigers, Sparky more than ever preferred eating in his room over dining out. Once in a while we ordered room service. More often than not, I was the designated runner for takeouts brought back to the room. I became familiar with the nearest Burger King, McDonald's, or other similar fast-food outlet closest to the hotel in every city.

In New York it was a tiny round-the-clock deli that made the largest egg salad sandwiches anywhere in the United States. In victory or defeat, I always had to make a run there.

After a complimentary continental breakfast in a designated hotel dining room that accommodated select guests, we normally walked for about an hour or at least until the number of autograph seekers grew too large to handle. We would return to the hotel for Sparky to nap while I completed my media preparations for that evening's game.

By the time the team bus from the hotel arrived at the ballpark about two and a half hours before a game, Sparky and I had already spent at least a couple of hours at the park. For Sparky, there was no better place to relax than in a clubhouse. It was home. It was where he felt he had to be.

Sometimes our early excursions presented their own little peculiar problems. Before a Sunday afternoon game in Toronto we found ourselves at the park before it even opened.

Having risen early and after our second cup of coffee, we decided we might as well go to the park. Once there, we discovered that the entrance to the visiting clubhouse was still locked. Then we spotted the stadium director arriving in his car.

"What the hell are you guys doing here at seven o'clock in the morning?" he asked.

Sparky simply shrugged his shoulders and said: "If you get to where you gotta go early, you don't never have to worry about bein' late."

The answer made enough sense for the stadium manager to unlock the door. We went to the clubhouse, and I brewed a pot of coffee even before the clubhouse manager arrived.

Sparky understood the power of his position. He was well aware of every baseball record that he held and the influence it afforded him wherever he traveled.

He preferred, however, to let it speak for itself.

Power, he lectured me many times, is often misunderstood even by those who have it.

"Power ain't somethin' where you get a license to push people around and have them doin' everything for you," he explained. "Those kinda guys don't know nothin' about people. Eventually, they trip over their own feet.

"The man who knows he has power and doesn't have to show it . . . that's the guy you wanna have in control. That's the guy who understands how people work and the right way to treat them."

Sparky wisely chose how to use the power he enjoyed. He allowed his coaches to freely become the center of dinner conversations. And he certainly didn't need a piano in his hotel suite to prove the power he had.

But that beautiful baby grand certainly made for a good laugh during the first of our last three days together.

9

★

Shopping with Sparky

There was a time, no doubt, when Sparky would have snickered at the mere notion of becoming a regular customer at Albertsons supermarket.

While sitting at the kitchen table, though, Sparky broke into a large warm grin the moment I mentioned the name. After his retirement, the supermarket became an almost daily obsession. And no one enjoyed strolling the aisles and teasing all the hired help in the market more than he.

Shopping with Sparky was a TV reality show waiting to happen. Or at least one of those hilarious slapstick comedy scenes in a Woody Allen movie. Every time I entered the store I smiled to myself. I imagined the absurdity of two such comical characters crashing shopping carts in the aisle of a crowded supermarket.

With Sparky at the handle of a cart, a crash was never far behind.

World order for Sparky had changed in retirement, almost as if his life had unfolded in reverse. For 42 years straight out of high school, Sparky's everyday work suit had been knickers and a baseball cap. He worked tirelessly hard and put in brutally long hours. And he cer-

tainly reaped unimaginable rewards such as three World Championship rings and a plaque that hangs in the Baseball Hall of Fame.

Now he was learning to deal with some of life's more mundane
matters, all those little things that most men had mastered while
Sparky was busy carving his path into baseball immortality.

Sparky had the curiosity of a child and the energy of a jack-in-the-
box on steroids. His life in retirement was filled with spontaneous
discoveries that could turn the mundane into the magnificent, the
ordinary into the sublime. He had already done it in baseball. Now he
was learning to make sense out of the ordinary world.

And for those he met along the way, he always had a smile and a
few kind words. For anyone needing a shot of encouragement, he was
an inspiring sight to see.

One day a few years before, each of us carried two supersized bags
stuffed to the top with groceries and miscellaneous household supplies. They were heavy enough to force a shortcut through the garage
to drop them onto the kitchen table.

And that was just the first trip. Six more bags were waiting in the
backseat and the trunk of the car.

There was enough food to feed half the neighborhood. When finished with that feast, we could have scrubbed all of their floors, baths,
counters, and kitchens and probably all the windows with the surplus
of cleaning supplies we brought home from the supermarket.

Moderation, to say the least, never was one of Sparky's virtues.

"Carol," he shouted proudly as she slowly walked down the stairs.
"I saved $8.42."

He sounded like a little boy who has just found a quarter he forgot
that he'd stuck in the secret pocket of his pants.

It wasn't about the money. Most of the time he never looked at the
price of any item. It was about his sense of accomplishment, a feeling
of self-worth. It was coupon Thursday in the local paper that day, and
Sparky had made sure to clip each one before we started on our rounds.
"I'm the master when it comes to shopping," he proudly claimed. "Self-
taught. Ain't no one better. Just ask all the girls up at the market."

As the self-appointed director of purchasing for groceries and
miscellaneous household supplies that lined each wall of his garage,

his choice of supplier was always Albertsons. Maybe it was a shade farther from home than a couple of other supermarkets, but Sparky's loyalty to special places, things, and especially people never wavered. Albertsons was where his daughter, Shirlee, had worked part-time while still in high school. Sparky believed that a part-time job was a giant step toward gaining maturity and independence. This is where, on rare occasions in the past, he shopped when Carol was unable.

"I know all the people at Albertsons," he used to say proudly. "I know their names, their families, everything about them. They all love me."

And indeed they did.

That's what Sparky loved most about his frequent shopping sprees. It was always about the people. He always had a show for them. Even if those workers knew what was coming, they enjoyed each moment as if it were being played for the first time.

Sparky never simply walked into the market and selected a cart for his trip up and down each aisle. When he burst through the door chirping like a singing messenger every employee on the floor knew that his or her smile for the day had just arrived.

Sparky was as familiar with each aisle as an airline pilot is with the runways of major airports. He knew each shelf as well as the stock boy who kept them filled.

The first stop was always at the fresh fruit tables, where he squeezed melons, plums, peaches, bananas, and various other daily offerings that happened to catch his eye.

I always teased him that with as much fruit as he ate, his head was going to turn into a melon with two strawberries for eyes.

"You don't get an Olympic body like mine without eating enough fresh fruit," he would shout back with his arm bent at the elbow to show his muscle.

From there he moved to the freshly cut meat and fish displays, where he often joked with Roberto that most of those pieces had been sitting on that same ice since the week before. "Better get some fresh stuff in there, Roberto," he would crack. "That old stuff's turnin' green."

Stock boy, butcher, druggist, cashier, janitor, store manager . . .

Sparky knew them all. He made sure to call each by his or her first name—Lisa, Roberto, Ted, Kathleen, Nancy, Tommy, Jimmy, and so many more—and all smiled brightly, feeling as if they were his best friend.

He had a different story every day for each one. He knew those he could tease and those who needed a little lift. He also knew those who merely waited for a simple hello. They never tired of the acknowledgment they enjoyed so much from their Thousand Oaks neighbor who just happened to be a member of baseball's Hall of Fame.

"Your Dodgers got no pitchin'," he would jab Jimmy. "How's your team supposed to win a pennant with no pitchin'?"

Jimmy would smile and say they'd always be his team even if they did struggle.

"Is UCLA really gonna show up to play my Trojans?" Sparky would tease Tommy.

"Not only show up, they're gonna make USC throw up," Tommy would shoot back. Sparky scrunched his face as if he had just taken a bite out of a fresh lemon.

The grateful smiles of all the workers were all Sparky asked in return.

Sparky elevated his routine whenever I was in town. Even after so many years, all the workers asked me if this was the way he had acted when he was in the big leagues.

"No," I told them. "He talked a little more back then."

"This is my best friend Daniel I always tell you about," he began one of his favorite stories. "He's from Detroit. He's one of 'the boys' that puts cement shoes on the bodies before dropping them into the river. Somehow those cats never do seem to come up anymore."

Everyone laughed despite having heard the story and having met me at least a hundred times before. Then we moved to the next aisle, where often the same story was repeated, word for word.

Sparky courteously returned each greeting he received from each customer he passed. He rarely was asked for an autograph in the store, because almost everyone was already familiar with seeing him there. Of course, he might tell people a joke if he had recently heard a new one.

The only time he got serious in the supermarket was when it was time to pay the bill. Even when one of the cashiers offered to help hurry him through an unoccupied self-scanning lane so that he wouldn't have to wait, Sparky always refused. "You know me better than that," he would politely tell her with a smile. "One day that self-scanner is gonna take away a lot of jobs and you know I ain't goin' for that. I'll wait my turn in line. Besides, I can talk to all of you pretty ladies a little bit longer."

After getting home—and despite many overflowing bags of groceries—we sometimes discovered we had forgotten one of the principal items for which we had gone to the store. Upon returning to more smiles, he would point toward me and tell the first worker he spotted: "This guy can't remember a thing."

We stocked all groceries and supplies in the refrigerator, cupboards, and garage before preparing for our day at the golf course. Almost always we played at Sunset Hills.

The most pertinent question facing Sparky each day was which hat to wear from his eclectic collection, which filled one-half of the floor space in his closet. There were more than 300 baseball hats from which to choose. Every color, every professional team, every major university, and a variety of miscellaneous hats were rotated throughout the year. He never wore the same hat twice in a year. Some went untouched for a couple of seasons.

A hat was never chosen simply to match the color of his shirt and pants for the day. In fact, often the colors of his shirt and pants didn't quite match. A hat was something sacred. He picked it by "feel" rather than for color coordination.

One Christmas I sent him a pair of hats—one from the U.S. Military Academy at West Point and another from the U.S. Naval Academy at Annapolis. Sparky wore those for special occasions. They were never to be worn for just another day on the golf course.

Just as at the supermarket, Sparky would greet at least 50 club members each morning before taking the first tee. He addressed each by first name and usually had a little story customized to each individual.

He took particular pride talking to the members of the grounds crew. They were mostly Mexican American immigrants who seemed to search out Sparky's morning greeting. Most spoke limited English. But a smile or a laugh doesn't come with an accent.

Before Christmas, Sparky stuffed a little money into the shirt pocket of each one. "Feliz Navidad," he said to each. Except for "sí" and "señor," that was the extent of Sparky's command of Spanish.

It never mattered how we scored on the course. The most fun for Sparky was mixing with the people.

After golf, we made our almost daily post office run. Again Sparky attached a litany of names to the right faces and added a personal greeting to each postal employee working the counter.

Sparky tried to stay current with the basketfuls of mail directed to his postal box day after day after day. The letters were all requests for autographs, and most asked for three or four.

A postal worker once asked Sparky if his fingers ever got numb from signing so much material.

"Numb?" Sparky asked with genuine surprise. "Sometimes my fingers get so tired I can't even feel 'em."

Upon returning home, Sparky started frantically ripping open each envelope and box sent to him. He was vigilant never to miss even one day of signing. If he did, it could back him up for as much as a week.

On special days we would drive to Westlake for a visit to Costco. He loved the juicy hot dogs smothered in mustard, onions, and sauerkraut. Once in a while he would share pizza with Carol. All three of us, though, never left the store without feasting on a smoothie.

Sitting at the picnic tables adjacent to the kitchen, Sparky was fascinated by the mixture of people he watched walking in and out of the door.

"There's an awful lot of old-timers that just come out to be part of the crowd," he said.

Carol and I smiled at each other.

"Yeah," I said. "And a whole lot of them are younger and seem to be staring at us."

Later in the day, when we got home, evening meals were usually prepared by Carol, who too often underestimated her culinary skills. "I hope you realize how good of a cook she is," I once taunted him. "You'd be eating McDonald's and peanut butter sandwiches every day if it wasn't for her."

Sparky didn't counter. He was wise enough to know just how fortunate he was.

Despite the glut of upscale restaurants in the city and the surrounding area, Sparky, Carol, and I preferred a handful of anonymous places where we knew Sparky wouldn't be expected to perform. We ate deli sandwiches at Roxy's, Chinese food at the Sesame Inn, fish and chips at the Thousand Oaks Fish Market, and pasta at a little hole-in-the-wall Italian restaurant that really didn't have a name. It was basically a carryout pizzeria; the tiny dining room had just enough space for two tables, which seemed to be used rarely except by us. It was the perfect place for uninterrupted conversations, and a place where nobody would expect to find Sparky. It was an ideal spot to share pasta, memories, and plans for the next day.

"How about shopping, golf, the post office, and dinner?" I would always offer.

Sparky would stare at me from across the table. He would wrinkle his brow and slowly shake the index finger of his right hand in front of my eyes. "Daniel, my boy," he'd say slowly, "now you're gettin' with the program. I think you got a chance."

Performing at sold-out stadiums across the country had long since become a thing of the past. For the most part, so had all the cameras, and the hungry press corps that fed upon each word he uttered.

Sparky didn't need the spotlight anymore.

Sparky's new life still offered plenty of opportunities to create some smiles for anyone wishing to feel good. Doing so meant more to Sparky than it did to those he was trying to entertain.

Now, as he looked out the window to see where the sun was, Sparky nodded his head a few times before making a suggestion.

"Maybe we'll go to Albertsons tomorrow," he said.

I smiled and placed my hand on one of his shoulders. "Let's see what the morning brings," I answered. "We don't need to have a schedule."

Sparky nodded and gave a thumbs-up sign.

We didn't go. But I'll forever remember all the good times we enjoyed at that market. I'll forever remember that to receive a little kindness, even from strangers, all you have to do is give some in return.

Sparky understood that. He had plenty to share.

10

★

82 Balls

I picked up a putter that was leaning against the side of the book-case in the family room. I bent over and took a few passes at an imaginary golf ball. I wanted to get Sparky talking about his lone hole in one, which had happened about eight years before on the 160-yard ninth hole at Sunset Hills.

He popped a 5-wood high into the air. The ball bounced once only inches in front of the green and proceeded to roll into the center of the cup as if riding on tracks.

His excited voice on the other end of the line after rushing home to call me sounded as if he had just won the lottery. It was a whisper, though, compared to a later time when he called to tell me he had just set a Sunset Hills record.

"Eighty-two!" he proudly shouted before even telling me what he was talking about.

"You shot an 82?" I yelled back in shock.

"No, you dumbbell," he reprimanded me. "You know I can't shoot 82. Eighty-two balls, Daniel. Eighty-two balls! No one will ever come close to beating that."

And once again on that first of our last three days together he almost dismissed the hole in one to talk about his passion for finding lost golf balls. As much as Sparky loved to golf and socialize at the club, nothing provided as much pleasure as the hunt for lost balls.

He groped through thorny bushes till his arms dripped with blood. He wandered desolate out-of-bounds areas like he was a professional hiker. He dipped down into barrancas into which he often tumbled. He fished his hands through streams and too often found himself near a rattlesnake nest.

No obstacle was too intimidating to prevent his daily challenge.

He would take the golf balls home, scrub them in the tub in his garage, place them in carefully marked boxes, and then give them to his golfing son Lee and all of his friends at the club. He knew the type of ball each player used. None bearing a scratch or smudge was given. He used those himself.

Once when I was leaving for home after a visit, he stuffed my duffel bag with as many balls as possible. The bag was bursting with an assortment of every golf ball manufactured. My ball of choice was relatively simple—white, orange, or yellow, dimpled, at least somewhat rounded . . . and above all free.

At the airport, a security agent asked what I was doing with so many golf balls. I just shook my head and told him he wouldn't believe it even if I tried to explain. I still have so many balls in one closet that only a few loose shirts have room enough to hang.

Once after finishing a round, a member asked our foursome how we had played.

Vinny said: "Great, 83."

Bob said: "Great, 84."

I said: "Great. I only hit six out of bounds."

Sparky said: "Great. I found 26 balls."

Not even Sparky knew for sure when his bent for finding lost balls turned into a passion. Sometimes even he was amazed at the number of balls he had in his garage. He certainly didn't need them. Each Christmas he received a boxcar full of balls from friends around the country.

"I just never understood why people don't take the time to find a ball that sometimes was lying right under their nose," he said.

More than anything, finding golf balls became a challenge. If he couldn't score better than some of the players at the club, he could surely whip them, hands down, at loading his golf bag full of perfectly good once-used balls.

And then at giving them away.

Once in a while he'd come down the side of a hill after scouring the brush with blood dripping down his arms and legs from the cuts he'd suffered on broken tree branches. Before going into his house he washed his arms and legs clean with the lawn hose so that Carol wouldn't know of yet one more hunting expedition.

A couple of times he tumbled down the side of a steep hill. Fortunately, he never broke an arm or a leg. But there was no way to hide those little adventures.

Sunset Hills is one of those sleeper courses that look innocent but that cleverly hide all kinds of sinister tricks. It's not extraordinarily long, but it features enough traps and trees and turns and tricky greens to challenge even the most prepared golfer. With mountain views on all four sides and a forest of lush green trees in the middle, it's a meretricious temptress that can lure an unsuspecting believer into a small slice of hell.

The first time I played Sunset, about 20 years ago, I made a par 4 on the first hole to set myself up for heartbreak. I scored no more pars until my third time out and could sense that the course was sneering defiantly at me.

Less than a five-minute drive from Sparky's home, Sunset Hills is considered to be a "stepping-stone" club, somewhat less affluent than Wood Ranch or Moorpark. Sunset members include some senior executives, some junior executives, an assortment of professionals, blue-collar workers, and retirees.

Sparky certainly wasn't looking to step up to or step out of anything. Sunset was his home. He wasn't going anywhere. He loved the course. He loved the people. And he knew almost everybody by his or her first name.

Sparky was the most celebrated member of the club and had been accorded honorary membership many years before. Without annual dues to pay, he distributed generous biannual checks to each staff member, including the entire grounds crew. He always had an affinity for every average worker who performed professionally behind the scenes.

During his daily march from his usual parking place at the end of the lot, he had a joke or a story for every person he passed.

There was no mistaking Sparky's arrival.

Some called him Sparky. Some called him George. But everyone knew he was a Hall of Fame legend who walked with all the players they had grown up with or watched on TV.

Vinny was Sparky's most regular golf partner. One day he asked Sparky if his brother, John, visiting from New York, might play with them the next morning. John was a longtime baseball fan who was well aware of Sparky's legend.

That morning, Sparky had just left the pro shop when he noticed both brothers walking toward him.

"Sparky, I'd like you to meet—" Vinny began, but Sparky cut him off: "Save all the small talk."

Sparky grabbed John's shoulder and yanked him a few feet away as if to say something very important in private to him.

"John, I'm telling you," he began, speaking loudly enough for Vinny to hear. "Your brother is not very well liked at this club and if it wasn't for his wife, Willy, they woulda kicked him out by now."

Then he broke into his characteristic smile and wrapped an arm around John. "John, it's my pleasure to meet you," he said. "Have a good time, 'cause after our round, you're buyin' the beer."

Of course, that wasn't true. Sparky bought as usual.

Sparky always arrived at the club about an hour before his scheduled tee time. Unlike most members, who hit a bag of balls to warm up, Sparky enjoyed kibitzing with employees in the pro shop, mostly about how beautiful the course looked and how ugly his game was.

On one morning a young man who worked in the cart barn happened to be in the pro shop practicing with a putter while Sparky quietly examined the merchandise. He overheard the pro tell the young man that he would sell the putter to him with the employee discount. Even with the discount, the young man said, the putter was out of his price range.

The next morning the young man was playing with the putter again. When the pro asked if he still liked it, he answered, "More than yesterday."

"Take it," the pro said. "It's yours. Someone bought it for you."

The young man was astonished and wanted to know who the generous person was.

"He told me not to tell you," the pro said. "He said only for you to use it well."

Under threat of never buying another item from the pro shop, Sparky had instructed the pro never to reveal the purchaser of the putter.

Over the years Sparky gave many little tokens of appreciation to the employees of the club. When he made a commercial appearance anywhere in the country, he almost always returned with a box full of hats from the sponsoring organization. He liked to give them to "the boys at the club."

He wasn't quite as generous to himself as he was to others. Once he showed up at the course with one of those oversized-head, high-tech drivers. He was bragging to anyone who would listen about how his new toy was going to slice a half dozen strokes from his handicap.

"Got it from Target," he proudly stated. "Cost $19.99. Now who thinks I don't know my golf business?"

He used the driver quite successfully for a few months. Then he purchased another during another Target sale.

I am fortunate to have played Sunset Hills more times than any of the courses around my house. Because of the nature of its design and natural setting, it's like playing a new course every day.

One of my fondest memories from there, however, has nothing to do with golf.

Sparky and I were sitting on the porch of the pro shop as a new member to the club approached from the parking lot. He already knew that Sparky was a member.

"Hello, I'm George," Sparky said. "Welcome to the club."

The newcomer smiled at him and said: "Did anyone ever tell you that you look a lot like Sparky Anderson?"

Sparky smiled and winked. "But you can still call me George if you like," he said.

Even when Sparky began to fail physically, he visited the club simply to chat with his friends. Once in a while he would grab a cart and drive out on the course to play a couple of holes before returning home.

The week after Sparky died, a large group of members gathered in the dining room one afternoon to share a toast to Sparky.

The club also created a plaque to honor him. It hangs on locker number 10, which is never to be used again. Sparky had worn the number 10 on his uniform as manager of the Big Red Machine in Cincinnati. On May 7, 2011, the club hosted a tournament in Sparky's name that raised a modest amount of money, which was donated to Sparky's charity for underprivileged children in Detroit.

Sparky would have liked that. He liked everything about Sunset Hills, where he could be Sparky or George or whatever character he chose.

I already knew how well Sparky treated people. But it was fascinating to watch how he interacted with every member, guest, and employee of the club. It was almost as if he felt responsible for the happiness of every person visiting the club on any given day.

Sparky could probably have chosen any club in Southern California to give him an honorary membership. But he had been given that privilege many years before by Sunset, and his allegiance to that generosity would live forever.

For Sparky, there was never any compromise on any matter of loyalty.

Sparky's loyalty was never overlooked by any of the club members. And it certainly wasn't overlooked by me.

The only problem with Sunset Hills now is that there are a lot more lost balls lying around the course that remain ripe for the picking.

11

★

"The Plug Puller"

Sparky rose from his chair and walked around the table to take the putter from my hand. He made the one step down into the family room and took a few passes at an imaginary ball of his own.

While watching him, my mind wandered back about five years to when we were sitting at the kitchen table, where we handled most of the world's problems early each morning before he and I headed to the golf course. Better to straighten out the world first before facing the humiliation of a golf problem we could never fix.

This particular precious memory was better to savor silently myself than to talk about at the present time.

Sparky and I had finished our daily walk and I was sipping on my second cup of coffee. I poured Sparky another half cup.

There may as well have been a Do Not Disturb sign hanging on one of Sparky's ears. He was perusing the newspaper for box scores from the baseball games played the night before. He rarely read any accounts of the games. The box scores and the league standings told him all he needed to know.

Carol and I were discussing a local story in the newspaper about a suspicious-looking older man hanging around the playground of a nearby elementary school.

"He wasn't a skinny five-foot-eight white-haired older man, was he?" I teased her.

She asked if either of the two of us ever took anything seriously. She told me George did have a serious question to ask me. She had to shout his name twice before he lifted his nose from the box scores.

"I'm supposed to ask you if you wanna be the guy who pulls the plug on me," he said, his eyes shifting back to the box scores.

I looked quizzically at Carol to see if she knew what he was talking about. She said that was just George trying to be funny. He wanted to know if I'd consider being his end-of-life health care agent.

"You mean he wants me to pull the plug?" I said with a cackle in my voice.

"You two are just like," she answered. "You deserve each other."

When the teasing ended, the three of us drove to a nearby notary public's office. Sparky had already had the legal document drafted. I was to serve as his representative in the event that, for whatever reason, Carol was unable.

Then Sparky and I hit the links. The sun was shining brilliantly that day, and surprisingly, both of us were playing quite respectably. I couldn't let an opportunity like this slip away, however. When he was lining up a tricky putt, I was particularly pointed with my quips. And I was relentless.

"Just put that plug in my hand," I cracked. "I can't wait to give it a yank. I'll be the last guy you see before you start floating up to the clouds. Now isn't that something to look forward to?"

The easiest way to deal with somber matters such as this is with the help of a laugh. At least it is for a couple of friends who spent a career together in the irreverent world of major-league baseball.

Even though we both had reached an age when a matter such as this was more the norm than the exception, I was slightly concerned over the fact that it had even been raised.

"I'm just a little bit concerned," I said without any hint of humor. "Is there something wrong with you that I should know about?"

"Yeah . . . that I was dumb enough to put you in charge of the plug," he replied, reverting to good old-fashioned baseball sarcasm.

At the time, he appeared to be perfectly healthy. I dismissed my concern as totally needless worry.

There were a couple of scares in 1999, however, that always kept the family on edge. In February of that year, Sparky survived a serious stomach rupture that could have cost his life. In July of that year, he suffered a heart attack that almost caused one in me.

I had everything planned for Sparky's annual 10-day visit to my home in the summer of 1999. There were two celebrity charity golf tournaments in which he was slated to play. I also scheduled a couple of leisurely rounds at courses near my home. I purchased enough burgers to barbecue to last us a month. I had plenty of suntan lotion for relaxing by the lake. And I had scheduled an evening at a local place that was his favorite Italian restaurant in the United States.

One thing I hadn't planned was the heart attack he was hospitalized for on the second day he was in town.

I felt inexplicably guilty. Who invites a friend to visit 2,000 miles from home and then allows him to suffer a heart attack? Especially if that someone happens to be his best friend!

It was a totally illogical feeling, but that's precisely what struck me.

There's no easy way to explain what was going through my mind. But then a lot of things Sparky and I did together were not easy to explain. Although his illness was terrifying at the time, Sparky and I had plenty of time to laugh about the awkward situation over the next 11 years.

The first charity tournament was a favor to Bo Schembechler, who was always busy raising funds to find a cure for adrenal cancer. The second, one week later, was Sparky's annual fund-raiser for CATCH, the charity he had formed to help underprivileged children in Detroit.

Sparky had been feeling ill for about two weeks before making the trip on a Sunday. Carol tried to persuade him not to go. Of course, he refused to listen. Before I left for the Detroit airport to pick him up, I received a call from Carol, who was returning from taking him to the Los Angeles airport. She said they'd had to stop along the freeway to allow him to vomit. Under no circumstances, she emphatically stated, was I to allow him to play golf the next day.

The next morning Sparky's face looked as white as his hair. Nevertheless, he pleaded to be taken to Bo's tournament in Ann Arbor. I conceded, but told him his golf clubs were not allowed in my car. His resistance was meek: a plea for him to take his putter.

"That's all," I told him. "And you're not going to putt on every hole."

When our foursome reached the first green, Sparky dropped a ball to putt. After meticulously lining up the relatively straight putt, he hit the ball completely off the green, at about 90 degrees away from the hole.

I looked at Bo, who happened to be standing on the green. "We're leaving right now," I told him. "I'm taking him to a doctor."

Upon our return home, Sparky removed his shirt and plopped into a lawn chair on my patio as I slipped into the back room of my house.

I called a friend who happened to be a physician. After I described Sparky's condition, he told me to bring him to the emergency room, where he would have someone waiting.

I anticipated Sparky's resistance and told him we were just going to visit the doctor, whom he also knew. I told him that perhaps the doctor would provide a prescription so that he would feel better for the rest of the week.

The look on his face as he slowly lifted his head remains forever etched into my mind.

"You better not be lyin' to me," he said.

The hospital staff was waiting and immediately rolled him into a room for a series of tests. He was then rolled back into another room, where I had been told to wait. Sparky was still feeling guilty about leaving Bo's tournament early. As I was assuring him that Bo completely understood his early departure, another doctor entered the room.

"Mr. Anderson"—he spoke directly in a low, even tone—"you've suffered a heart attack."

Sparky just seemed to stare into space while I was busy fighting off a heart attack of my own.

There has to be some kind of mistake, I told myself. My thoughts became jumbled. If I hadn't brought him to the hospital, I thought, maybe none of this would have happened.

"Are you sure about this, Doc?" I finally blurted.

The doctor was kind and smiled as he told me he was a cardiologist who had been practicing for years.

He explained that Sparky had suffered what is termed a "silent heart attack." It could have occurred anywhere from the day before up to two weeks ago. The doctor explained that Sparky had to be moved to the hospital's main campus near downtown Detroit for treatment. He chuckled when I told him I would drive Sparky there immediately.

"Out of the question," he said. "Your friend will be transported by ambulance accompanied by a member of the staff."

Before leaving the hospital, I told Sparky I would meet him there. First I had to face my next dilemma. I had to call Carol.

"George is all right," I immediately began. "But he's suffered a heart attack."

Quickly, the words I had just spoken flashed through my mind. They didn't seem quite right. Nevertheless, Carol was as solid as ever and said she wasn't surprised. We quickly arranged a flight to Detroit for early the next morning. We drove to the hospital, where we remained until visiting hours ended, then returned to my house, where she could consider the proper decision to make.

It had been determined that Sparky required surgery to repair four arteries. The question was whether to have it done in Detroit or at home in Thousand Oaks. After discussing the matter thoroughly, Sparky and Carol decided to return to Thousand Oaks. The rehabilitation process would be lengthy and burdensome on the family if conducted 2,000 miles away from home.

Through Bo's association with Northwest Airlines, special boarding arrangements for Sparky were made. From the Los Angeles airport, Sparky was transported to Thousand Oaks' Los Robles Hospital, where he was immediately admitted and underwent successful surgery that evening.

As expected, Sparky outperformed almost every patient in rehab. If told to walk a mile on the treadmill, he would walk two. If told to walk 20 minutes, he would walk 30.

He pushed himself to always finish on top. And he did so with the same bubbly enthusiasm he could always summon when performing for the fans during his career as a manager.

On my first trip to Thousand Oaks after the surgery, he made the rehab center the first stop on our daily itinerary. He wanted to introduce me to the rehab specialists who were helping him to make his heart strong once more.

"These are my girls," he said proudly. "They all love me over here."

Once he completed a formal rehab program, he was instructed to maintain his exercise at least on an informal basis.

Nothing was a mere formality for Sparky. Everything became a ritual. Even during trips for speaking engagements or commercials, he packed his walking attire and never skipped a day of walking.

Through rehab, he began his daily walks around the neighborhood. It was from these walks that he made friends he kept for the rest of his life. A regular group of neighbors religiously walked the neighborhood each morning. Sparky became a regular and brought me into the group for my regular visits.

He felt proud of the way he attacked his rehab program and boasted about it to anyone willing to listen. I shared his pride and then I teased him: "Next time, though, pick another place for your heart attack or you're going to give one to me."

Until that October Sunday in the kitchen that always felt so reassuring, I had never thought about having signed that legal document to serve as Sparky's end-of-life health care agent, a commitment that is a mutual expression of ultimate trust.

Sparky and I chose a lighter approach toward dealing with everything in life. That's why official "plug puller" made more sense to us than "end-of-life health care agent," which sounds like an overly pretentious insurance agent.

Rarely did Sparky and I discuss anything about our friendship. We were too busy doing what friends do together. That's why the only thing we mentioned with any regularity was the fact that there would never again be another friendship like ours in baseball.

The distance between our homes never eroded the strength of our relationship. If anything, at times it strengthened the bond.

During our careers in the game, rarely did we go more than a day during the off-season without speaking on the phone. In retirement, when we weren't traveling together for one of his appearances, there were stretches when one or the other would call every day.

We talked about baseball, but not nearly as much as when we were in the game. We both loved college football. On fall Saturdays we took turns calling at least a half dozen times to rave about a spectacular play or an upset neither of us had anticipated.

Sparky was a diehard University of Southern California fan. One year he was given the Tommy Trojan Trophy from USC. My allegiance was to the University of Michigan. We looked forward to seasons when both were in the Rose Bowl. One-dollar bets can be pretty exciting.

Except for when USC was playing Michigan, Sparky pulled for the Wolverines. He loved Bo and knew how his heart bled every time his Wolverines lost.

Each summer between Sparky's charity golf tournament and our annual trip to the Hall of Fame in Cooperstown, we drove to Ann Arbor to visit with the coaches and talk to the players. We also made a stop there before going to spring training.

On one occasion, Heisman Trophy winner Desmond Howard happened to be in the football building. Sparky was spinning a story about how he was called "Sweet Hips" in high school for the way he could run with the football. "When I was goin' up the middle and some guy tried to tackle me from the left, I'd swing my hips to the right," Sparky said while twisting his hips in dramatic fashion. "If someone came from the right, I'd swing my hips the other way."

Howard's eyes got wider as Sparky's story grew. His lips broke into a football-wide smile as Sparky finally took the ball into the end zone. "I didn't know you played football, Sparky," Howard excitedly blurted.

There was a pregnant pause.

"Actually, I didn't," Sparky said matter-of-factly. "But that's the way I *woulda* done it."

On another occasion, Tom Brady was in the building.

"They tell me you got a chance to be pretty good," Sparky said.

Brady smiled and said he hoped they weren't wrong.

Time, obviously, has proven the speculation correct. Sparky liked telling the story about meeting Brady to his friends at home. It usually finished with him saying: "I taught that young Brady everything he knows."

At one time, Sparky and I were rabid boxing fans. A couple of days before significant championship fights, we exchanged phone calls constantly.

I rented one championship match on HBO and called him after each round to tell him who was winning.

The NCAA men's basketball tournament triggered a lot of back-and-forth phone calls the closer it got to the final rounds.

Inevitably, our conversations wound up with at least a little dab of politics. From Reagan to Bush, Bush to Clinton, Clinton to another Bush, and finally Obama. Sparky was well equipped to argue contemporary politics and—not surprisingly at all—was never shy about expressing his opinion.

Over the years, we had plenty of disagreements. But I honestly cannot remember any argument that didn't end with a smile.

I never agreed with all of the decisions Sparky made as a baseball manager. But I always regarded him as the best manager I had ever seen.

Of course, I remember all of his record-setting years. It's strange, however, that the longer we were out of the game, the less it mattered what we had done for so many years.

We were friends. That was good enough. And it felt so good just reminiscing about all those times.

12

★

Sparky's School

Sparky walked from the kitchen to the bookcase in his family room. Most of the shelves were filled with framed pictures of his three children and all of his grandchildren. The bottom row was lined with books that had been given to him over the years.

He picked out the three that he and I had written together. He placed them on the kitchen table and said he was "proud of these three." He opened the flap of each book and silently read what I had inscribed to him on the books we had exchanged.

"I remember the press conference for the release of this one," he said while holding his copy of *They Call Me Sparky*.

At that press conference, in 1997, Sparky set the tone and drove the crowd into laughter with his answer to the first question.

"What kind of books do you like to read, Sparky?" The question was innocently posed.

He glanced quickly at me for a little help and then decided to simply tell the truth.

"Except for the Bible, I ain't never read a book in my life," he honestly admitted. "But I know one thing . . . I met a lotta good, smart people that are just like me."

The initial hush of the crowd immediately turned into polite applause. Then came the laughter. From his quick and straightforward answer, the people knew that what they would read in his book would be the truth.

"At least they found out real quick I ain't ashamed of nothin' I did," he said as memories of so many good times sprung back to life in our hearts during our Sunday reminiscing.

He also told the audience that once he left Dorsey High, he never stepped into another schoolroom again. "I think God blessed me with enough common sense to put some things together, though," he added.

Sparky enjoyed a lifelong link to the University of Southern California after living in the shadow of the school while growing up. He rooted for the Trojans in every sport, and in his youth he was a batboy for the baseball team for several years. He became a great friend of legendary coach Rod Dedeaux, whose teams ruled the NCAA baseball tournaments for decades. Once his baseball career was over, he often was asked to address the football team at a practice during the week before a pivotal game.

Although he never took a step into any of its classrooms, California Lutheran University (CLU) became the school closest to his heart. CLU was the recipient of a lot of unselfish fund-raising by the celebrated individual who just happened to live in the neighborhood.

CLU is a private liberal arts school with an enrollment of just over 2,000 students. The picturesque campus is only a five-minute walk from Sparky's home.

I teased Sparky often about how that would be the closest to a university that he would ever get.

"Yeah, you got a degree or two," he conceded. "But you ain't got no baseball park named after you."

For decades Sparky helped to raise money for the baseball program and awareness of the school by hosting an annual celebrity golf tournament. He also appeared at several fund-raising functions and loved to talk about his favorite university from one coast to the other.

"I gotta be the only Catholic raising money for a Lutheran university and never spent a day in college in my whole life," he used to joke.

It wasn't until after his heart attack in 1999, however, that he became more familiar with the campus through his rehabilitation program of walking.

Prior to that, I had become quite familiar with the university when I walked the campus alone during my visits to Thousand Oaks. When he started his walking routine, he circled the perimeter of the school without actually entering the heart of the campus.

I invited him to join me on the paths on the gentle green hills surrounded by a variety of trees, bordered by grass so green and lush it almost looked artificial. He thanked me for the tip and soon discovered he spent more time on the campus than some of the students who commuted to the school.

"I can honestly say I go to school every day," he joked. "But I don't think they're gonna be givin' me no degrees. It ain't big, but it's one of the most beautiful campuses anyone will ever see."

A Division III school in intercollegiate athletics, CLU boasts a full menu of varsity men's sports including baseball, football, basketball, swimming, soccer, golf, and track. Except for football and with softball instead of baseball, women participate in their own varsity programs.

Baseball, of course, garnered most of Sparky's attention. After retiring, he became a frequent visitor to the CLU games. Walking to the games he often said: "Daniel, this is what baseball really is all about."

He became a magnet at the ballpark as soon as he was spotted walking up from the parking lot. Encountering Sparky at a grocery store or gas station was one thing. But seeing him at a ballpark stirred a special jolt of emotion.

After his induction into the Hall of Fame in 2000, he was greeted by a standing ovation every time he set foot in the park. Visiting teams taking batting practice used to pause to get a glimpse of a true Hall of Famer.

There were autographs to sign. Pictures to be taken. Handshakes to be given. And honor to be received. Modestly, Sparky accommodated every person. This was his home. These were his friends. And this was a baseball park where he always belonged.

When he wanted a little quiet time simply to watch the game being played, Sparky would slip down to the gate that led to the field and sit at the end of the dugout bench without saying a word. He did not feel comfortable making any suggestions to any of the coaches.

Sparky not only became good friends with head coach Marty Sliwak and his assistants; he also made sure to memorize the names and faces of each player on the team. Every year.

Imagine the thrill felt by a 19-year-old Division III baseball player receiving acknowledgment from a Hall of Fame legend who lived up the street and just happened to know his name.

Although he never interfered with the coaching, Sparky was an immense recruiting tool for Sliwak when he was trying to convince a high school senior to come to CLU for a good education and a chance to play some competitive college baseball. All Sparky had to do was show up, shake hands, and give the potential recruit a wink and a pat on the back, and Coach Sliwak wound up with another player.

Sparky's loyalty to his neighborhood's school led to a distinguished, unexpected honor four years ago. For all the time and commitment he had given to the school, the renovation to the ballpark enjoyed a perk even larger schools don't enjoy.

The renovated park, with an impeccably manicured infield the equal of any major-league diamond, would forever be named the George "Sparky" Anderson Park.

Sparky choked up at the dedication ceremonies. But he managed to tell everyone he didn't know how to repay such an honor. As Coach Sliwak and everyone else in the program assured him, he already had.

Coach Sliwak must have learned some of the lessons in loyalty that Sparky loved to talk about from morning to night. Since the passing of Sparky, he calls on Carol often merely to inquire if he can help get something done or run an errand.

At the opening game of the 2011 season, a moment of silence was observed in Sparky's memory before the flag was raised to half-staff. On a sleeve of their uniforms, players and coaches wore a red patch featuring the number 10 Sparky wore when he became a legend managing the Cincinnati Reds.

Just to the home dugout side of home plate, a plaque honoring Sparky was placed in a seat never to be used again.

The players that were treated to his presence over the years have memories to tell their grandchildren many years from now. Those future players yet to set foot on the CLU campus will form memories of their own from the spirit Sparky left.

Not bad for a guy who "didn't know nothin' about no college," as he used to say.

He will always be a part of CLU.

"I think I did a little to help the school as best as I could," Sparky mentioned that Sunday afternoon with evening quickly approaching.

I corrected him quickly.

"You did more than anyone will ever know," I said. "More than all the books can tell."

There's a whole lot of knowledge to be learned from all those books at any university. But wisdom is acquired by experience. And Sparky provided so much to me.

13

★

"I Can't Talk?"

Browsing through the bookcase that Sunday, I discovered a plastic box containing a tape. It was a copy of a national Ford Motor Company commercial that Sparky had filmed more than a quarter century before.

While Sparky was leading the Tigers to the top of baseball's mountain in 1984, he spent a day on a real San Francisco mountain midway through Detroit's charge to a World Series Championship.

On Monday, the day before the All-Star Game was to be played in San Francisco's Candlestick Park, he was perched almost at the peak of the breathtaking 2,571-foot Mount Tamalpais just north of San Francisco's Golden Gate Bridge.

The majestic mountain is covered with groves of redwoods and oak woodlands. As morning crept slowly toward afternoon, a friendly sun burned gently through the clouds to offer a spectacular view of downtown San Francisco, the Bay, and the hills and cities of the East Bay.

The Tigers dominated the American League squad with six selections, including three starters. Sparky was asked by Baltimore Orioles manager Joe Altobelli to serve as one of the two coaches.

Sparky and I flew into San Francisco after the Tigers game on Sunday. On Monday I was scheduled to take Sparky to the mountain for the filming of the commercial. The producer of the commercial happened to have played for the same American Legion baseball team I did as a kid.

Because of the Tigers' meteoric record-setting start of the season, their fans were talking about the World Series shortly after Mother's Day.

Even without all of the national attention, Sparky was a hot commodity for endorsements of all kinds. With his trademark white hair and sharp facial features that looked like they had been carved with a hammer and chisel, Sparky had a singular, unmistakable look. He had an identity that led him to be featured on a variety of television comedy shows.

He was a sponsor's dream. He smiled easily, his teeth looked like polished ivory, and he had just enough gravel in his voice to make even strangers listen. He could call a different emotion to his face as quickly as switching stations on a TV remote. He had an inexplicable aura about him that invited everyone to be his friend.

Despite working in a pair of cities known for sweat and grease, he was a born poster boy for commercials of almost any product. It's scary to ponder how much money he might have made if he had managed in New York or Los Angeles.

This time the commercial was for Ford. Representatives of the advertising agency picked us up in a limo in front of the hotel for the relatively short drive to Mount Tamalpais.

"Hurry up," I remember him teasing the driver. "I don't like people seeing me ride in somethin' fancy like this. Beautiful car, but it ain't me."

The limo took us to the peak of the mountain. Just before meeting with the producer, we decided to ease any preshooting jitters with a practical joke Sparky and I had devised during the drive.

I introduced the producer to Sparky and told him that Sparky had always driven a Ford product . . . but he just didn't like the script that had been written for him.

The producer looked puzzled and showed the early signs of desperation.

"What do you mean he doesn't like the script?" he asked, almost panic-stricken. "He doesn't have to say a word. All he's got to do is ride down the mountain."

That's when Sparky jumped in. "Yeah, but I gotta say somethin'. You know how much I love to talk. I've been thinkin' up lines since we got on the plane last night."

Obviously, the producer had never encountered a commercial spokesman upset about not having to memorize a scripted sales pitch. Sparky and I looked at each other and then broke into a laugh. The relieved producer was happy to be the target of the joke and knew that the shoot was bound to be successful.

What Sparky was requested to do was ridiculously simple. Too simple, he thought, for the money he was being paid.

Sparky was seated behind the steering wheel of a Crown Victoria whose front underside was attached to an eight-foot steel bar. The bar was hitched to the backside of a pickup truck that pulled Sparky's vehicle down the winding road of the mountain.

The camera switched back and forth between the side of the vehicle Sparky looked to be driving and the paradisiacal landscape with a view of the Bay in the background. All Sparky had to do was keep his profile toward the camera and look as if he had full control of the wheel.

Upon reaching the final destination, Sparky was to turn and stare squarely at the camera with a "What did you think I'd be driving?" look on his face.

Not a single word was spoken. He could save all of those for the story he would be able to tell all of the players when he went to the park.

Sparky became the king of commercials for sponsors in Detroit. For about his final dozen years, he was featured in Metro Detroit Ford Dealers Association commercials. His identifiable white hair landed a TV spot for a local chain of barbershops for men.

The first commercial he did soon after his arrival in Detroit was for a long-standing family-owned pizzeria called Buddy's on the east side of the city. Although this is not necessarily the result of the commercial, Buddy's has since expanded throughout the entire metropolitan area. Ironically, the ball club was subsequently owned by two different national pizza chains during Sparky's last 12 years.

Sparky thoroughly enjoyed shooting commercials when he was free to ad-lib. When something sounded awkward to his ear, he asked the director if he might switch a few words to make it sound more like him. No one knew the Sparky character better than Sparky. Rarely did a director object to any change Sparky made.

On a shoot in Toronto's SkyDome for Gillette of Canada, Sparky was asked to deliver eight one-liners for eight different scenes in the park. After the director reviewed all eight at the end of the shoot, he agreed that the four that Sparky had switched had more punch than the scripted originals.

Sparky was always more concerned about the products he was asked to endorse than about the final negotiated fee for his service. We both had a good idea about how much his image was worth to a prospective suitor.

"Don't nickel-and-dime 'em, Daniel," he would once in a while remind me. "Be fair to 'em once and they might come back for more."

There wasn't a payday big enough, however, to make him compromise his commitment to endorse only products he felt comfortable with.

Early in his Detroit career, for instance, the owner of a restaurant-bar in an upscale suburban hotel called to ask if Sparky might consider putting his name on the establishment. I informed the owner that I doubted Sparky would agree. But with an initial offer of $100,000, I owed it to Sparky to let him make the final decision.

"Absolutely not!" he said. There was no hesitation. "They could double the offer and the answer would still be no."

Sparky anticipated the possible problems. The establishment would want him to visit a couple of times a week. "I never went to no bars and I ain't startin' now," he said. "And suppose there was trouble in the bar one night. Who do you think would get all the publicity?"

Over the years, Sparky rejected several offers to promote alcoholic products. "I got a pretty good hunch the mamas and papas of all the kids who love baseball wouldn't appreciate me pushin' beer on the public," he said. "There's enough companies out there, Daniel. We can lay back and do the right thing."

Throughout the years, Sparky generously donated his time to record innumerable public service announcements for charities and an assortment of other worthy causes around the state.

Surprising to Sparky, but certainly not to me, was the recognition he received even outside of the United States. On seven different cruises to the Caribbean with him, he was always recognized by at least a few dozen of the natives.

Baseball has exploded throughout South America. An ambassador such as Sparky is impossible to hide.

Sparky not only became the face of the Tigers for almost two decades; he was an unofficial baseball trademark throughout his career.

"That mug of yours has fooled a lot of people," I used to tease him.

He'd wink and smile. "I just know how to use it," he'd say.

Before moving to another story on that Sunday I couldn't help thinking about how fortunate both of us had been. Throughout all of our years together, there was never a scandal involving Sparky. Not even a controversy.

I learned from Sparky that even in the business world honesty and courtesy are the surest tickets to success.

14

★

God Is Watching

I teased Sparky by asking if he had said his prayers that Sunday morning.

"'Yea, though I walk through the valley of the shadow of death, I will fear no evil: for you are with me; your rod and your staff they comfort me,'" he responded without hesitation.

The 23rd Psalm was Sparky's favorite. Sometimes he would throw it out of nowhere into a conversation for no other reason than to allow everyone a moment to catch his breath.

Sparky was not a religious zealot. Not even close. Religion to Sparky centered more around the Golden Rule of treating people right. "That's the most important rule to God," he often said. "There ain't nothin' God loves better than to have all of His people treated right."

Sparky was one of the few major-league managers—maybe the only one—to have met the pope. He was friends with Detroit archbishop Edmund Szoka, who was instrumental in arranging a papal visit to Detroit by Pope John Paul II in 1987.

Countless thousands crowded all the streets of Hamtramck, a heavily Polish city surrounded by Detroit. The crowd exploded with wild cheers when Szoka presented Sparky to the pope on the outdoor stage that had been constructed for the papal address.

Speaking to Szoka in Polish, the pope asked: "*Co to jest*, Sparky?" The English translation is: "What is this, Sparky?" The pope was fluent in several languages. Sparky knew a little about English and a whole lot more of what we called "Sparkyese." That wasn't a language the pope had mastered. Or even knew anything about.

Szoka explained that he was the manager of Detroit's baseball team and a beloved figure in the community. Sparky was humbled by the experience and even received a baseball signed to him by the pope. It was probably the first baseball ever signed by a pope. That put John Paul II only a couple of million behind the number Sparky signed throughout his career. The surprise gift was arranged by Szoka.

Sparky smiled and bowed reverently as the pope put a hand on his shoulder.

"This sounds crazy, but I never saw nothin' in my life like the look in the pope's eyes," Sparky told me. "I can't explain it, but his eyes really did twinkle. It was the most peaceful look I ever saw in my life."

Sparky kept the signed baseball in a safety-deposit box in Thousand Oaks. Upon his induction, he donated it to the Hall of Fame.

Sparky did believe in God. But, far more than with words, he practiced his spirituality by treating each person he encountered with respect.

The closest he came to any mention of religion was his usual goodbye to those who were nearest to him—"Just remember . . . God loves you."

Sparky was converted to Catholicism during his playing and managing days with Toronto, which then was part of the International League. He was counseled and baptized by a priest named Father Joe, a soft-spoken, gruff sort of character who could have made a good longshoreman or a lumberjack had he not opted for the wearing of the cloth.

I got to know Father Joe at the breakfasts the three of us shared at least once during each series when we played the Toronto Blue Jays after they joined the American League. He was a jovial fellow who enjoyed talking baseball as much as any spiritual matter. He enjoyed exchanging memories of the old days when he and Sparky met. He always sought some encouraging words about his beloved Blue Jays.

Sparky always provided an optimistic picture, almost as if he were delivering his own sermon.

Before he left the breakfast table, Father Joe would give us a "carryout" absolution for all of our sins! It felt kind of neat to receive a house call absolution in the middle of a restaurant where people were finishing their scrambled eggs.

And we didn't even need to confess all of our sins!

Sparky was a parishioner of St. Paschal Catholic Church, about five miles from his home. During the season while managing, of course, he was unable to participate in any parish activities. During retirement, however, he could usually be found in the back of the church, on the right side, for nine o'clock Sunday Mass.

He chose the back to avoid causing any distractions. He knew almost every parishioner. After each Mass he had to shake as many hands as did the priest.

Sparky enjoyed a healthy interpretation of spirituality that eliminated any ill-conceived feeling of guilt while endorsing the rewards for living an honest and decent life.

"I can talk to God any time I want to," he told me many times. "It don't have to be in no church. And you don't gotta be fallin' down to your knees for Him to listen. He's got better ears than all of us. He's gonna hear you and He's gonna listen to what you have to say. How can He not hear you? He's God!

"If I can make it to Mass I go there. And if I can't, I tell Him why. He ain't gonna send me to hell just 'cause I didn't go to church to talk to Him. He knows what's goin' on inside all of us. So I suggest we better do right by people 'cause that's what He cares about most."

Throughout many years of being a parishioner at St. Paschal he befriended a few different pastors of the church. He had great respect for Father David, who now serves the parish. Of course, Sparky shared a slice of his personal religious feelings soon after the pastor's arrival.

"I just wanna let you know," Sparky began. "I ain't afraid of you. I ain't afraid of any man. I'm only afraid of that man up above. That's the guy we all gotta do right by."

Sparky was almost always involved with a variety of activities to raise money for the parish. He was called upon to play as a celebrity in the annual church golf tournament. He was called upon to serve at the various pancake breakfasts—obviously for his celebrity and not for his baking skills!

Unless he had a prior commitment, Sparky never refused. He knew that wouldn't get him closer to heaven. He just knew it was the right thing to do.

It didn't matter that Sparky had been unable to attend Mass on that Sunday. He had spoken to God. And he knew that God had listened.

The strength of his conviction certainly made a lifelong impact on me.

15

★

Spring Training Memories

One of the pictures I saw standing in Sparky's bookcase featured the Old Man, George McCarthy, smiling brightly under Florida's scorching spring training sun.

"We did a lot of bitching about how long spring training lasted," I told Sparky. "But wouldn't it be neat to slip back in time for just a couple of days?"

Sparky smiled and shook his head. "We had our time," he said. "Now it's time for the young people."

They'd be in for a little surprise when getting a taste of the spring training that unfolds daily away from the park.

Lizards and rattlers and a menu full of other tasty delicacies speckle the back roads of central Florida from the Gulf Coast to the Atlantic Ocean. Those back roads are long. They're desolate. And they're scorching hot even before the sun revs up to full power late in the morning. There's nothing glamorous about traveling to road games during the spring training exhibition season.

I know. Over the course of about 25 spring trainings in the middle of the state, I think I traveled all of them.

Those wearisome morning drives to meaningless exhibition games now mean so much more when looking back through the years. They made for myriad precious memories.

After calling up a few during our Sunday session, Sparky and I laughed till tears formed in the corners of our eyes. The memories remained etched permanently in our minds.

After a couple of years with the Tigers, Sparky rode to all exhibition road games with me. We left after the team bus had departed so that he could get a longer look at minor-league prospects who were working out in Lakeland.

I was responsible for filling the tank with gas, packing the trunk with a couple of coolers of soda and juice, taking a handful of packaged snacks, and grabbing enough towels from the clubhouse to sponge up all of our sweat.

The tricky part of the trip was leading Sparky through a line of autograph seekers waiting outside of the clubhouse and then leaving with enough time to arrive at the park so that he could kibitz with the press for a few minutes before the game.

Sometimes we had guest passengers. There was my son Dan Jr. There was the Old Man. Once in a while we were joined by Pat Zier, who covered the Tigers in spring training for the *Lakeland Ledger*.

On one trip we were joined by movie star Tom Selleck. Selleck is a native Detroiter who kept his allegiance to the Tigers. He occasionally showed up for a few games in Florida.

"I hate when you show up here, Tom," Sparky used to tease him. "All the young women mistake me for looking so much like you."

The rules for conversations driving to and from the games were simple—there were no rules. No topic was off-limits. And anyone who didn't get a chance to say enough had no one to blame but himself.

At times our drives were filled with music. Some from the radio. Some from a CD I carried. And some sung by Sparky, who couldn't put two proper notes together if the first one had been given to him.

Out of nowhere, at times, he would break into a chorus of Rodgers and Hammerstein's classic "You'll Never Walk Alone." As soon as he started the first line—"When you walk through a storm"—I quickly flipped the radio on and turned it up as loud as possible.

"That's such a beautiful song," I used to tell him with a clear tone of sarcasm. "If you really like it that much, I suggest you never sing it again."

He winked at me, smiled, and just continued to sing. After a few more lines, I knew my point was missed and turned the radio off. When he reached the final line—"You'll never walk alone"—he upped his tone a couple of decibels, and he repeated it even louder as I glanced out the window to make sure no passing car might hear him.

One spring I had purchased a CD containing a collection of songs by Mary Chapin Carpenter. The only Carpenters Sparky was familiar with were those of the Pennsylvania family that once owned the Philadelphia Phillies.

Perhaps I played the CD too much. After a couple of trips, Sparky actually got to liking the songs, particularly one titled "Passionate Kisses." Whenever it played, he accompanied Carpenter with as many words as he could remember. It's impossible for me to hear that song today without falling back to a time that felt so much more complete.

On a longer trip home from Vero Beach, Sparky called for an unscheduled stop to use the restroom. When informed that this was a nonstop ship we were riding, he simply stated that he'd just have to relieve himself inside the ship.

I immediately reconsidered my refusal and pulled into the first service station we approached. Watching through the front window of the car, I noticed a collection of patrons emerging from the food aisles to gather near the counter.

After all, it's not every day that a little man with white hair dressed in a full Detroit Tigers uniform—except for cap and spikes—walks into a filling station in the middle of Florida and asks where the men's room is.

And especially not when the man is a spitting image of Sparky Anderson.

Familiar with the routine I knew was about to follow, I turned off the ignition and walked into the store. By the time I reached the counter, Sparky was surrounded. He was dripping with sweat and dirty from the dust of the game, but there he was spinning yarns and signing autographs.

When he glanced up to see me, he looked relieved.

"I can't talk no more," he courteously told the crowd, and pointed at me. "That guy over there will kill me. He's gotta get back to Lakeland as fast as we can."

I can't recall how many times we played that same scene. Strangely enough, I was always the bad guy.

On most drives back to Lakeland after a game, the roads were filled with traffic. Because of the game and all of the natural energy he exerted throughout each day, often Sparky would lay his head on top of the rolled-down window, with his white hair flapping in the wind.

Many passengers in passing vehicles did a double take. It must have struck them that the older man with white hair and his head hung halfway out the window, who was wearing a Detroit Tigers uniform, looked a lot, coincidentally, like Sparky.

Could it really be him?

Those that did recognize him when he was awake tooted their horns or waved wildly, asking only a small sign of recognition in return.

Sparky always accommodated. As they drove by happily yelling "We love you, Sparky," he clenched his fist high out the window and yelled back: "Go, you Tigers." It was just a kind token of appreciation for the fans, who stored those chance encounters permanently in their memories to share with friends, neighbors, or even their grandchildren sometime down the road.

After arriving at Lakeland's Marchant Stadium, Sparky darted from the car into the clubhouse to shower and prepare for his "glamorous" dinner with the coaches and me. We usually dined at a cafeteria near the team hotel. Customers paid by the item or plunked down $6.95 for all they could eat.

It's impossible to measure how many seemingly unimportant moments such as these we shared. They become even more precious with each passing day.

Sparky's boundless enthusiasm taught me to appreciate each day as a special moment in time that will never be lived again. He showed me how sometimes the ordinary truly does become the sublime. He also showed how one tiny slice of kindness to a stranger can make a lasting memory for that person, as well as for people like me who were privileged to share in such moments every day.

16

★

Kindred Spirits

Another book I spotted in Sparky's bookcase that Sunday afternoon was the one I had written a few years prior with Michigan-raised former college and professional football legend Ron Kramer.

"Did you ever read this book I gave you?" I asked.

"No," he said.

"Are you ever going to?" I followed teasingly.

"I'm workin' up to it," he settled the issue.

But the mention of the book made Sparky want to talk about the visit we made to Kramer's house a couple of years before.

It was always fun to be around Kramer. He was a colorful character who never cheated himself out of one minute of life, either on the football field or away from the park.

Visiting him at his home was always an almost otherworldly experience, especially for first-time visitors.

Kramer was a football legend, a throwback to those lovable swash-buckling days of professional sports when players played as hard at life as they did during their games on the field.

Kramer was so perfectly robust at filling his role that he would have stretched the imagination of Damon Runyon.

Kramer was an All-Pro tight end for the legendary Green Bay Packers coached by the immortal Vince Lombardi. Featuring household names such as Paul Hornung, Bart Starr, Jim Taylor, Boyd Dowler, Ray Nitschke, and Max McGee, among others, the Packers established an NFL dynasty perhaps never to be equaled.

Lombardi loved Kramer and called him his "12th man on the field." Not only did Kramer possess the soft hands of a pickpocket, he had the battering power of a tank that provided the key block on the Packers' celebrated "Green Bay Sweep."

Before being drafted by the Packers, Kramer was an All-American tight end for the University of Michigan. He was on a straight line toward a spot in the professional football Hall of Fame before injuries cut short his career.

I was going to prepare Sparky for the unimaginable sight he was about to see in Kramer's house. Then I realized no amount of warning was sufficient to describe how the end of the world might look one day.

We were driving north to Fenton, about 60 miles from downtown Detroit. The area is filled with trees, apple orchards, lakes, streams, and gently rolling hills. This picturesque slice of country is stolen from the dreams of men who wear beards, jeans, plaid shirts, boots, and baseball caps.

We were going to the home of one of them. He was born and raised in the city but was perfectly placed in seclusion, where homes need no fences and locks on doors are optional.

Kramer and I had been friends for many years. He expected my arrival but was unaware of the mutual friend I was bringing.

I walked through the front door yelling at Kramer to put on some clothes, just in case he had decided to be as natural for the day as his animal friends running around outside. That often was the dress code of the day in Kramer's house.

"Somebody's waiting for you out on the front porch," I told him. "Better go see who it is."

Kramer wasn't used to guiding people into his home. Most simply entered and shouted: "Kramer, I'm here."

His curiosity piqued, Kramer shouted as he neared the door: "I don't know who in the hell you are, but get your ass in here."

Immediately the door opened and there stood Sparky.

"What the hell are you doing here?" Kramer barked.

Kramer then lifted Sparky from under the armpits and bowed his head so he could kiss Sparky on the top of his head. That was Kramer's normal greeting. Departing guests he really liked were in for a special treat: a kiss on the lips and a hearty "I love you." Sparky, of course, always qualified for the special farewell.

"I was walkin' around the neighborhood and thought I just might drop in to say hello," Sparky said.

Kramer was a giant of a man, close to double the size of Sparky. His body blocked Sparky's view of the living room until Kramer set him down at the edge of the adjoining kitchen.

That's when Sparky got his first glimpse of the ruins of Armageddon . . . or at least a vision of what to expect.

Kramer's living room exploded with a mishmash of at least 32,348 items of sports memorabilia, equipment, posters, pictures, signs, balls, trophies, trinkets, and other unknown items that have yet to be named. They sat on tables. They were attached to the walls. They stood on the floor. They hung from the ceiling. They covered a couch and a pretty close to matching chair.

It was impossible to scratch your head without an elbow bumping into some sort of trinket, figurine, trophy, or other "valuable" piece of memorabilia Kramer didn't even know was there.

These were all collected throughout Kramer's colorful career and the equally colorful life he led after hanging up his football cleats.

A male's dream and a female's nightmare. That was life according to Kramer.

"How do you like my collection?" Kramer asked Sparky.

Sparky took time to peruse the entire room.

"The collection looks great," he said. "But where in the hell is the living room?"

Kramer was particularly proud of the wooden duck that quacked a variety of obscene messages whenever someone approached the kitchen. "Looks just like the duck on the old Groucho Marx show,"

Kramer said proudly. "But my guy is funnier. Women sometimes don't know how to take him, but what the hell? The damn duck is funny."

On one wall hung a framed number 87 University of Michigan football jersey. It was the last one Kramer wore before the number was retired by Coach Bennie Oosterbaan after the 1956 season. At Michigan, Kramer won three letters in football, three in basketball, and three in track when freshmen weren't eligible to play on the varsity.

He was a born athletic freak and a certified "only visiting this planet" alien.

With Sparky's proclivity for order and all things being put into their proper places, I thought his stomach might be doing flip-flops as he continued to gaze around the room.

"You okay?" I asked. "I told you this is what the end of the world looks like."

"I'm okay," he said. "Just afraid to move. I don't wanna step on nothin' that just might explode."

Kramer took us outside for a walk around the property, including an overview of Lake Kramer. "I swim every day when the weather is right," Kramer said. "Just walk out here naked and dive right in. Nobody comes around. If they do, what's the difference? It's all part of nature."

Despite the differences in their personalities, the differences in their sports, the differences in their physical sizes, and maybe the differences in their perspectives on life, Kramer and Sparky shared a kindred spirit. Both lived life with a passion; both loved people; and neither could refuse any request to support a charity . . . especially one that benefited kids.

Sparky got to know Kramer almost from the first year he came to Detroit. Everybody involved with any sport in Detroit got to know Kramer.

Except for one time because of illness, Kramer participated in every golf tournament Sparky hosted for his charity. Sparky came to love the eccentric big kid who did more for Detroit area charities than anyone will know.

"Football players are really different from athletes in any other sport," Sparky remarked on the drive home.

"For sure, that one is," I said, referring to Kramer. "The world isn't big enough to have two like him."

Sparky always looked forward to visiting with Kramer each summer. Because of failing health, Kramer could not play in Sparky's golf tournament of July 2010.

Less than two months later, on September 11, Kramer died at the age of 75. And less than two months after that, on November 4, Sparky joined his friend.

I never did tell Sparky about Kramer's passing. I wrestled with it in my mind and discussed the matter with Carol. We decided that with the battle Sparky was fighting, it was better left at keeping Kramer as still one of his dear friends.

I felt good to have taken Sparky on that peculiar visit a couple of years ago. None of us could have guessed it would turn out to be the last meeting between a couple of such precious souls.

On that Sunday as we spun all of our yarns, it was best that Sparky believed Kramer was still around.

17

★

Special Walks

Because it was Sunday, Sparky's regular group of walking buddies took the day off. The group was a mongrel mix of personalities—just the kind of followers Sparky naturally attracted.

Gerry was a retired Lutheran pastor. His wife, Jan, who has passed away, was a tenured English professor at California Lutheran University. Mary and Ike were retired elementary school teachers. Both ladies came from the Midwest and shared a house together. A Cleveland transplant, Paul, was a retired flight attendant.

Sparky, by the way, was the only retired major-league manager and Hall of Fame member of the group.

We referred to them simply as "the walkers." They all lived within a half mile of each other, and Monday through Friday, they walked the neighborhood beginning at 6:30 a.m.

Sparky's involvement with the walkers sprang from the rehabilitation program prescribed after his heart surgery in the summer of 1999. Because of his hyperactivity and determination to excel, he promised himself that no one would walk longer than he on any given day.

He was bulldog stubborn about becoming the healthiest man in the neighborhood.

They all came to understand Sparky's drive, and it was amusingly all right with them. I became an honorary member of the walkers through my many visits to Thousand Oaks. Other stray visitors occasionally joined the group, but not on a permanent basis.

On several occasions throughout the years, a walker would comment about Sparky's heightened sense of anticipation as my arrival date drew near. The feeling, of course, was mutual.

I was living validation of all the colorful baseball stories only Sparky could tell.

"You don't know how lucky you are," I used to remind them periodically. "Sparky gets a lot of money to spin those tales at dinners all around the country."

Sparky was the master at spinning baseball tales. No matter how many times he told the same story, there was always a fresh little twist. He had a natural sense for drama and often came up with a more sparkling conclusion to a story he may have told several times before.

"Are all those stories he tells us true?" one would occasionally ask.

"Of course they're true," I answered. "As true as baseball allows them to be. That's the magic of the game."

The group never tired of any story Sparky chose to tell. With me around, they often said, Sparky seemed to spice each story as if it had happened just a few days ago.

Each member of the group was curious, insightful, and kind. They appreciated the sense of baseball history unfolding before them as told by a legend who had helped to write so much of that history himself.

They never tired of asking the same questions that they had posed many times before.

Is Pete Rose the toughest player you ever managed? Is Johnny Bench the best catcher ever to play? Is Alan Trammell really as nice as he appears to be? Is Jack Morris the meanest pitcher you had?

Sparky never tired of answering each question as if being asked for the first time. And with each little detail he cleverly added, it sounded like a story they had never heard before.

Some in the group expressed concern over the rising price of going to a major-league baseball game or any of the professional sports.

"Me too," Sparky would answer, and then unload some personal theories about how to return the game to the average working family.

"They're all gonna price out the little man," Sparky lamented. "Baseball used to be the game for the average workingman and his family. Well, it ain't that way no more. I feel sorry for all those people. They oughta let each family that buys four tickets to a game get into the park for free for another game."

Discussions were never limited to baseball: the president, the economy, health care, education, the United States' involvement in any number of wars—each took a turn at being the topic of the day.

As a professor of American literature, Jan shared many book titles and authors with me. I was impressed by a seminar she had taken under the direction of Wallace Stegner at the University of California at Berkeley. There was a time when I was fascinated with Stegner's body of work, and it was refreshing to listen to one of his students provide her perspective on the author.

Days with Sparky began at about six o'clock. Because I was still functioning on eastern time, I was usually the first one in the kitchen. I brewed a pot of coffee and had a half cup waiting for him when he came downstairs.

Sparky was a fruit junkie. He ate any kind of fruit, from apples to papayas to everything in between. I teased him almost daily that he ate more fruit in one week than a monkey does in a month.

"Ain't no monkey healthier than me," he answered.

He then mixed a couple of fruit juices like cranberry and grape in an oversized bottle filled with ice to drink during the walk. Then it was time to go.

Before joining the walkers Sparky would scamper across the street to pick up the newspapers lying in the driveways of three neighbors. He placed one in front of each door. It was one of those rituals he insisted on following every day.

"Just a little thing," he said. "Maybe that'll be the nicest thing to happen to them today."

During my visits, I handled the first two houses. Sparky finished with Pinky's house on the corner. About two years ago, however, Pinky died. Pinky, along with Sparky and Carol, was one of the last original homeowners in the subdivision, which was built more than 40 years ago.

The first destination for the walkers took us out of the subdivision along Moorpark Road to pick up Ike, Mary, and Paul before returning to Sparky's sub, which comprised the largest part of our route. The rest of the group joined us as we passed their houses.

There were no standards concerning the direction or speed of our walks. The leader of the pack turned onto streets of his or her choice. The pace of the walk was decided on an individual basis. At times the group walked in a pack. At other times the group was strung out in pairs almost a half block long.

Those walkers inclined to cut the route short one day simply retired to their homes as the rest continued down the street. There were no rules, no stringencies attached.

Except for one. And that was self-imposed.

If the last walker finished after 45 minutes, Sparky would push himself to 50. If someone bumped up to 55, Sparky kept going for an hour.

Each walk centered around the quaint campus of California Lutheran University. The picture-postcard campus looks as if it were lifted straight out of a *Better Homes and Gardens* pictorial. Rosebushes, tulips, mums, lilies, and orchids speckle the lush green hills. Walking paths slice through an orchard of trees from one edge of the campus to the other.

Recently completed athletic facilities are more functionally equipped and aesthetically engaging than those at many universities competing in Division I athletics. There are two Olympic-size outdoor pools, a new football field, two gymnasiums, and a host of other indoor facilities. And, of course, there's George "Sparky" Anderson Park.

After all the walkers had dispersed for the day, Sparky and I often returned to the campus by car. For a while he developed a penchant for surreptitiously snipping flowers to make bouquets for Carol and two of the walkers, Mary and Ike.

In the backseat of his car, he carried a pair of garden scissors, gloves, and a towel for protection from the thorns of the rosebushes. I served as a sentry while he crawled into a garden to snip the stems and then quickly threw them onto a pile to be loaded in the backseat.

It was a harmless clandestine exercise that allowed us to play James Bond for a few moments. All of the gardeners, whom Sparky knew by name, smiled and looked the other way upon seeing his car approaching.

It was merely the excitement of the game he played that made the exercise so innocently endearing. He already had donated so much time and effort to the school that the president would have sent him an invitation to snip till his fingers hurt had he known.

After arranging the flowers so that each color was in its most stunningly dramatic position, we placed it on the front porch of Mary and Ike's home before ringing the doorbell and dashing to the car for a getaway unseen by anyone.

When Sparky wasn't collecting flowers, he was heisting rocks for his front yard garden. Because of construction for all of the new athletic facilities, the campus was littered with rocks of all sizes. Following the same strategy we used for snatching flowers, we loaded the trunk with rocks ranging from marble-sized to as big as bowling balls. In the course of one week, we had enough to fill two blocks' worth of rock gardens. Still not enough, of course, for Sparky.

I miss those walks with all of those good people. I miss that peculiar bond that only we had shared. I miss our clandestine schemes to secure flowers and rocks that the university would have delivered to his door if only Sparky had asked.

But I can remember. I can still feel the excitement. And I'll never forget.

There are walks around my home. There are flowers to pick and rocks to be touched. But they don't feel the same.

Peace, I discovered, is more easily found in such free and simple activities shared by friends than in anything more elaborately contrived.

I miss those walks immensely.

18

★

A Beautiful Day

The first of three days in October had come to an end. And it had been a beautiful day. One we both wished could have lasted forever.

We shared memories and feelings accumulated over more than three decades. The memories were vivid. The feelings were so alive.

And they belonged only to us.

Each story confirmed a conviction I had formed many years ago. The best baseball stories often aren't about the game at all. The games serve merely as a stage for the stories to come to life. For players. For managers. For fans. And, most of all, for friends.

Long ago I had realized the impact Sparky had had on my life. Now, with humility, I came to appreciate how much I had meant to him. For the first time in my life I fully accepted what Carol had told me many times over the course of many years—Sparky considered me to be his best friend.

As we told those stories, I could feel the love and trust both of us shared. It was different from any other friendships we had accumulated along the way.

Our friendship was born out of baseball, but was unbound by the game.

"I wonder what woulda happened if that jerk of an agent in Cincinnati hadn't kept that money he owed me," Sparky said as we wound up our visit for the day.

This was the story we had dissected many times. It was because of that breach of trust that Sparky asked me to handle all of his business affairs shortly after he joined the Detroit Tigers.

Since I was public relations director for the team, our jobs already shared a link. Almost immediately, we established an efficient and enjoyable working rapport. He used to pepper me with questions about the organization, the history of the club, and the city of Detroit. I used to tease him about finally joining the major leagues.

"You're in the American League now," I chided. "No more National League softies for you."

From our professional positions grew a business relationship that evolved into a friendship that got stronger each day.

"Just be honest with me and all of our clients," he said. "You got good instincts. Follow your gut. I trust you."

That was it. There were no questions. No rules. No contract. Not even a promise of what to expect. We both took tremendous pride in the fact that we didn't need any scribbles on a piece of paper to know what one expected of the other.

"If you need a lawyer and a contract to do what two people who trust each other do, then you ain't got somebody you can trust," he explained.

Sparky also took pride explaining our agreement at commercial shoots and dinner appearances at cities around the country when introducing me to the hosts. "This is my man Daniel," he would say. "He's handled all my business for 32 years. And here's the agreement we have."

He would then extend his right arm as if to shake a hand.

"We don't need nothin' more than that," he would say. "He's my best friend."

We both shared similar ethics. We both came from blue-collar families that taught us honesty and the beauty of hard work. We both loved baseball and were able to laugh at ourselves.

As time went on and Sparky's celebrity continued to grow, I became his shadow, particularly after our retirement from baseball, when we were free to travel more extensively.

He was the teacher—not only of baseball, but of living the right way. He taught me all the unwritten rules. Not merely through words, but through the way he lived.

I learned the right time to allow people to approach him. I learned when it was more appropriate to keep them away. I came to gain his trust in all the decisions I made.

There certainly were times when we disagreed on matters of baseball, business, politics, and the various complexities that everyone faces in life. But we disagreed only for the sake of one protecting the other.

I usually ended all such discussions by teasing him: "Down deep you know I'm right."

Sparky had a photographic memory for all the games he played on those rock-filled minor-league diamonds and from his one season in the big leagues with those brushed infields. That was 1959 with the Philadelphia Phillies. He batted only .218, but at least he was there. He vividly recalled each hit he had.

"It wasn't that hard to do," he laughed. "There weren't that many."

He maintained total recall of all the games he managed in the major and minor leagues. He could recall specific plays that changed the course of a game. He had vivid recollections of certain moves he made to force an opposing manager's hand. The moves he should have made and regretted for not having done so were even more painfully etched in his memory.

He loved swapping those old baseball stories with longtime baseball cronies and members of the media who kept such stories alive.

He just didn't spend much time reliving a whole lot of the past that had nothing to do with the games. He lived very much in the moment. He always maintained that "there's no future living in the past."

For these three days in October, however, he felt peaceful reminiscing: not merely about "the good old days," but about what those days meant to him, to his family, and to his friends.

None of the stories we told were epics. Most were simple serendipitous moments that touched both of our hearts.

Reflecting now over the different stages of our lives together, it becomes as obvious as the pug nose on Babe Ruth's face how much our already time-tested friendship grew after we retired from baseball.

And neither of us ever took that blessing for granted.

It took me a few years to thoroughly appreciate the difference between the personality of the character everyone knew as Sparky and the man I came to love simply as George.

Sparky was the engaging character who could overwhelm a ballroom full of people with the simple flash of a smile. It didn't matter who else was in the room. Sparky always became the focus of attention.

Sparky had charisma. Charm. Presence. Personality. He could make a Wal-Mart suit look like it had been tailor-made at Brooks Brothers. He could make every person he touched, even for a moment, feel as if he or she were his best friend.

George was the guy who lived down the street of every neighborhood. He preferred pizza and burgers to steak and shrimp. He did yard work and watched TV instead of performing and appearing on TV.

Each character needed the other in order to survive.

George loved people as much as did Sparky. They just happened to express it in their own distinct ways.

George felt more comfortable at home. He enjoyed telling stories to neighbors and running errands to the supermarket. He was as flamboyant as a wet shirt hanging on a clothesline.

Sparky was always onstage. He was the ultimate showman, who could mingle with the "beautiful people" and capture an audience as big as a ballpark crowd. He preferred, however, talking baseball with one of the men working the line at the Ford River Rouge plant.

He was able to mix both characters so well that it took me a while to realize how taxing on him each transition could be.

At the core, however, the person was still the same. He was a regular guy who happened to hit it big without surrendering the values of a blue-collar background.

The stories that afternoon showed how much he cared for people. They also reinforced how strong our friendship had become.

During my plane ride early that morning I couldn't imagine what to expect after I arrived. Perhaps I should have realized that no matter how low George was feeling, Sparky was going to deliver a show.

I just never would have guessed how a collection of almost trivial stories so precisely defined our unshakable bond.

Shortly after seven o'clock, Sparky said he was tired. He had picked at a dinner Carol had prepared though his appetite by then was no more than those of the birds he fed daily from the feeder in his backyard. He was exhausted. Yet, we were both exhilarated. We had fed each other a significant slice of a lifetime that our stories captured so well.

And it felt good.

Lying in bed, I anticipated what Monday would bring. He had said we were going to talk baseball. Just like the old days, when there was nobody better than Sparky orchestrating a game.

I was anxious for Monday to come. Yet I didn't want the minutes to pass. Only two days in October were left. We had to cherish each moment.

MONDAY

★

Talkin' Baseball

It was darker than a Halloween midnight nightmare when I awoke obscenely early Monday morning. The clock next to my bed flashed four o'clock. My body told me it was seven where I had come from the day before.

I was too anxious to go back to sleep and too restless to simply lie in bed.

Quietly I arose, showered, and shaved. It was too early for the newspaper to be lying on the driveway, so I picked up a magazine I had brought from the plane.

At least I was back in the kitchen where Sparky and I had spent all of Sunday afternoon and part of the evening. It felt good to know that in a couple of hours I could watch sunlight slowly swallow the darkness.

Like on Sunday, we had no specific plans. We had agreed to let the day unfold as naturally and gently as a lazy pop fly to shortstop. No time schedule. No agenda. Just talkin' some baseball and grabbing a few laughs along the way.

By the time Sparky made it to the kitchen, I had already brewed a pot of coffee. As Sparky used to do, I had delivered the newspapers from the driveways to the front doors of the neighbors across the street long before any of them had arisen. I had a half glass of orange juice waiting for him on the table.

"About time you decided to join the real world," I teased him.

Sometimes there's no better medicine than good old-fashioned baseball irreverence regardless of the seriousness of a situation.

I was anxious to hear some old-fashioned baseball stories. Listening to them is sometimes more fun than watching a game. Especially the stories only Sparky could tell.

All of the stories happened just as he told them . . . or at least close enough for his message to be unmistakably clear. Between the lines of each story lay a deeper message. Listening to them carefully, you could always discover a valuable lesson about life. That's what meant so much to Sparky. That's why his stories must live forever.

Over the past few years, we had talked far less baseball than most people might imagine. The myriad corporate changes were difficult for either of us to accept, but our love for the game in its innocence remained unshakable.

That's why Sparky's gift, delivered to me almost nightly over the years in his office after the clubhouse cleared and in hotel suites on the road, was a priceless treasure that enhanced my appreciation for the purity of the game.

That's when Sparky stripped each game—sometimes each play—to the bone. I was learning the game from the master.

Step by step, from the first inning through the last, he tested and corrected me till I came to understand baseball on a level I hadn't even known existed.

It was as if I were learning the intricacies of the computer from Bill Gates. Or the essence of the blues from B. B. King.

Sparky was a thorough teacher. He was patient. He was direct. He had a sense for what a student might or might not know. He could tell I was eager to learn. And it was obvious he was willing to share.

His lessons went beyond the game. He taught me about all the unwritten rules that apply as much to life as they do to sports. The unwritten rules aren't found in a textbook. They're not even found in a prayer book.

They're all about how we treat people and what it means to be a good person.

Sparky liked to joke about his limited playing talents. But he did survive playing 17 minor-league seasons when the system had more than twice as many teams as it does today. He played in the major leagues for just that one year. But that was when there were only 16 big-league clubs.

So Sparky did have some playing talent. And it might have been good enough to land him in the big leagues had he played today.

Sparky, though, was born to manage. Even before he got his first minor-league assignment, he thought like a manager. He talked like a manager. More important, he acted like a manager.

Right behind the positions of president of the United States, a five-star general in any branch of our military, and the pope, no job was more revered by Sparky than that of a major-league manager.

Managing is taxing, trying, testing, and tumultuous, but Sparky loved every second. Throughout history, only a handful of managers have had more impact on the game than he.

Reflecting upon all of our years together, I still feel privileged to have learned from such a historic character, who also doubled as one of the greatest showmen in the history of the game.

Obviously, as good a teacher as Sparky was, my insight into the game was far less than his. Much of Sparky's success originated in the gut. That's a gift that can't be taught. And he knew how to use it.

Sparky could have managed and performed in any era. That's one of the ultimate yardsticks of greatness in baseball or any sport.

I felt myself being thrown back into one of those late-evening sessions in a quiet hotel room where nothing mattered but Sparky, the art of baseball managing, and me.

Of course, we began the session at that old reliable kitchen table. Except for maybe a clubhouse, there was no better place to be. We paused only briefly for a few breaks in the backyard under the pleasant autumn sunshine.

Again, the stories bounced gently from one subject to the next. This conglomeration of baseball stories defined one of the most accomplished managers in the history of the game.

Of all my baseball learning sessions I treasure this one the most. I knew it was my last. I knew my teacher expected my best. I couldn't let him down.

And thanks to a teacher who refused to accept mediocrity, I still carry those lessons today.

19

★

Something to Smile About

Sparky's eyes were twinkling. A smile covered his face.

Even though it had been a few years since we had talked about managers and their opportunity to make a difference in a game, there was no subject closer to his heart.

Despite his weakened physical condition, I was sure I heard that familiar cackle in his voice. Even the squeeze of his hand on my shoulder told me these stories were going to be good.

The mere opportunity to manage anywhere in professional baseball was a privilege for Sparky. To have managed for 26 years in the major leagues was a blessing Sparky never took for granted. In fact, he treated that honor more like a holy mission than a profession in which he had few peers.

A teacher at heart from his 17 years in the minor leagues, Sparky enjoyed face-to-face training, one player at a time. "I never was big on clubhouse meetings," Sparky said. "If you have two a year, that's one too many. Clubhouse meetings are for college and high school kids. Big-league guys are supposed to be pros."

Unlike most managers, who sit in the dugout during batting practice watching players hit balls all the way into the next county, Sparky preferred to roam the infield and outfield for brief personal talks with the players. He called those visits "house calls." By the time it was the other team's turn to take the field, Sparky had completed his rounds.

Maybe he had noticed that a player's hands were too low on the bat, or that he was standing too deep in the batter's box.

If an infielder was having trouble turning a double play, maybe he needed a little tip about how to make his feet move quicker around the base.

If a player was hitting and fielding generally well, Sparky almost always just waved at him and kept walking.

"I got nothin' to say to you," he might joke with that player. "I'm gonna stay out of your way and let your bat do all the talkin'. I hope I don't have to talk to you for the rest of the season."

I uncapped a bottle of water and placed it in front of Sparky. I popped the top from a can of diet soda pop, took a swig, and prepared myself for a final lesson on baseball, one like I had never had before.

Sparky began with typical simplicity.

"Get the best players," he said. "Keep 'em healthy. Put 'em in the lineup every day. Stay out of their way. And don't forget to pat 'em on the back once in a while just to let 'em know you care. Ain't it funny how the good managers seem to get all the good players and the bad managers get all the bad ones?"

We both smiled. That formula would probably work 99 percent of the time. But it doesn't happen that way. No manager always comes up with all of the best players.

Of course, Sparky knew he was overstating his premise. Then again, what would anyone expect? Sparky was always the master of overstatement. He wasn't going to change now.

Sparky's underlying foundation for success was getting to know all of his players.

"If you don't understand people," he began, "how they act, how they react to certain situations, what their strengths are, what their weaknesses are, then you ain't got no chance to be a successful big-league manager."

Baseball players are no different from people in all other walks of life, he insisted. Some are significantly more talented than others. That's just the way life goes.

"It happens like that in all jobs," Sparky explained. "Some doctors with all those fancy extra degrees they got after their names ain't no better than a little old country doctor who understands people. I've run into some doctors who shoulda thought about becoming a vet."

By understanding people, Sparky believed, a baseball manager is giving himself the best chance to fully utilize all the talents that his players possess.

"Let's be honest," he said. "Some managers get stuck with teams that ain't got no more talent than Humpty Dumpty. Based on talent alone, some teams got more chance of hitting the $100 million lottery than they do finishing anywhere but at the bottom of their division.

"But if the right manager comes along and gets his players playing together and gets them to playing to the best their talents allow, maybe he can steal a few games and sneak up a notch or two in the standings. There's nothing more anyone can ask."

Any major-league manager is capable of recognizing talent. Not all, however, are equipped to understand the potential and limitations of each individual player.

Although I had heard his managerial credo many times before, it was refreshing to hear the master run through his litany one last time. He began:

- Understand each player as a person. "Every player has a personal life that affects the way he performs on the field," he said. "Make sure everything is going right at home for each player or it will show up on the field."
- Get to know each player's family. "They have wives, children, even dogs and cats," he said. "Get to know their names. Get to know who they are. It makes a difference when a manager shows concern for the things that matter most to a player."

- Keep the door to your office open. "Every player must understand that the manager is concerned with their futures," he said. "If there's a problem, that player deserves the opportunity to discuss it with the manager."

- Maintain the confidentiality of manager/player relationships. "A player must feel confident that what's said in confidence remains in confidence," he said. "There were things I discussed with players in Cincinnati that I never told [general manager] Bob Howsam. It was the same situation with Jim Campbell at Detroit. It was up to me and the player to handle the situation, and nobody else needed to know."

- Never speak derogatorily about a player to the media. "The player has enough on his mind without worrying about his manager berating him in the press," he said. "If you got a problem with a player, keep it behind closed doors. The player's gotta know that."

- Never ask a player to do something both he and the manager already know he can't do. "If a guy ain't laid down a bunt even in high school, how can you expect him to do it in the big leagues?" he asked. "If you want a guy to hit a three-run homer in the ninth inning and he can't even get the ball to the warning track in batting practice, how in the hell can you expect him to do it now?"

- Don't be afraid to lose a game. "Better to lose one game than to put yourself into position to lose three or four more in a row 'cause you wasted all your pitchers," he said. "Be wise and handle this one with care."

- Make a move one batter too soon rather than one batter too late. "Wait too long and you might look up to see that one batter you had to get out is trotting around the bases," he said. "That ain't the pitcher's fault. That falls on the manager."

- Pick out one player you refuse to allow to beat you. "Before each series I picked out the one guy I simply wouldn't pitch to in a tight situation," he said. "George Brett still claims half of his intentional walks were ordered by me. And he was

right! He already proved he could beat me. I finally put a stop
to it."

- Always demand that players act like major leaguers . . . on
and off the field. "Being a major leaguer goes way beyond the
field," he said. "A player's gotta look like a big leaguer, talk like
a big leaguer, and most of all act like a big leaguer. Anything
less is not acceptable. The rest of the stuff will take care of
itself on the field."

Sparky was an uncompromising believer that a manager runs his
teams almost identically to the way that manager runs his personal
life. The two are inseparable. There's no other way.

If a man enjoys taking risks in life, he's going to gamble in tight spots
during a game. If a man is conservative and usually moves cautiously,
he's almost always going to employ a one-base-at-a-time attack.

"You know that old sayin' about a leopard not changin' his spots?"
Sparky asked. "Well, there ain't enough bleach in the supermarket for
that to happen. You gotta study the other managers. You gotta get to
know 'em. They'll send a signal about what they're gonna do. You just
gotta be ready to jump all over it when it happens."

Sparky was a little different from almost every manager he competed against. He was unpredictable to the point that once in a while
even his own coaches were uncertain of the direction he was headed
from one inning to the next.

I remember an incident in one of Sparky's early years in Detroit
that neither the coaches nor I had ever seen before.

With runners on first and third and one out, Sparky called for a
hit-and-run with right-handed hitter John Wockenfuss at bat. The
runners broke on the release of the pitch. Wockenfuss hit a ground
ball to the second baseman, whose only play was at first base as the
runner scored from third.

Nobody calls for a hit-and-run with a runner on third!

But Sparky did. And it worked to perfection. Sparky had studied
Wockenfuss and was impressed with his ability to hit-and-run.

After the game I asked first-base coach Dick Tracewski if he had ever seen such a play. Tracewski had been a player or coach for more than 30 years.

"Never," he said. "But Sparky must have felt pretty strongly that it would work. On my way to the shower, I stuck my head into Sparky's office and asked about that play. Sparky just smiled and winked."

That unpredictability was one of Sparky's strongest weapons. He never tried anything outrageously illogical. But every opposing manager knew that Sparky knew as much about everyone on the opposing side of the field as he did about those in his own dugout. He was always well prepared and refused to be tricked by anyone.

To label Sparky strictly as a hunch player would be insulting to the profession and the preparation he poured into every game. "Hunches are for racetracks," he said. "You better have more than just a hunch in a ball game or you ain't goin' to last too long. Sometimes, though, your gut knows a little more than your head."

Sparky was unafraid to play any hunch because the homework he did usually put the odds for success in his favor.

Sparky used to scour the opposing roster before each new series. He picked out at least one player that he would not allow to beat him. "I think he led the league for ordering intentional walks to certain players every year," Tracewski said.

Although Sparky modestly minimized a manager's role, he was clearly aware of his impact on every game. "I ain't never seen no manager hit a home run or make a great defensive play or strike out a batter to win a game," he said so often. "But I have seen a lot of managers lose plenty of games that his players already had won."

Beneath the humility, he knew how the game really unfolds.

At the start of each season, Sparky figured that every team could write in 60 wins and 60 losses. "It's what you do in those other 42 games that will tell the story," he said.

Even good managers can't win every game. They just don't lose games they're supposed to win. And the great ones steal a few extra along the way.

For the first six innings of a game, Sparky believed, a manager should find a good seat in the dugout and enjoy watching the game. "He already did all he could up to that point," he said. "He turned the lineup into the umpires and sent his players onto the field, and now all he can do is wait."

Come the seventh inning, though, the pressure shifts to the manager's shoulders. "If a manager has a lead in the seventh inning, he's supposed to win that game," he said. "His players already done enough for that W. No manager should ever lose a game that his players already gave to him. Do that enough times and your next stop is Paducah."

A manager's role, though, stretches far beyond the foul lines. There are more intangibles that must be addressed than there are misinterpretations to the infield fly rule.

He must be able to instill enough confidence in his players so that each one performs to his ultimate talent level. He must look like a manager and dress like a manager. He must treat all the fans as he demands that his players treat them.

A big-league manager is a composite of myriad elements. He's a teacher. He's a parent. He's a drill sergeant. He's a salesman. He's a cheerleader. He's a protector. He's a priest. He's a con man.

Sparky was a little bit of each. He was a regular street guy who knew how to run a game.

And Sparky had another weapon that some managers don't enjoy. He loved all his players. And all his players loved him.

After Sparky managed in Detroit for a couple of years, the Tigers made a player trade with the Philadelphia Phillies during spring training. One of the Phillies coaches who had known Sparky for several years visited him in his office before an exhibition game. He began to give Sparky a scouting report of the former Phillies player's talents and personality.

"Stop right there!" Sparky commanded. "He's my man now. Don't go talkin' about one of my players. I'll make my own decisions on what I see and how he acts."

Taking everything that Sparky had taught me about baseball and managing over the years, it was plain to see that successful management in baseball parallels successful management in most other professions.

"There ain't that much difference," Sparky said. "You gotta know your people."

When it was time to take a break, the smile on Sparky's face was as bright as when he first taught me this lesson so many years ago.

I was smiling too. There was little new about what we had covered. It had just sounded simple and clear and had triggered many warm memories from a time when we were still young.

Just talkin' baseball with Sparky. At least for the moment, we were young again.

Sparky (*front row right*) was a proud batboy for the
University of Southern California team.
National Baseball Hall of Fame Library, Cooperstown, NY

Sparky enjoyed his one year as
a major league player with the
1959 Philadelphia Phillies.
*National Baseball Hall of Fame
Library, Cooperstown, NY*

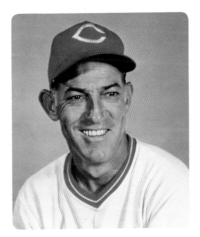

Sparky was the leader of Cincinnati's Big Red Machine. *National Baseball
Hall of Fame Library, Cooperstown, NY*

Always pondering the next move.
National Baseball Hall of Fame Library, Cooperstown, NY

Sparky loved playing with the media. *Photo courtesy of Detroit Tigers*

"Please, just listen to what I have to say."
Photo courtesy of Detroit Tigers

Sparky knew the rule book from cover to cover.
Photo courtesy of Joe Arcure

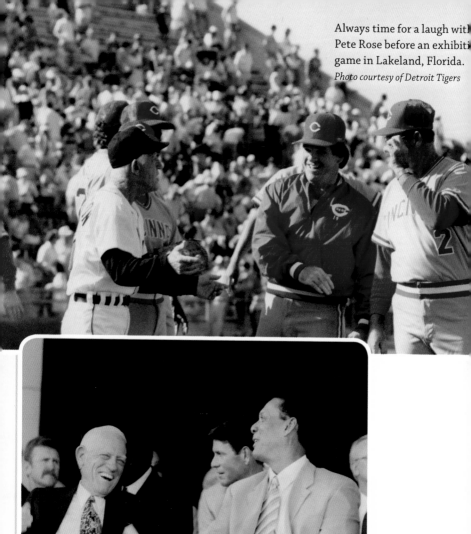

Always time for a laugh with Pete Rose before an exhibiti~ game in Lakeland, Florida. *Photo courtesy of Detroit Tigers*

A little bit of warm-up to his Hall of Fame acceptance speech with Tony Perez. *Photo courtesy of Detroit Tigers*

No better feeling than that victory dousing after winning the 1975 World Series in Boston. *Associated Press*

That ol' Sparky charm was part of every autograph show.
Photo courtesy of Detroit Tigers

Johnny Bench and Sparky kept the postal workers in Cincinnati busy with all the fan mail they received. © *Bettmann/Corbis*

No time was more precious for Sparky than that shared with the kids.
Photo courtesy of CATCH

Sparky loved one-on-one teaching sessions with players such as David Concepcion.
© *Bettmann/Corbis*

Sparky and Dan swapping stories and sharing a summer day in Detroit. *Photo courtesy of Nick Posavetz*

You don't swing with a putter, Sparky.
Photo courtesy of CATCH

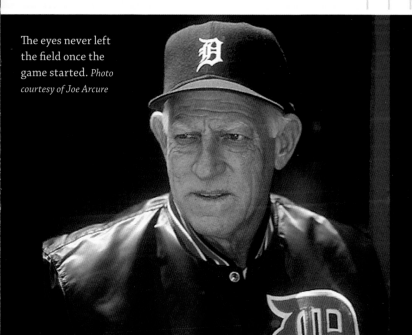

The eyes never left the field once the game started. *Photo courtesy of Joe Arcure*

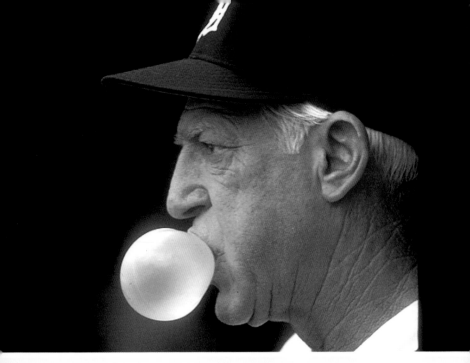

Wonder what's behind the eyes and the bubble during a tight game?
Photo courtesy of Joe Arcure

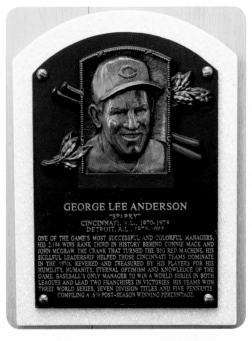

The plaque that hangs forever in Cooperstown. *National Baseball Hall of Fame Library, Cooperstown, NY*

20

★

From the Players' Lips

Sparky never had to boast about the respect he had earned from his players.

They did all the talking. And over the years I collected a treasure chest full of tributes I had already shared with him many times.

On that Monday morning talkin' baseball in the kitchen, however, they needed to be stated one more time.

The contrast between the team Sparky inherited in Detroit and the one he so masterfully ran in Cincinnati was wider than any differences between the Democrats and the Republicans in Congress today.

Cincinnati had a lineup full of Hall of Famers when Sparky led them to two World Championships and annual playoff contention. With veterans like Johnny Bench, Joe Morgan, Tony Perez, and Pete Rose, the Reds enjoyed a dynasty that chewed up the opposition throughout the '70s.

At Detroit, Sparky inherited a mother lode of dazzling young talent that needed time to mature into World Champions. Some of the brightest prospects were still in high school when the Reds were busy ravaging their way through the National League.

The two teams had completely different personalities, and Sparky wisely and carefully guided both to their full potential and baseball's ultimate reward.

I was already with the Tigers when Sparky was hired to manage. As a writer I had interviewed all of the Cincinnati stars. I got to know them better when I shared time with them at various events through Sparky. Knowing them provided me with the insight to appreciate how much the players from both teams respected Sparky.

The contrast in teams was staggering. Sparky proved he could ride a seasoned thoroughbred to victory without a serious challenge. Or he could guide a collection of untested, unproven, and unpredictable kids through a major-league dogfight and come out on top.

Particularly significant were the players' strikingly similar observations of their manager, who finished his career as one of the most charismatic characters in the history of the game.

Each player performed to the peak of his potential. Each individual matured into a responsible citizen and a genuine man.

Sparky cared as much for developing his players into responsible human beings prepared for life after baseball as he did for coaxing their physical talents to the top. He was keenly aware of his managerial talent. But he was even more proud to help shape the lives of those he led.

He understood the intangible responsibilities of his position. Unlike many of today's sports figures, he welcomed the opportunity to be a role model. He understood the game of baseball and all of its tradition. He loved the kids who came to the park, and he smiled as brightly as the star on top of a Christmas tree when they asked for his autograph.

"If you wanna leave your mark on the game, you better embrace every part of it," he used to tell his players. "You can't just do it on the field. You gotta do it in every part of your life to be a real big leaguer."

Sparky was always armed with a ready answer for fans who asked how many good players it takes to win a championship. "A couple of good players and 25 good men," he said. "I'll take my chances with the guys who have guts and character."

Sounds simple and too good to be true. But Sparky believed deeply that the measure of character of each man dictates how much each team can achieve.

Sparky cared about his superstar players, and about those who only got the chance to play during lopsided games. "Just 'cause some don't got the talent of others don't mean you hang 'em on the clothesline to dry," he said. "Those are the guys who need the most help. Those are the guys no manager should forget."

All he asked in return was for their full effort on the field and professional responsibility when they were away from the park.

And so he led. By words and by actions.

"No question about it," Hall of Fame catcher Johnny Bench said. "He loved all his guys and made sure they understood that the games don't go on forever. One day they all would be out in the real world. He got to know the families of the players and made sure they felt part of the whole show."

Those same sentiments are often echoed by Rose, Perez, Morgan, and all those unforgettable Cincinnati players.

"Sparky knew each player, inside and out," Rose said. "He knew what made every man tick. He knew when to pat a guy on the back. He knew when to let a guy alone. And he knew when to give a guy a kick in the ass. He could have been a leader in any field he chose. He just happened to choose baseball."

After Sparky came to Detroit, the young Tigers players learned quickly what the more experienced Reds already knew.

"Sparky took time to talk to all of us about the importance of accepting the responsibility of being a good man, a good husband, and a good father," said former Tigers great Alan Trammell. "The things he taught us we carry today. That's why Sparky's spirit will always be around. I can't walk into a ballpark without feeling his presence somewhere in there. That's a special kind of rush. That feeling will never leave. It lives in all of our hearts."

Although I had relayed some of those comments by his former players several times to him over the years, I watched a smile spring softly upon his lips and tears form in his eyes as I spoke. He looked as if he was hearing them for the first time.

He stared off into space, and I couldn't help thinking that all the time he had spent with so many youngsters and all the sacrifices he made to help shape them as players and men had been worth all the time and effort.

Silently, he nodded several times as if giving his final approval.

There were so many names. So many faces. I could see all of them flashing through his mind as if all had decided to visit him that morning. He would have welcomed all by name. He would have told them "job well done."

Sparky understood that any credit for enriching the players' lives on or off the field belonged to the players themselves. They accepted the challenge. They followed the program. They became the good citizens and fathers Sparky pushed them to be.

All that mattered to him was that he made at least a little difference. I certainly appreciate the difference he meant to me.

21

He Had Potential

Sparky rose slowly from his kitchen chair and walked to the refrigerator to grab a bottle of water. He needed a moment to regain his composure after listening to the words his players had said about him. The peaceful expression that formed on his face was a portrait that had come to life. I wanted him to savor the feeling for as long as he wanted before we resumed.

His sense of peace was contagious; I felt it too. I decided to resurrect an old story that we had shared so many years ago. Real baseball stories like these are better than anything that happens on the field.

I asked if he remembered the time I asked what might be the saddest epitaph to be chiseled onto a tombstone. Just as he did when I asked the question several years ago, he scrunched his nose and forehead for a moment before suggesting: "He was a jerk."

I jokingly told him I wasn't referring to his personal tombstone before offering my opinion.

"He had great potential," I told him. "Are there any sadder words than those?"

He looked at me with his head cocked and a mischievous smile on his lips. "Daniel, my boy," he said, "sometimes you're not as dumb as you look."

That was Sparky's way of conceding acceptance. He liked the line.

"I might steal it for my own," he joked. "I still got time to use it someplace."

Sparky may have borrowed the line about potential occasionally, but he knew the meaning of its essence longer than I did.

In fact, of all Sparky's baseball magic, I believe his ability to extract full potential from each player he touched was one of his mightiest managerial weapons.

He could make a marginal major-league player usable. He could lift a usable player into a starting role. He could drive a good player into becoming great. And, once in a while, he could nudge a great player into becoming a legend.

It didn't always work. Baseball was made to break people's hearts. Over a long period of time, however, he got more out of all of his players than any of the managers he competed against got out of theirs.

"Potential" is a nebulous word, connoting that someone exhibits promise that exceeds the present results. It's the ice-cold bottle of beer in a scorching desert with no opener around. Somehow the cap has to be lifted without doing damage to the contents inside.

It's easy to say the potential of the Cincinnati Reds that Sparky inherited was the kind that comes around only once every two or three decades. The nuclear-powered lineup was a ticking bomb just waiting to explode.

But would they have thrived as much without the climate Sparky had created for them? Would they have pushed themselves to the limits of their abilities without perpetual prodding from Sparky?

Bench used to tease Sparky that if he just kept his feet out of the aisles and didn't trip anyone on the plane rides, the Reds would make him a star.

Sometimes bombs misfire, though. Sometimes they fizzle out before getting off the ground.

The four big Reds of that Cincinnati dynasty—Bench, Rose, Morgan, and Perez—were four totally different personalities who happened to share a similar trust in Sparky. They learned that beyond all of his chatter, Sparky was a man worthy of their trust.

Even without Sparky, Bench most likely would have become one of the greatest catchers in history. Rose probably would have become the all-time hits leader. Morgan would have become one of history's finest all-around performers. And Perez would have been a deadly clutch hitter no pitcher wanted to face late in a game.

Even that much talent, though, needed someone to lead. Bench scoffs at the notion that just anyone could have managed the Big Red Machine.

"We had a lot of talent," Bench explained. "And we had a lot of egos. Not everybody can handle something like that. It takes a real leader. Sparky was the man. He had a talent for reaching each player in a totally individual way. There's an old saying about there being a lot of ways to skin a cat. Sparky had all the cats carrying the knives to him."

Sparky had an instinct for measuring a player's potential. He knew he'd been dealt a winning hand with the Reds. But he had to play it wisely.

Sparky loved the yearly challenge of taking 25 players of differing baseball talents and working tirelessly toward having each perform to full potential. He believed one of the most important jobs of a manager is to understand what each player can or can't do.

"You can't ask a player to do something he can't, 'cause he can't do it anyway," he told me in typical Sparky logic. "He'll fall flat on his face. Now you got everyone lookin' bad.

"You gotta know what goes on in every player's mind. Some like to get up to the plate when the game is on the line. Some like to hide under the bench and hope nobody sees 'em. That ain't their fault. It ain't their mama's fault and it ain't their papa's. That's just the way they are. It's up to the manager to know that, and don't put 'em in a situation you know they can't handle."

His drive to make each player reach full potential was complemented by his fascination for discovering the personality of each player on his team. There are many similarities with players. It's the differences that separate the ones who reach their potential from those who don't.

Sparky loved the challenge and was rarely wrong.

"You gotta know the person inside just as much as knowin' how well he can play," he explained. "It's not up to the player to get to know the manager. It's up to the manager to get to know the player. The manager must understand that young player in order to make him a better player and a better man."

The Reds believed in Sparky. They knew he was as good a manager as they were players.

"We never had any trouble," Bench said. "The respect we had for him made us want to follow everything he said. We wanted to do things right for him. We wanted to please him. Nobody wanted to let Sparky down."

Sparky inherited a different situation with the Tigers, a richly talented young team with tremendous promise. They just didn't even have a clue about what their potential was.

"We had a lot of raw talent when Sparky came to Detroit," said slugger Kirk Gibson. "We just didn't know what to do with it. We still had to mature as men. We had to learn how to handle both of those challenges. Sparky was always big on that."

Right from the start, Sparky made sure all of his players understood a simple formula: Those who refused to give their best wouldn't be around too long.

The players are accountable to the manager. The manager is accountable to the general manager. The general manager is accountable to the owner. And everyone is accountable to the fans.

"A player must give all he's got on every play and in every game," Sparky said. "It don't matter if the score is 10–0 or if a team is 20 games out of first place. Even if there's just one person sitting in the stands a player owes it to the fan to play as hard as he can. That fan paid for that ticket. The players' full honest effort now belongs to him."

As he did with the Reds each spring training, he began his Tigers tenure with his lecture about respect. No player needed to like him. Furthermore, he never asked for their respect. "You guys owe me nothin'," he told them bluntly. "I only get respect if I earn it. And the same goes for all of you."

Eventually, the message clicked for the youngsters. After a few seasons they learned to appreciate how their actions away from the park affected their professionalism on the field.

"We're gonna play hard every day and we're gonna win our share of ball games," Sparky told them. "But if we don't win it all, we're still gonna act like professionals. On the field, in the clubhouse, and away from the park."

It took Gibson a session on the bench for the picture to become clear in his mind.

"I was bullheaded and wanted to do it my way," Gibson admitted. "I finally realized what Sparky was doing for all of us. He wanted all of us to be proud of what we brought to the team and proud of the persons we were away from the park. We were husbands, fathers, and citizens. He expected us to act accordingly. He helped me to become the man I am today."

As manager of the Arizona Diamondbacks, Gibson said he tries every day to pass along to his players what Sparky had given to him.

"I think about Sparky every day," Gibson said. "The most important thing he taught me was to remain humble."

Gibson recalled one long-ago incident that he keeps close to his heart.

"Where's Babe Ruth?" Sparky asked Gibson.

"He's dead," Gibson answered.

"And the game goes on," Sparky made his point.

Gibson said he lectured all players about the importance of recognizing that it's an honor to wear a major-league uniform. Sparky told them the players aren't the most important people in baseball. Neither is the manager.

"It's not about us," Gibson said. "The most important people are the fans."

Sparky was relentless in his drive to develop better players who accepted the challenge of becoming better men.

"All the players that any manager has are gonna be out of the game eventually," he said. "They're gonna be out in the real world with real jobs and real problems. I want 'em all to know how to handle things like that. If they can learn to reach their potential on the field, there's a good chance they'll be able to take that into the real world."

The enthusiastic professionalism of Sparky's conduct made a deeper impression on his players than a daily sermon. Once Sparky earned the respect of the players, they learned to manage themselves.

In 1984, Sparky, the players, the Tigers organization, and the entire community reaped the fruits of that maturation process by winning the club's first World Championship since 1968.

Not every player reached his potential, but none stopped short of giving their best. They got the message. Nobody wanted that message of having "great potential" chiseled on his tombstone.

Even though I never wore a uniform, Sparky pushed me as hard as he pushed his players. There were times I wondered how much more he could demand. There were times that I knew I had let him down.

He simply refused to quit on people he truly loved. When I realized he did it more for me than for himself, I promised myself never to compromise. I vowed to reach the potential he had seen in me.

Again some tears of pride formed in Sparky's eyes when reflecting on what some of his players accomplished once their playing days were completed. He was proud of Trammell, Gibson, and Rose, who went on to become major-league managers. He was equally proud of those who became coaches and instructors, as well as of those who moved into other professional fields as productive citizens and family men.

In turn, each player who had the opportunity to work under Sparky is grateful for the experience. None of them wanted to walk away from the game with the reputation of having great potential.

Sparky made sure they understood the consequences. I'm grateful he made sure I did.

22

Half-Cup

It was time that morning for a little changeup. Time for a funny story. One to make both of us laugh.

All it took was the mention of a nickname I had pinned on him as a joke about a half dozen years before he retired.

"How ya doin', Half-Cup?" I asked, and he broke into his million-dollar smile.

Nicknames aren't as popular in modern baseball as they were in what is termed the game's "golden age." Some are based on a player's physical appearance. Others evolve from a player's quirky habits.

The name I stuck on Sparky referred to the half cups of coffee I poured for him in his office after games at home and on the road. Once in a while I used the name when pouring coffee at his house or mine.

The name originated from a physical condition that caused Sparky's hands to shake. Doctors explained that even though the condition imitated Parkinson's disease, there were no grave consequences.

Unless, of course, a desk full of drenched papers or—even worse—a crotch full of boiling hot coffee might be considered a grave consequence.

We had a team rule that prohibited the media from entering the clubhouse for the first 10 minutes after each game at home or on the road. Win or lose, that little respite allowed Sparky just enough time for a quick jolt of caffeine to help him through all the interviews until the reporters finally conceded that they had had enough.

"Here you go, Half-Cup," I used to tease him. "Don't burn that golden tongue. Tonight the coffee's really hot."

Sparky would smile, then lift the cup carefully with two hands.

"Not too high and keep both hands on the cup," I reminded him.

After a win or a loss, the degree of shaking remained fairly constant and manageable. Unless the game was close and intense. Then the hands started to pump faster than the fingers of Jerry Lee Lewis on an old upright piano.

Sparky loved tight games. He lived for them. With the final out of the fifth inning of a tight game, Sparky started to prepare for the seventh, eighth, and ninth innings just in case the situation remained tight.

With a one-run lead from the seventh inning on, Sparky was the master. With a one- or two-run lead late in the game, he wasn't afraid to lift his setup pitcher for his closer with more than three outs to go.

"A manager should never lose a lead late in the game with his number one guy sittin' in the bullpen," he insisted. "The boys done gave me a lead that I'm expected to protect. Well, there ain't no better protection than my number one closer. So I'm either sealin' the deal or goin' down with him. Those are the games a manager is supposed to win."

Of course, Sparky hated to lose. Even in defeat, though, he loved a tight game. It put him nose to nose against the manager in the other dugout. It gave him the chance to put his fingerprints on the outcome.

Being on top of the division or looking up at all the other teams never affected the way Sparky managed a game. Each game became the most important one of the season. It stayed that way till the first pitch of the next game.

All managers claim to be the game's hardest loser. That kind of makes one wonder what the other guys are doing by not taking the game so seriously. Although Sparky bled less after a loss late in his career, there once was a time when winning was an obsession.

After a tough loss to Los Angeles in Dodger Stadium while he was managing Cincinnati, he made a mistake for which he never really forgave himself. He had left tickets for his father, his mother, and a few other relatives, who were told to wait for him in the parking lot after the game. Upset with the loss, Sparky went straight to the team bus for the ride to the hotel without stopping to say hello.

"Can you imagine that?" he said, shaking his head. "My mother and father! What was I thinking? I had to be the biggest jerk in the world."

Even when he was older and his passion for winning mellowed slightly, it was never extinguished.

Late in his career the Tigers were short of pitching talent . . . considerably short. We were starting a three-game series in Boston, and that's a recipe for disaster at hitting-friendly Fenway Park.

In the first game, Sparky had to run through most of his staff in a humiliating loss. With two games left before we could get out of town, Sparky was puzzled about whom he could rely upon to pitch at least five innings in each of the next two games.

Sitting next to him on the team bus for the ride to the hotel, I heard him mumbling quietly to himself. Though the words were almost indiscernible, after listening carefully to about 20 repetitions, I knew what he was saying.

"Who the hell am I gonna pitch tomorrow night?" he kept repeating. "Who the hell am I gonna throw out there on the mound?"

We had left some soft drinks under ice in the sink of my room for our nightly postgame session. Win or lose, it was impossible to fall asleep immediately after a game.

Sitting in the parlor that separated our bedrooms and with the television blaring in the background, he resumed the mantra he had started on the bus. After about 30 minutes, I noticed that his head was drooping. I walked him to his bed. Upon laying his head on the pillow, he looked up at me and said: "Who the hell am I gonna throw tomorrow?"

At 6:30 the next morning he was scheduled to appear on his daily flagship radio report. Hearing the phone ring about a dozen times in his room, I dashed across the living room to answer and told the producer Sparky would be with him in a moment.

I covered the mouthpiece with one hand and shook him awake with the other. He was startled and looked at me as if I were a burglar. I told him the radio station was waiting on the line.

He twisted his face and took a sweeping look around the room. Sometimes on the road, it took a couple of moments to remember the city in which you went to bed the previous night.

"Okay . . . okay," he mumbled. "But who the hell am I gonna pitch tonight?"

Although his voice crackled like a scratchy 78 rpm record found at the bottom of a trunk in an old uncle's basement, Sparky made it through the interview. The host at the other end of the line sensed some sort of dilemma and mercifully cut the discussion short.

I told Sparky he owed the host a super interview the next morning.

Upon reaching the breakfast room I poured Sparky a half cup of coffee and told him I'd bring another after he finished the first. He thanked me and smiled. He gave me that look that said I knew what he was about to say.

"Now who the hell am I gonna pitch tonight?"

That was Half-Cup. He could always make me laugh.

23

No Future in It

The sun was now shining brightly through all of the back windows of the house. It was daring us to step outside and sit on the patio in its warmth.

Though tempted, we preferred to remain in the kitchen. We had our table. Our stories. And each of us had his best friend by his side. We glided easily from one story to another. There were still so many to share.

I glanced into the family room and scanned the mantel holding some of the awards Sparky had gathered over his career. Of course, they were pleasant reminders of his storybook career. But he rarely spent much time reminiscing.

"I've got my faults, but livin' in the past ain't one of 'em," he once told me. "There's no future in it."

That's classic Sparky. Nakedly simple. Amusingly wise. Rarely does a conundrum sound quite so profound.

One of Sparky's most remarkable qualities, I learned over a long period of time, was his uncanny consistency in focusing on the moment.

There was no half cup about anything he did except for drinking his coffee.

He respected the past. He learned from it. He didn't simply disregard it. When it came to anything pertaining to baseball, in fact, he enjoyed almost total recall. And he never worried about the future. He was too busy handling anything unfolding in any particular day.

He was the perfect poster boy for the Serenity Prayer. Who cares if he didn't know all the words? He knew how to live them.

Victory or defeat had a brief shelf life with Sparky. Game after game. Season after season. One award after another. I marveled at his gift for becoming immersed in the moment.

My first real appreciation for his incurable drive to move straight ahead without looking back occurred after the Tigers beat the San Diego Padres to capture the World Series in 1984. The day after the city celebrated with a victory parade for the team, Sparky and I left on a weeklong promotional tour for his book *Bless You Boys*—his diary of the championship season—which I had written religiously day after day.

I can't imagine another manager leaving immediately for such a taxing tour following the grind of such an epic season. I was certain he was going to ask for a couple of weeks at his Thousand Oaks home before fulfilling his promise to the publisher to tour.

Confetti from the parade still littered the downtown streets when we left. And he was crowing louder than a carnival barker to the long line of fans that waited at every tour stop.

"If you make a promise, you keep that promise, Daniel," he said. "There's a lot of off-season left when we'll be lookin' for somethin' to do."

After he received his most distinguished individual honor—induction into baseball's Hall of Fame in 2000—we toured a number of cities and states for an itinerary packed with speeches, promotions, dinners, and commercial projects.

Sitting in the airport waiting for his flight to Los Angeles and mine to Detroit after 10 excruciatingly long days, he looked at me and winked. "Now what's up next?" he asked.

There was always something next. Always something more to do. It had nothing to do with money. It had everything to do with the challenge.

Those awards he had already earned made for pretty pictures standing on the mantel. Pictures, though, represent a piece of the past. There were no reruns for Sparky. There was more mantel space to fill.

Looking back, I realized that his gift for leaving the past behind was part of the blueprint for his managerial success. He learned a little something new from each game, especially from the close losses. He just didn't allow them to interfere with the job he had to do today.

No job was more important than the game he had to manage on any particular day. Not the game he had won or lost the day before. Not the one scheduled for tomorrow. Nothing mattered but the game that belonged to the moment.

Sparky was an unpredictable manager, not afraid to make bold and sometimes unconventional moves. Each inning offered a new challenge. He never allowed the success or failure of a previous inning to dictate what his gut told him for the inning of the moment.

If a hit-and-run failed in one inning, he wasn't afraid to call the play again in the next. If a batter followed an intentional walk with a home run, he wasn't afraid to intentionally walk the same batter again.

For Sparky, there were far more innings that went right rather than wrong. Either way, he refused to let the past steal the potential of the present.

Even though Sparky looked tailor-made for a giant city such as New York or Los Angeles, he felt blessed to have managed in two mid-major markets such as Cincinnati and Detroit.

He loved playing the role of David against any Goliath. He respected the work ethic of both of the cities he represented. Playing David forced him to live in the moment. There wasn't much time for lingering in the past. He embraced the role of an underdog. And he lived for each new challenge.

That was the way he managed. That was the way he lived.

"Give me nine guys full of spit and vinegar I can run out on that field every day and I'll take my chances against anyone," he said. "When you look at the big picture, that's what the people of Detroit and Cincinnati have to do every day. Those are good, tough, generous people. We were the lucky ones. We got to wear a baseball uniform."

And he never went to work worrying about yesterday . . . and certainly not about tomorrow.

24

★

Sacred Sanctuary

If Sparky had to pick just one place to be other than in the kitchen of his home that special Monday morning, it would have to be a baseball clubhouse anywhere in the United States.

After spending 17 years in the minor leagues, 26 in the majors, and a few winter seasons in the South American leagues, Sparky had spent more time in a clubhouse than he had in the bedroom of his own home.

Among the many lessons learned and habits formed in the game's most sacred sanctuary, there were a few Sparky simply couldn't surrender.

For him, disorder was intolerable. It had to be fixed immediately.

A couple of days before Sparky's annual summer visit to my home, I picked the front and back yards clean of every weed. Except for one scrawny weed squeezed into the skinny seam of two concrete driveway slabs, the yards resembled the freshly brushed green felt of a billiards table.

Each year, a decrepit single weed was left by design. I wanted to measure its lifespan after returning home from picking him up at the airport.

The life expectancy of any weed was usually measured in seconds with Sparky around. Just long enough for him to retrieve his suitcase from the trunk of my car and quickly scan the landscape for any unwanted intruders.

One year the outlaw weed survived till almost the evening of the next day. Every rule of nature and man, it seems, must sometimes endure an inexplicable aberration.

For Sparky, that, no doubt, was one of those times.

We replayed the scene year after year. He knew it was coming and so did I. A withered old weed turned into a game. It always drew a laugh and offered gentle assurance that some things should just never be changed.

Sparky had a compunction for having all things in order. Animate or inanimate, it didn't matter. If something was out of place, he moved quicker than a light switch. If something didn't belong, he eradicated it like squashing a pesky bug.

His penchant for order carried throughout his life. His compulsion for cleanliness would have made the board of health proud.

Within the first few days of Sparky's arrival as manager of the Tigers, the players got a not so subtle message that order in the clubhouse would precede any changes on the field. From that day forward, the clubhouse was to be treated with the same respect that players would be expected to show to the homes of their parents.

The clubhouse is baseball's most sacred sanctuary. It's where confidences are shared and trust is formed. Where lessons are taught and lessons are learned. Where boys become men and where, once in a while, men can feel free to be boys.

Sparky had been raised to respect the clubhouse. Except for the field, there is no more hallowed ground for the true professional baseball player.

Respect for the clubhouse began with order and cleanliness. No exceptions were allowed. Not for the most celebrated player on the team. Not for the coaches. Not even for the manager himself.

Sparky had never seen the Detroit home clubhouse before his first day on the Tigers job. Compared to the penthouse luxury of those in new parks throughout both leagues, the home clubhouse in Tiger Stadium looked, at best, medieval.

It seemed smaller than the parking space necessary for a half dozen of the luxury vans that today's multimillion-dollar players hold on to for a month or two; a player could almost stretch an arm to touch a teammate at a locker on the opposite side of the room. Lockers were made of fencing wire and bulged with clothes, uniforms, spikes, hats, gloves, rubber-soled shoes, shower shoes, and miscellaneous pieces of equipment that seemed to grow in number each year. Milk stools were used for seating, although no discerning cow would ever wander inside that clubhouse.

The ceiling was an eclectic combination of pipes, electrical wire, and sheet metal. Two stalls and a urinal constituted the "necessary" facilities. The trainer's room featured a single trainer's table and a cabinet full of medical supplies. There were four showerheads in the shower area, which was about the size of four home bathtubs.

The ambience of the room was enhanced by the aroma that had been trapped in the walls for about a half century. Particularly on steamy summer days and nights, the sense of tradition was heightened by the sweaty scent of Hank Greenberg and Charlie Gehringer, which never could find a way to escape.

None of those conditions bothered Sparky as long as some semblance of order was maintained. Regardless of the spartan environment, this was a major-league clubhouse, and Sparky decreed that its dignity must be preserved. "I never liked those new clubhouses where there were so many places a player could hide," he said. "So what if it got a little tight in Detroit? At least all the players got to know each other."

After his first few days in Detroit, Sparky detected a disturbing pattern. He noticed that before heading to the showers, players had dropped jerseys, undershirts, pants, socks, and jocks to the floor in front of their lockers. After drying from the shower, they dropped the wet towel on the same pile of sweat-soaked uniforms.

Sparky called the relatively new and young clubhouse manager, Jim Schmakel, into his office to inquire about the policy for dirty laundry. Schmakel looked somewhat surprised. He informed his new manager that there really was no policy. This was the practice that had been established since before he arrived.

"Well then, Jimmy," Sparky said. "As of right now we're 'unestablishing' the practice. We're gonna come up with something new to give the clubhouse the respect it deserves."

He ordered Schmakel to have two large clothes bins set up in the middle of the clubhouse before the next game. Before the team took the field for batting practice that day, Sparky called the players to circle around him in the middle of the room.

"Gentlemen, we've got a laundry problem on this team and this is how we're gonna fix it," he said. "Startin' tonight and runnin' till the day I'm gone, uniforms will be dropped into this bin, whites and towels into the other. I expect Jimmy to assume that any clothes left on the floor don't require washing. Jimmy then will leave those dirty clothes in front of the locker to be worn by the player the next day.

"And if I happen to see Jimmy covering for someone who thinks the rules don't apply to him, then I'll take care of Jimmy and the guy who created the problem by myself."

On one occasion soon after the rule had been established, by accidental force of habit, one starting player had left all of his dirty laundry in a pile in front of his locker before leaving for home.

Schmakel was getting ready to dump them into the bins just as Sparky appeared. Sparky always seemed to have a sixth sense about where a problem might arise.

"Leave 'em right there," Sparky ordered. "I want him to see them when he gets here tomorrow."

Upon arriving the next day, the player asked Schmakel why his uniform hadn't been laundered.

"Orders from the boss," Schmakel said. "He wants to see you."

The player promptly walked into Sparky's office and was asked to shut the door.

"Maybe you didn't understand the rule for dirty laundry I explained a few days ago," Sparky said.

After repeating the rule, Sparky assured him that his uniform would remain unwashed every time it was left on the floor after a game. "It might get a little smelly after a couple of games," he added.

With Sparky's rules, once forgotten was always remembered. And players actually discovered that the new policy made them feel a little better about themselves.

"That's what rules are for," Sparky said. "They're designed to make the players disciplined. I wanted them to become the well-rounded professionals I expected them to be."

A few days after rectifying the laundry issue, Sparky decided to establish rule number two.

The limited space of the clubhouse tested a player's ingenuity for comfortably eating even the most basic postgame meal. It would have been easier to use chopsticks to eat chicken chow mein straight out of the box on a crowded subway car than to dine gracefully in the clubhouse.

The postgame meal that evening featured chicken wings and salad, as evidenced by the bones, crumbs, and lettuce leaves littered in front of all the lockers.

Again before the next game, Sparky called for a brief meeting. He conceded that the facilities were not conducive to dining room etiquette. But bones, crumbs, and any semblance of leftovers must be deposited into one of the trash cans. It was up to each player to clean his own mess.

"If you're gonna eat like a pig, you're gonna act like a pig," Sparky reasoned. "I don't want no pigs runnin' around in my clubhouse."

Sparky believed that even such a subtle slice of discipline might be carried somehow onto the field.

"If you're gonna be a big leaguer, then you gotta act like a big leaguer," he often used to say. "This ain't the minor leagues. You gotta respect that. Mama ain't around no more to pick up after all you guys. And neither is Jimmy, so you better learn to handle things yourself."

We ran a rather restrictive clubhouse. Only uniformed personnel, specific club officials, and accredited members of the media were granted access. I was responsible for governing such access, with Sparky, of course, serving as the ultimate judge.

Sparky believed the clubhouse was a place for players to prepare themselves to perform at their highest level. It was a place for establishing unity within the team.

No family members, no children, no friends, were allowed. Sparky appreciated how long it had taken him to gain access to a big-league clubhouse, and how hard the climb had been. He was not willing to compromise the reward of acceptance.

Even society's so-called celebrities needed Sparky's dispensation for a rare look inside the Detroit clubhouse, which was granted to only a few.

Rock star Ted Nugent, a native Detroiter and diehard Tigers fan, attended a Tigers game with his agent. The agent was a friend of long-time coach Dick Tracewski. He asked Tracewski if the pair might enter the clubhouse to meet Sparky and a few of the players.

Tracewski asked me what I thought, and I referred him to the boss. After getting approval and just before Tracewski left the manager's office, Sparky asked: "Now who is this Ted Nugent guy again?"

Over the years there were other dispensations. But they were few and brief. Rocker Bob Seger was the friend of a few players and became an occasional guest. So did Alice Cooper, without the garish makeup he used in his shows.

One of the most interesting visitors, and a lifelong Tigers fan, was Elmore "Dutch" Leonard. Leonard is the author of a library full of crime novels, with several having been turned into celebrated full-length movies. All the players wanted to hear about the filming of *Get Shorty*. Especially about Rene Russo, who was one of the stars.

A frequent visitor at Tiger Stadium and at spring training in Lakeland, Florida, was Tom Selleck. Sparky and Selleck, in fact, developed a friendship. They lived within 20 miles of each other in California and occasionally happened to meet during the off-season.

"Yeah, but my side of the tracks is a little different from where Tom lives," Sparky clarified.

Even on the road, Sparky demanded a restrictive clubhouse.

The day before the internationally famous rock group the Eagles were scheduled to perform a concert in Texas, I received a phone call in my hotel room from lead singer Glenn Frey. The Tigers were playing in Arlington that evening in the first of a three-game series.

Frey asked if he could come to the park early to meet a few members of the team he followed religiously when he was growing up in suburban Detroit. I knew the players would enjoy his visit, so I arranged for tickets and a place to meet Frey.

Wishing to respect Sparky's rule for clubhouse admission, I decided to introduce Frey to all the players on the field during batting practice. To make Frey's visit special, I arranged to have Sparky sitting at the end of the dugout just before batting practice was complete.

"Now you're in for the big one," I told Frey.

I had briefed Sparky with the titles of a couple of well-known Eagles hits.

"'Hotel California'!" Sparky shouted, and pointed his finger at Frey as we slowly inched toward the dugout. Frey looked flattered by the recognition. Later that evening, Sparky asked me if he had remembered the title correctly.

Even through the most frantic periods of a season, I always made sure my desk was in order before Sparky stopped in my office on his way to the clubhouse each day.

"Inspection passed?" I would teasingly ask.

"For today," he might answer. "But that one pile of papers in the corner is gettin' a little out of control."

Under Sparky, big-league jobs demanded big-league attention. It didn't matter what they were.

And through personal experience I must admit that orderliness makes any job a whole lot more fun.

25

★

No Weeds Wanted

Just recollecting the clubhouse made Sparky smile. Anyone who spent a career in one knows that the attachment is forever. The Tiger Stadium clubhouse was retro chic. That made the attachment even stronger.

Sparky shook his head and rolled his eyes when reminded about the condition of his team during his early days in Detroit. He took a swig of water and explained his plan for molding a talented collection of kids into legitimate major leaguers.

He didn't change his method of managing. He was always confident about that. He had been unaware, however, of how much rebuilding would be necessary to lift these young Tigers to a level that even approximated that of the powerhouse he enjoyed at Cincinnati.

"I shoulda worn a construction helmet," he joked. "That's how much rebuilding we had to do. But just like anything in life, if you believe what you're doin' is right, you just go out and do it one day at a time. That's what we did in Detroit."

Sparky got schooled about the perils of managing prospects who didn't know how to act like big leaguers, let alone play like them on the field. That wasn't what he'd had in Cincinnati, where postseason participation was as expected as the playing of the national anthem before each game.

First on Sparky's to-do list was to weed away any existing problems.

"I never let weeds grow in my garden," he told his players soon after his arrival.

As inexperienced as these youngsters were, they were wise enough to realize he wasn't talking about horticulture.

"A baseball season is too long and too tough to have to put up with a jerk the whole year," he explained. "Better to get rid of the problem before it starts to infect the whole team."

In 1981, only his second full season in Detroit, the players got an up-close look at how serious Sparky really was about keeping his garden fresh.

Before a night game, Sparky was in his office sparring yet another round with the press. He loved to tease and tantalize the writers. He was congenial, as usual, but it was evident that something far more serious was weighing on his mind. Suddenly, he jumped from his chair and asked to be excused for a moment. "I'll be right back," he said. "I gotta straighten someone out."

Sparky had heard the voice of a particular player who had violated perhaps the manager's most inviolate rule. No player, no coach, not even the manager himself, was ever allowed to mistreat a working colleague regardless of that person's job.

The victim of the indiscretion was one of the high school clubhouse boys, frequently referred to as "clubbies." Clubbies are hired by the clubhouse manager to perform such "glamorous" duties as cleaning and polishing spikes, distributing clean laundry to all members of the team, and running for hot dogs or sandwiches for hungry players. The long list of mundane duties designed to make the players' lives less encumbered is actually comical to any person who's been trained to take care of himself.

On the previous night, one clubbie had been falsely accused of stealing equipment by this particular player. In front of a clubhouse full of players and the entire clubhouse staff, the player had unleashed an obscenity-laced berating of the young man, who had been reduced to tears.

Upon hearing about the indiscretion early the next afternoon, Sparky was furious and waited anxiously for the player's arrival. A player humiliating a young man who had no means of defense was a transgression Sparky simply refused to allow.

Sparky didn't yell. But the razor blade in his tone of voice cut cleanly through the silence of the clubhouse.

Sparky lectured the player that no clubhouse manager, clubbie, assistant, batboy, ball boy, concessionaire, or other honest, hardworking person deserved such treatment. Just like everyone else, that clubbie had a job to do and must not be humiliated.

He told the player that if he did his job as well as all those other people did, he'd be leading the league in hitting.

Wearing a uniform carried no special privilege, he continued. In fact, the responsibilities demanded were even greater. No one was a big leaguer unless he acted like one.

"If I ever so much as hear your voice again in this clubhouse, I'll send you so deep down into the minor leagues, a postage stamp won't reach you for a month."

Obviously, this player did not understand the message about the weed in the garden. Or maybe he just didn't care.

After the game that evening, the same player provoked another incident that probably kept Sparky awake all night.

This one transpired in the parking lot at Tiger Stadium where players and club officials were allowed to park their cars. The lot was a disjointed pie-shaped piece of concrete into which guards were forced to squeeze triple the number of vehicles it should handle.

The lot resembled a vehicle version of the old circus routine in which about a dozen clowns squirmed their way into and out of a tiny Volkswagen. The crowd would roar with laughter as they managed to disembark . . . with all arms and legs still attached and the rest of their bodies in one piece.

After a game, Harry Houdini would have had trouble escaping that lot without at least a couple of thousand dollars' worth of scrapes, scratches, and broken glass from windows, headlights, taillights, and mirrors.

Patience was the only sure way to leave the lot with a vehicle unscathed. What kind of magic the guards used to clear the space as quickly as they did still remains a mystery to all those who parked there.

Patience, evidently, was not a quality that one young Tigers player ever bothered to learn.

Upon entering the lot through the tunnel under the stands, the player spotted his car surrounded as tightly as a single tablet in the middle of a bottle full of aspirin. He wanted to leave immediately and screamed at the guard to move all the surrounding cars so that he could quickly drive away. When the guard tried to reason with him, saying he'd have to wait until at least a few vehicles in the front rows departed, the weed began to grow.

The player unleashed a litany of obscenities at the guard, who happened to resemble Dick Butkus. He was walking toward the player when another guard intervened. After the obscenities subsided, the second guard led his partner away.

Sparky was always one of the last to leave the park. When informed of the incident while walking to his car, Sparky apologized for his player's unacceptable behavior and promised the guard the matter would be addressed vigorously the next day.

The following day, Sparky visited general manager Jim Campbell in his third-floor office. The two consulted briefly, and before Sparky left for the clubhouse he was carrying that player's assignment papers to a minor-league affiliate.

Sparky waited impatiently for the player to arrive. He called him into his office and shut the door. He told the player he had a lot of growing up to do before he would ever set foot in a major-league park again. He then phoned the parking lot to tell one of the guards to have this player's car waiting in front of the exit.

"This player has to leave early tonight and won't be coming back," he said.

Maybe it was the way Sparky had been raised. Or maybe the odds he'd had to beat to find success in baseball made the difference. For whatever reasons, Sparky loved an underdog. He showed his support at every opportunity.

He loved anyone who had to perform at a level above his or her natural talents to achieve success. The profession of a person never mattered to Sparky. He thoroughly admired people who did ordinary jobs in extraordinary ways.

Sparky was a people watcher in and out of the park. He was especially fascinated when able to watch people work. It could be a waitress in a restaurant. A doorman at a hotel. Or even one of the frenzied brokers working the chaotic floor of the New York Stock Exchange, where he was once invited to hammer the close of a day.

The guys who worked in the factories to feed their families and give their kids a better chance in life were always special to him. That's one reason why Sparky fell in love with Detroit. It's always been a blue-collar city with a gold-plated work ethic. "If these ain't good people, then I don't know where all the good people are," he often said of the Detroit fans. "It's a great city. You have to live in Detroit to appreciate the love there."

Sparky was fascinated by people who could do things with their hands. As long as they worked hard, he loved them all. He called them the "regular people" and supported them however he could. "Without regular people we ain't got nothin'," he often said. "Every one of my players better remember that these are the guys who are payin' our salaries. Say good-bye to them and it's lights-out for everybody. And how long do you think the players would stand for that?"

Maybe that's why he spent extra time signing autographs. Maybe he understood a simple smile from him could make a difference in someone's day. Making people feel good made Sparky feel even better than them. "Sometimes one smile at the right time can make a person feel that somebody out there really cares about him," he said.

Sparky made his point on a bus trip to the airport after a steamy Sunday afternoon game in Texas. Dressed in the coats and ties mandated by Sparky, the players were sweating profusely as the air-conditioning struggled to circulate throughout the bus. Texas sweat seems different from all other kinds. It has a nasty way of penetrating right to the bones.

"Hey, driver," one of the players shouted from the back. "Turn up the AC."

Some of the players gave their teammate a hand.

A few moments passed and again the player shouted: "I told you to turn up the AC, driver. It's burning back here."

Now the players were hooting and whistling.

After his third call, Sparky had heard enough. He rose from his seat and turned toward the back of the bus.

"This driver has a name." Sparky spoke deliberately. "In case anyone didn't look at the sign above his head, it's Herman. Now Herman is doin' the best he can. So if you wish to say anything else to Herman, I suggest you call him by name."

As the players departed the bus at the airport, Sparky remained seated until the boisterous player from the back approached. He grabbed the player by his sleeve and suggested it might be wise to apologize to Herman.

The player wisely apologized, and Herman smiled at him in return. Herman also thanked Sparky for the consideration he had shown.

Just one of those little things that meant so much to Sparky.

At dinner in Baltimore one evening following an afternoon game, we were seated next to a table where a customer was complaining to the waitress about the service being too slow. The young lady apologized and told him she would check with the chef in the kitchen to find out how much longer the wait would be.

After being informed it would be another 15 minutes, the impatient diner began to berate the scared and speechless young woman. Only a few seconds into his tirade, Sparky had heard enough.

He rose from his seat and took a few steps toward the other table. Staring straight into the surprised customer's eyes, Sparky politely told him the lady is doing her job the best that she could. If he was so upset, why not walk into the kitchen and voice his opinion to the chef himself?

Suddenly, a surprised look of recognition covered the man's face. "Aren't you Sparky Anderson?" he blurted.

At the moment, Sparky wasn't in the mood for any sort of acknowledgment.

"It don't matter if I'm Sparky Anderson, Pete the Plumber, or the Shah of Iran," Sparky said. "Just think about how you just treated someone who didn't do nothin' to get you so mad. You gotta tell me what she did to make you so mad at her."

The man sat tongue-tied.

"She might be a mother workin' this job to put food on the table for her kids," Sparky continued. "Now how can you get mad at someone like that?"

Fortunately, the disgruntled customer was appeased for the moment and sat quietly until his meal was served. He whispered something to the waitress after she properly placed the plates on the table.

Was it an apology? Had the man really heard the words that Sparky had delivered? No one knows for sure. But the smiles on both of their faces as we left drew smiles from us in return.

While Sparky managed in Cincinnati and for the first couple of years in Detroit, Carol maintained a part-time job working as a cashier in the Thrifty Drug Store only a couple of blocks from home. Sparky was always cognizant of treating people in those positions as he wished for his wife to be treated.

And if he caught someone trespassing, he let that person know exactly how he felt.

A church still stands on a corner of Michigan and Trumbull across from where old Tiger Stadium once stood. It's a refuge for homeless people in the neighborhood. Throughout the summer and into early autumn, the vagrants sleep on the streets or in the alley behind the church. They sustain themselves with food provided by generous donors. In winter months filled with snow and ice storms, they scramble for shelter in designated sanctuaries, or at least in an abandoned building where maybe the wind doesn't blow so hard.

These are all among Sparky's regular people. Maybe their lives had taken just one bad turn. Maybe their lack of good fortune wasn't their fault at all.

Sparky was always moved by those people who spent endless hours simply staring into space. He studied their faces and watched their defeated motions. It was easy to see that they had given up. Life had become far too difficult. He wondered which turn or inexplicable twist of fate had landed them where they were.

We often talked about circumstances that might have led us to where they were instead of to the other side of Michigan and Trumbull, where the worst thing that could happen was to lose another ball game.

Once each homestand, Sparky popped out of his car to deliver a donation to the pastor of the church. He walked in quickly and left with few words exchanged. It wasn't necessary for anyone to know that the visitor had been Sparky Anderson.

He lectured his players to look across the street before pulling into the parking lot every day. He wanted them to appreciate the talents with which they'd been blessed. He wanted them to know that these were people too.

If a player was fined for breaking a team rule, often Sparky sent him across the street to put that money to good use. It was easy for Sparky to identify with those people. He was always a "regular person" himself.

I often drive by where the old park stood. I fill a couple of cardboard boxes with packaged and canned food to leave on the steps of the front door to the church. Driving home, I think of Sparky.

He wouldn't have cared how much or how little was given. Remembering the "regular people" was all that mattered to him. If his lesson made a lifelong impression on at least one player, then it was worth all the time.

I know it made a difference for me.

26

★

A Uniform Is a Uniform

Perhaps because Sparky was a character that comes around only once in a lifetime, he appreciated individuals that operated a little bit out of the norm. On that Monday morning, I could see him rifling through his mind to pick out a couple who had wound up close to his heart.

Pitcher David Wells was one of the closest.

Sparky, as usual, was worried about his starting pitching throughout spring training of 1993. On the day before the regular season started, however, he received quite a surprise.

So did Wells. In fact, Wells wound up getting what he considers the biggest break of his major-league career.

We were playing our final exhibition game in Vancouver, Canada, on our way to open the regular season in Oakland, California, the next evening. Shortly before the game ended, the Tigers agreed to terms with the free-agent pitcher. Wells was scheduled to meet us in Oakland that evening.

Sparky was ecstatic with the deal. He admired watching Wells pitch when we faced him playing the Toronto Blue Jays. An imposing figure at 6 feet 4 and somewhere around 230 pounds, Wells looked intimidating on the mound.

Making the deal even sweeter, Wells was left-handed and was unafraid to throw strikes.

"He don't walk nobody," Sparky used to say. "And he ain't afraid to move a batter off the plate. At least your fielders get a chance to make a play."

Sparky could tolerate any pitcher giving up a reasonable number of hits each game. He simply had no tolerance for pitchers who chose to ignore one of the basic unwritten rules of baseball: "You walk . . . you lose." He didn't like nibblers who looked as if they actually feared throwing the ball over the plate.

Wells was fearless about everything he did in life. The glass was either full or empty for David, nothing in between. On or off the field, he had an insatiable appetite for competition and good times. His voracious hunger for baseball history centered around the New York Yankees. He was convinced God had sent Babe Ruth down to earth to save the game.

Anyone who idolized Babe Ruth was going to be all right with me.

Wells is an outgoing, offbeat, and sometimes outlandish character, a truly free spirit who is honest, brutally blunt, and humorous. He could never hide his passion for the game.

That's all that mattered to Sparky.

Shortly before the game ended, general manager Jerry Walker told me to inform the press about the signing.

As soon as the writers reached the clubhouse they peppered Sparky with a barrage of questions. How did Wells fit into the starting rotation? What did he like most about the lefty? Did he think the team had a chance at signing him?

And the big one: "What are you going to do about the earring David wears?"

Wells was among the first wave of major-league players to sport an earring. As soon as the deal was announced, the writers started to sample their one-liners about what the manager would say about the diamond sticking out of David's left ear.

When the question was asked, Sparky flashed one of his devilish smiles. "I guess you'll just have to wait and see."

Upon arriving at the Oakland airport, Sparky instructed traveling secretary Bill Brown to contact Wells and send him to Sparky's suite for his official welcome. Sparky then told me to find the nearest coffee shop and buy enough sandwiches and beverages for Wells, him, and me.

Sparky was a throwback to 17 seasons in the minor leagues when ballplayers looked more like lumberjacks than a version of some wannabe rock star. As a major-league manager he had served two general managers who shared his philosophy.

At Cincinnati, Bob Howsam often sat in the grandstands during batting practice. He monitored how each of his celebrated Reds looked in uniform. Once in a while after returning to his office, he called Sparky in the clubhouse before the game. He "suggested" that he remind a player or two that baseball pants were to be worn in traditional baseball style with a length that ended midway between the knee and the ankle. And, he added, he expected to see it in that evening's game.

Detroit's Jim Campbell wasn't quite that meticulous, but he expected his team to act and look like major leaguers on and away from the field. Baseball to him was as much a ritual as firecrackers on the Fourth of July.

For Sparky there was no higher calling in life than playing in the big leagues. So many tried and so few survived. Those who did were expected to follow one of Sparky's simple dicta: "If you're gonna play in the big leagues, then you have to look like a big leaguer."

Traveling on the road, players were required to wear a suit or a sport coat with a dress shirt and a necktie. On the field, they were expected to look like ballplayers and to act like men. "Act like your mother is somewhere in the ballpark watching every move you make," he told his players.

Changes in social styles and mores, however, effected changes throughout society. And even America's most traditional game was not immune to the cultural revolution. Rock star hairstyles began to replace military cuts. Though not encouraged, neatly trimmed facial hair became acceptable.

But an earring? We all wondered what Sparky was going to do.

Soon after Wells arrived in the manager's room, it was obvious that the left-hander was captured by Sparky's charisma. He had schooled himself in baseball history, and the aura of his new manager, only half his size, filled the room. Wells was dazzled by Sparky stories the manager could dish out like he was dealing a deck of cards.

Sparky told him about all of his wonderful years with the Big Red Machine. He told Wells he would have loved to watch how hard Pete Rose played day after day. He talked about the 35-5 start that his 1984 Tigers nursed into a World Championship. From a seat in the adjoining room, I was treated to a lesson in subtle persuasion that a professional psychologist would be proud to claim.

"You know, David"—Sparky's voice suddenly dropped a decibel—"a lot of people think I'm old-fashioned. They don't think an old man like me can keep up with the times."

Wells wasn't sure about Sparky's direction, but his gut must have told him to listen carefully to every word.

"It's like that earring sticking in your ear," Sparky said. "A lotta people think I don't go along with all of the changes in society. I wanna tell you I don't care what a man likes to do or how he likes to dress. If you wanna wear an earring that's strictly up to you. In fact, you look pretty good with it."

A smile the size of a giant jack-o'-lantern's covered David's face.

"But *not* when you're wearing a big-league uniform." Sparky now raised his voice a decibel just to make sure Wells did not miss the point.

"A uniform is a uniform," Sparky said in typical fashion. "That's why it's called a uniform."

How could Wells argue with an argument as logical as that?

Wells smiled and shook his new manager's hand. Message delivered and message received. The earring never appeared when Wells pitched for the Tigers.

Wells later publicly stated that Sparky became more like a father than a manager to him. "I respect him more than anyone I was ever associated with in the game," Wells said shortly after Sparky's death.

Since childhood, Wells had been enthralled by the mystique of the New York Yankees. So when given the opportunity to play for them, he seized the moment.

"I'm not sure I could have played for them without everything I learned from Sparky," he said.

While managing Cincinnati, Sparky defused a similar situation involving utility players Ted Uhlaender and Joe Hague. The Reds were preparing to travel to Pittsburgh for the start of the National League Championship Series the following day. Neither player had shaved for four days.

Bench and Rose showed up in the clubhouse with fresh haircuts. Sparky called them into his office and then sent for Uhlaender and Hague.

He addressed Uhlaender and Hague by saying the other two players in the room were critical to the Reds' success. "And so are you," he said.

Then he proceeded to say that if they weren't neatly shaved by the next day, "don't even bother to show up for the flight."

Needless to say, the next day the faces of the pair were cleaner than the cheeks of a young altar boy.

"He knew people," Rose said of his former manager. "He knew how to get their confidence. He knew when they were struggling with something. He knew how to make them feel good. That's why he was so successful."

Like all professions, baseball has a code of behavior that has nothing to do with the rules of the game.

It falls under those "unwritten rules."

A manager, for instance, never flashes the steal sign to a runner when it's late in the game and his team is more than a half dozen runs ahead. No player is expected to risk a season-ending injury diving for an uncatchable ball with his team enjoying a comfortable lead. And no manager worth his big-league uniform tolerates any kind of excessive celebratory behavior by his players that shows up the losing team.

"That don't get it," Sparky used to remind his players. "Not with me. Act like you've been there before. That other team knows they lost. Save the drama for the TV people. They like to turn every game into the Fourth of July."

We spent a lot of time talking about those unwritten rules. Not just the ones in baseball, but all of those we find in everyday life.

"It's all about how you act in different situations," Sparky explained. "There's a right way and a wrong way. You better learn the difference by the time you're in the fourth grade.

"If you make it to the big leagues and still don't know the difference, then there's something wrong. Then it becomes my problem and them that don't get it might wind up with a one-way ticket out of town. That's the most important job for a manager . . . making sure all of his men know how to act. And then going out and doing it."

No one knew that better than Sparky. And everyone knew exactly what to expect. Wells already understood those unwritten rules. And he wound up being one of Sparky's favorite players ever to play for him.

And all without wearing an earring when he pitched.

Through simple, honest communication, a mutually agreed upon solution is usually just a few words away.

Maybe some of our leaders in Washington could learn a lesson from Sparky.

27

"Close the Door"

Only three months before sitting in Sparky's kitchen reflecting upon the good fortune with which we'd been blessed, we were sitting in my kitchen when a surprise visit from former Tigers pitcher Dave Rozema generated some unexpected humorous memories.

Sparky had just finished signing his name on about a hundred collectible items such as baseballs, bats, pictures, books, and cards for a friend who owned a couple of sports memorabilia stores. Rozema—known as Rosey to his teammates and Tigers fans everywhere—had heard about Sparky's visit and called to ask if he could drop by. He wanted to say hello to his old boss, who had helped to shape his life.

Throughout his career, Rosey remained that mischievous little boy that trouble seemed to follow. His hand was caught so often in the cookie jar that we thought perhaps the jar was attached to his wrist. He was incorrigible, playful, sassy, flaky, and loquacious enough to make a monk break his vow of silence.

He still has that impish sense of humor that no one can resist. He laughs often and he laughs hard. He's polite, cooperative, and as harmless as a butterfly bouncing in the breeze. He's simply a genuinely good guy.

But in those days trouble followed Rosey like a shadow on a sunny summer afternoon. Regardless of what sort of trouble he might have stumbled into, it was impossible to remain upset with such a character too long.

Except for one particular incident when he nearly wrote his own career's far too early obituary in a godforsaken baseball park in San Juan, Puerto Rico.

Seated next to Sparky in the aisle seat near the front of the plane, I could feel his body temperature rising even under the air conditioner blasting from directly above.

It was spring training 1981. The Tigers had boarded an early-morning flight from Fort Lauderdale, Florida, to San Juan for a quick two-game series. Everyone was buckled into their seats, and the flight captain was waiting for final clearance before pulling from the gate.

Almost everyone, that is. One player was missing in action. And the type of action suspected as the cause of his absence was certainly not part of Sparky's guide to the making of a well-rounded major-league professional.

Unaccounted for was Rosey, the free-spirited pitcher whom no one, it seemed, was able to find. Sparky sat silently fuming as the team waited anxiously to see how the mystery would unfold.

I said nothing to Sparky. It didn't take a baseball genius to determine that silence, on this particular morning, was more in order than taking a 3-0 pitch with the bases loaded and two out in the ninth.

The story circulating among the players was that Rosey and a few other free spirits had spent the previous evening judging a wet T-shirt contest at a Fort Lauderdale tavern. That was the last anyone had seen of him, and the betting odds were high that he was still holed up fast asleep in his hotel room.

Before boarding the plane, a frantic team trainer exhausted all his change in a futile effort to make telephone contact with the missing pitcher. We were still in the dark ages when anything resembling a cell phone belonged only to characters such as James Bond.

The clubhouse manager, always adept at resolving even the stickiest unforeseen problem, phoned a bellhop at the hotel where the team had stayed. He asked him to go to Rosey's room and pound on the door until it was answered or the door fell off the hinges.

Obviously, the plan of last resort worked. Once Rosey had awakened, the bellhop summoned a cab and then called the clubhouse manager to say the tardy pitcher was on his way.

For Rosey, the real problem was yet to come. That struck suddenly when he finally reached the plane. And Sparky handled that situation swiftly and emphatically.

How Rosey managed to pack his belongings and grab a taxi that somehow snaked through early-morning traffic to get him to the airplane before it departed still remains a logistical mystery. Miraculously, the cabbie managed to complete his delivery while the plane was still on the ground.

That was the end of the miracle, however. Reality now fell solely into Sparky's hands.

Sparky had alerted a flight attendant to the situation. Under no circumstances, he told her, was the flight captain to wait a second past the moment he was cleared for departure.

Time was ticking quickly, and everyone on board was wondering if Rosey could finish the race.

"I don't care if you see him at the end of the Jetway," Sparky told the attendant. "Once you start to close that door, you close it all the way."

A few moments later the attendant did, in fact, begin to close the door, when she suddenly spotted a tall, disheveled stranger. He had a travel bag in hand, bloodshot eyes falling out of their sockets, and a frightened look on his face as he dashed down the Jetway. When the stranger made it to the closing door, there was just enough room for him to stick his head and blurry eyes inside.

If the attendant had any notion to quickly drop the door to allow the stranger inside, it was dashed with no uncertainty by the tone of Sparky's voice. "CLOSE THE DOOR!" he thundered.

The door was closed. The plane rumbled slowly to the runway. In a matter of moments it was airborne over the Atlantic Ocean. And Rosey was left stranded in the airport, desperately trying to secure a seat on the next flight to San Juan.

Fortunately for Rosey, there were several flights leaving on the hour. He booked a seat on the next departure and took a cab to the hotel where the team was staying for the night. He even arrived at the park ahead of the rest of the team.

He was the starting pitcher that evening against St. Louis. And no matter how effective or ineffective he happened to be, Sparky was determined to make him work till he was panting and his tongue was ready to fall from the back of his throat. Then he would work him a little bit more.

After pitching a few innings and serving up a bagful of line drives to every corner of the park, Rosey was removed from the game. Like all starting pitchers during spring training, he then headed to the outfield for his daily running just inside the fences while the game played to its conclusion.

I happened to be in the dugout late in the game when I overheard pitching coach Roger Craig whisper to Sparky. "You better let the boy come in," Craig said. "He's gonna drop dead out there."

Sparky looked at Craig and hissed through his teeth: "Let the son of a bitch die."

Huffing, puffing, and scuffling for the tiniest breath of air, Rosey finally reached the dugout, perhaps thinking it was his last trip anywhere. Ironically, it happened to be at the same time Sparky reached the dugout following a meeting with the home plate umpire. Sparky then accidentally stepped on a row of stacked bats and tumbled into the dugout. His tumble came to a stop when his body collided with the edge of the bench.

He started to wheeze and cough almost as much as his misbehaving pitcher. Coaches and players scrambled, not knowing what to do.

"Where are you hurt?" one of the coaches asked Sparky.

The manager rolled his eyes and coughed. "I just swallowed my chew," Sparky managed to grunt, obviously shaken by one of baseball's most embarrassing moments.

With adrenaline racing through every vein in his body, Rosey jumped from his own prone position. In an effort to dislodge the wad of tobacco that had stuck in Sparky's throat, Rosey started to pound Sparky on the back. After spewing what was left of the wad from his mouth, Sparky had no choice but to thank his unlikely, wayward hero.

The sight in the dugout must have looked considerably different to the members of the media perched high in the press box behind first base. They immediately raced to the field to investigate what they had mistakenly thought to be a fight between the manager and Rosey.

Convinced of their error by the evidential remaining wad on the floor, the writers moved into the clubhouse, where Rosey was recovering by lying flat on his back with arms and legs spread on the rat- and scorpion-infested concrete floor.

On the first day back in the Lakeland clubhouse, Sparky ordered one of the coaches to send Rosey into his office the moment he arrived.

Rosey tiptoed apprehensively into Sparky's office, perhaps remembering the days he was sent to visit the principal in high school. After shutting the door and before sitting down, Rosey deftly dodged the baseball shoe that Sparky fired across the room.

In what is now cleverly referred to as a "learning moment," Sparky fired another shoe in good old-fashioned frustration. Sometimes learning moments are best understood through the benefit of special effects.

When the commotion subsided, the lesson had been delivered. Naturally, Sparky was upset with the circumstances. But he reminded himself that this incident was precisely the reason the Tigers had hired him.

It would take a couple more years for all the young players to mature. The promising young talent sprinkled throughout the organization was definitely worth the wait. The team needed the right man to guide the process, and Sparky chose to handle the situation in his own way.

The lecture he gave Rosey was nothing the bright right-hander hadn't heard before. This time, though, it was delivered with an emphatic ultimatum even Rosey had to understand.

"One more episode like this and you'll be sent so far down into the minors nobody will remember you're still part of the organization," Sparky said. "How in the hell can you be a big leaguer on the mound when you can't even handle your own business away from the field? You don't get it now, but I'm gonna make sure you do get it or you'll be gone."

Sparky emphasized the responsibility that each player carries— not just to himself, but to every member of the team and every fan that buys a ticket. He told him this was the last personal lecture he would ever receive. If there was cause for another, it would have to be delivered by mail to "whatever club was dumb enough to be willing to take a chance" on him.

On that afternoon visit between Rosey and Sparky at my house, we laughed about that incident. We wondered where the time had gone and marveled at how much everyone had changed.

"You were a great group of guys," Sparky told him. "I'm so proud of you all."

Sparky asked about Rosey's family and smiled genuinely when told all were doing fine.

"David, my boy, you've come a long way," Sparky said. "There was a time when I wasn't sure you were gonna make it. I'm so happy that you did. Now here we are standing together and laughing about how it all began."

Rosey thanked him for his patience. He appreciated all the lessons that had helped him grow into a man. He asked Sparky for a baseball personally signed to him.

After signing the ball, Sparky rose from his seat. He said he would like a few sips of beer.

"Would you like to join me?" he asked his once recalcitrant pitcher.

The shock on Rosey's face was a picture no amount of words can truly describe. It was that same infectious boyish grin that stays forever young.

"Hell yeah!" Rosey screamed. "I can't believe all this. Here I am drinking a beer and swapping stories with Sparky Anderson. This'll be one for my grandchildren to hear."

When Rosey finished, he thanked Sparky for all he had done for him in life. He thanked me for the opportunity he never dreamed he'd have when he awoke that morning.

Looking back, Rosey probably was the last Tigers player on Sparky's teams to visit with their old manager.

This memory was far more precious than the one Rosey brought back from Puerto Rico.

28

No Flagpole, Please

Shortly before lunch, we wandered out of the kitchen and down the hall to a handsome three-level glass-lined china cabinet in the living room. Encased on each separate level were the miniature World Series trophies that Sparky had earned from his three World Series Championships.

There were two from Cincinnati and one from Detroit. Each was special in its own way.

"Because we led wire to wire, some people in Detroit probably thought this one was the easiest," he said as he pointed to the Tigers trophy. "They don't realize how tough that year was."

That magical 1984 season obviously was one of our most precious memories. There were so many treasures to keep in our hearts. One of my favorites occurred in obscurity. It happened in the darkness of the team bus just before midnight in an empty Anaheim Stadium.

Sparky was sitting in the customary manager's seat. First row, right-side window. We were parked under the right-field stands inside of the darkened ballpark.

Boarding the bus about 10 minutes before departing for the Los

Angeles airport, I hoisted my overstuffed case of record books, papers, and miscellaneous supplies onto the overhead storage rack. I tucked the last evolutionary link to the laptop computer—my reliable Olympia portable typewriter, which had faithfully traveled with me through all stops in the American League—on the floor under my seat. Then I collapsed into the seat next to Sparky.

As after every victory, players jabbered loudly in the back of the bus. A few blaring boom boxes must have been heard all the way to Newport Beach. The cacophonous blend of rock, country, soul, and Latin chords mixed magnificently into a fractured symphony symbolic of victory that only baseball players truly appreciate.

On that particular evening, the back-of-the-bus celebration was euphorically spirited. At one point I could actually feel the bus rocking. This wasn't like just any other win.

All the while, as if floating elsewhere in space, Sparky sat silently staring into the darkness of the tunnel through which the bus would soon depart. His eyelids never seemed to blink. His arms and legs were as motionless as a statue's. He looked catatonic, and I nudged him in the ribs.

"Hey, we just swept the Angels," I teased him. "That's nine wins in a row. Isn't that worth at least a smile?"

We had also started the season with a nine-game winning streak. Now we had a pair of nines and it was only May 24.

Inside, of course, Sparky was deliriously happy. Like so many others, he simply was having trouble putting together all the pieces of this mysterious season that kept unfolding the same way day after day after day.

Maybe it was some weird sort of dream. If it was, though, it had to be contagious, because everyone was dreaming the same thing. And there were no signs of its stopping.

Finally he stared at me with a look of never having seen me ever before in his life.

"I oughta tell this bus driver to take us to Las Vegas," he finally managed. "With the way things are goin', we might be able to break all the banks."

Neither Sparky nor all the gods of baseball could explain what the

Tigers were accomplishing in the spring of 1984. Whatever it was, though, no one had ever witnessed a start to a season quite like this. It happened so quickly and with so much thunder, even the players didn't really have a chance to fully appreciate what they were doing.

The three-game sweep of the California Angels upped Detroit's record to 35-5. No team in history had ever finished its first 40 games with an .875 winning percentage. The odds against such a start wouldn't even have made the Las Vegas betting boards.

Maybe that's why Sparky mused about heading to the gambling capital of the world instead of to Seattle. Or maybe Sparky had, in fact, sold his soul to the devil. Could there have been a little piece of Joe Boyd of *Damn Yankees* fame deep inside of him that I had never noticed before?

Whatever the case, there had to be some sort of ethereal answer to the numbers his team was running up.

In hindsight, the side trip to Vegas might have been a pretty wise decision. Although the Mariners wound up finishing the season 14 games under .500, they swept three straight from the seemingly invincible Tigers.

Despite the three losses to Seattle, the Tigers finished their West Coast swing by taking two of three games at Oakland. They returned to Detroit to start June with an inconceivable record of 37-9.

Hours before the first game in Anaheim, I had been sitting alone in the press box working on material to distribute to the media. A few minutes later, Gene Mauch quietly took a seat nearby. After serving 23 years as a major league manager, Mauch was working in an advisory capacity for the Angels.

Sparky's admiration for Mauch was superseded only by his respect for Casey Stengel. He thought Mauch possessed the sharpest baseball instincts of any manager he'd competed against.

Sparky always looked ahead on the schedule for the games against the Mauch-led Montreal Expos. Sparky knew his Cincinnati crew had far more talent than Mauch's Expos. But he also knew Mauch wasn't going to make any mistakes. And he was bound to throw in at least one surprise that no one in the park had anticipated, something like the double switch of players into the lineup that he had devised and that is now used by all managers.

It was the same when Sparky went to the American League, where he ran into Mauch managing the Minnesota Twins and later the California Angels. For Sparky, the battle was personal, a one-on-one chess match for blood between two of the game's most instinctive baseball minds.

Only 15 managers in history had managed more games in the major leagues than Mauch. Even at his own induction into the Hall of Fame, Sparky remained outspoken that his longtime adversary should have been enshrined before him.

"What are you working on there?" Mauch asked as he watched me pounding the keys of my typewriter. "Are you making preparations for the World Series?"

I was stunned by the question. Even in jest, managers are notoriously paranoid about counting victories before they're recorded in the books. Injuries happen. Slumps strike. Sometimes team slumps cripple for a month. And who knows? Maybe another team jumps up to finish the season on a 35-5 run.

Exercising respect for Mauch's credentials, I told him it was a little early for that. With an icy stare that Sparky so admired in his friend, his one-word answer ended any further response.

"Why?" he simply asked.

He then pulled out a pen and grabbed a sheet of my paper. He hurriedly scribbled a series of numbers and then presented his case to me. "Numbers don't lie," he said. "If you just split your last 122 games, you finish with 96 wins. Ninety-six will win your division. I've studied your team and watched all the other teams play. Believe me, your guys can win that many games just falling out of bed. This is no fluke what your team is doing. They're the real deal."

I thanked him for his encouraging words and finished my work so I could return to the clubhouse. I couldn't wait to tell Sparky what his old adversary had to say.

"You won't believe who I saw upstairs," I said. "And you sure as hell won't believe what he told me."

Sparky valued every word Mauch ever uttered. After listening intently, he was silent for a few moments.

"He really said that?" Sparky finally managed. "Maybe he was just foolin' around to stir things up a little."

Maybe somewhere deep down in his belly Sparky felt the same as his esteemed friend. Maybe he was just afraid to say the words out loud. Almost every manager has seen too many baseball goblins jump up out of nowhere to derail a parade before it had a chance to start.

Ironically, though, it was Sparky who started the bandwagon rolling after an Opening Day victory in Minnesota.

Jack Morris coasted to an easy 8–1 victory and Darrell Evans celebrated his Tigers debut with a three-run home run. During the off-season, Evans had become Detroit's first big-time free agent signing. Not only did he add some much needed left-handed punch to the lineup; he also brought a veteran presence to the youthful Tigers clubhouse.

The Tigers were still a collection of kids with a carload of talent. But they also were still learning how to win, and Sparky felt more comfortable having a veteran who had played in tight races when September rolled around.

Finished gathering quotes from various players after the game, a couple of writers congratulated me before returning to the press box to write their stories.

"What did I do . . . win the lottery?" I asked, bewildered by their best wishes.

They explained that Sparky had told them about the book he and I were writing about a championship season. I must have looked like Sparky did staring out that bus window in Anaheim. The only person not knowing about the project just happened to be me.

"We're gonna do somethin' special this year," Sparky finally told me after the clubhouse had cleared. "I can feel it. Trust me. We'll make it into a diary. I'll do the talkin' and you'll do the writin'. It'll be a lot of fun. Somethin' your grandkids can talk about forever."

A whole lot of fun. All that was missing was a story, a format, and yes, of course . . . a publisher. At the moment, I knew of no publisher to call and coldly ask if perhaps the company had been looking to publish a diary.

Sparky was convinced, though. Somehow we would get it done.

Both Detroit dailies ran a brief two-paragraph short about Sparky writing a book about the newly christened season. And somehow I had to come up with a publisher willing to take a chance on his promise coming true.

About a week later, I received a visit from a Chicago publishing representative who said her boss was willing to take that gamble. I immediately asked her for the contract. I wasn't going to let her leave town without both of our signatures firmly affixed to the dotted line.

The book—titled *Bless You Boys*—was, in fact, published. Primarily due to the euphoria of so many loyal fans over the Tigers winning their first World Championship since 1968, the book enjoyed multiple printings. A couple of days after the swift conclusion of the World Series, we made a weeklong book-signing tour.

The publisher arranged for a chauffeur-driven black Cadillac limousine to transport us to two or three stops daily in cities around Michigan and Ohio. Two-hour signing sessions often dragged into three as Sparky teased, cajoled, and entertained each determined customer who had endured the long lines that snaked throughout the bookstores and sometimes out onto the street.

In addition to Sparky's signature, some wanted a picture. Some wanted to shake his hand. And some asked for a kiss on the cheek. Sparky spent the extra time to accommodate every person in line. He especially enjoyed toying with the kids, some too young to know who the funny man with the white hair really was.

With scheduled stops almost always running beyond their allotted time, lunches and dinners were purchased at the drive-through windows of fast-food restaurants. We ate in the backseat of the limo, protected by frosted windows. It was impossible for Sparky to wander even a few steps from the car without drawing a crowd. Young cashiers at a couple of places shrieked with glee at the recognition of Sparky when he rolled down a back window simply to say hello.

The magical season provided yet one more insight into Sparky's managing mastery. He was used to the overwhelming-favorite role with his Big Red Machine Cincinnati teams. He had a Hall of Fame lineup that reveled in the bull's-eye they always carried on their backs. They were the bullies of the National League, daring all comers to give their best shot at knocking the chip off their shoulders.

This time Sparky was doing it with a collection of kids who had never been through such a war. And not even Sparky was convinced exactly how they were going to react once September arrived.

The 35-5 start was a blessing and a curse. It certainly put the Tigers into a lead they never surrendered. But it came with the caveat that anything less than a World Series in Detroit come October was unforgivable. Even during losing seasons, there's far less pressure on the manager of a team that isn't expected to win than on the heavy favorite.

The fans of this Tigers team started to prepare for October with the arrival of June. Nothing but complete victory would be accepted.

And the man with the most to lose? Of course, it was Sparky.

"When your guys give you a lead like the one they gave me, you ain't supposed to lose," Sparky said. "It's all on the manager to steer that team home. The boys had already done their jobs.

"Come August, every time I walked out of the dugout for batting practice at home the first thing I looked at was the flagpole in center field. If we didn't win the whole shootin' match, that was the place where those people were gonna run me up. I didn't think that was such a good idea."

The miraculous start did provide me the luxury of finalizing all World Series preparations shortly after the All-Star Game in July. It's not easy to book about 2,000 hotel rooms for sponsors, baseball officials, and media from around the world for the convention-rich month of October, especially for events as tenuous as the American League Championship Series and the World Series. Not to mention all of the ancillary accommodations for parties, press conferences, and other miscellaneous events.

Obviously, though, the hoteliers and caterers were swept up in the excitement. If the Tigers were to stumble, though, those hotels would be my flagpole.

After all plans had been finalized I told Sparky my job was finished.

"Thanks," he said wryly. "Now are you gonna keep me from gettin' run up that pole?"

Not frightening enough to cause panic, but scary enough to pop a few Tums for the tummy, was a nine-game stretch at the beginning of August that included three straight doubleheaders. Any doubleheader can be a rotgut mix of chocolate ice cream and anchovies to a pitching staff. Three in a row adds a splash of vinegar to the concoction.

The Tigers dropped four straight home games to Kansas City, including two on the day they traveled to Boston for a critical five-game series. A game at Fenway Park is a land mine waiting to explode for any visiting team. With doubleheaders scheduled for the first two days, Sparky couldn't shake the image of that flagpole from his mind.

As soon as we arrived in Boston, Sparky asked me to call some friends that he had made during the 1975 World Series when Cincinnati defeated the Red Sox. They treated us to a New England clambake during every visit to Boston. This time Sparky's stomach had trouble handling anything more than a bowl of diluted oatmeal. "I don't care if the president calls," he said. "I ain't seein' nobody this time around."

That was unusual for Sparky, but I knew exactly how he felt. Since the 35-5 start I was overwhelmed by daily media requests from around the world. It made me more appreciative of the agility and patience Sparky always displayed when dealing with the press.

After winning the opener, Sparky could handle a baloney sandwich during the between-games break. The Tigers won one more game in Boston before going to Kansas City for a three-game sweep, and suddenly Sparky's indigestion was cured.

The Tigers enjoyed a nine-game lead after the Kansas City sweep. They clinched the division championship at home on September 18 and finished the regular season with a 15-game lead.

The Tigers wasted no time clinching the American League pennant. In the then best-of-five-game series, the Tigers defeated the Royals twice in Kansas City and won the first game in Detroit. Now it was merely a matter of waiting to see whether the San Diego Padres or the Chicago Cubs won the National League Championship Series and the right to play in the World Series.

Although he carefully chose his words with the media, by then

Sparky was bubbling with confidence. He really wasn't concerned about who the opponent would be. He had watched his young players mature throughout the season. And he liked everything he saw.

Escorting Sparky to face the national media in the interview room after the first-game victory in San Diego, I discovered exactly how confident Sparky felt. "Daniel, my boy, this thing is gonna go really fast," he whispered to me. "We ain't comin' back to San Diego. We ain't gonna need seven games to take that big trophy home."

After the Tigers dropped the second game to the Padres, the teams returned to Detroit, where the Tigers swept all three. Before the final game on Sunday, Sparky addressed a small piece of unfinished business. "As soon as I walked out of the dugout for the first time, I took one last look at that flagpole," he said. "You ain't got me this time, pal. Better luck next year."

A few hours later, Sparky became the first manager in history to lead a team from each league to a World Championship.

And then the real celebration began.

I had worked and covered several World Series before 1984. This was my first as a participant. I had been seasoned by all of the media commotion since Opening Day. I wanted to perform my small role as professionally as the team on the field had done its job all year.

At least I knew exactly what to do. I just followed Sparky's lead. The wisest man doesn't possess all the knowledge. He just knows where to find it.

29

★

"Ah So"

Gazing at those two Cincinnati World Series trophies in the china cabinet sent Sparky back again in time: first to baseball limbo when he was out of a job after being fired by the Reds in 1978; next, to his 17-year roll as manager of the Tigers; and finally, to nearly embarking on a two-year stint in Japan as manager of the Hanshin Tigers before he decided it was best for him to remain stateside and wait for his call from the Baseball Hall of Fame.

Sparky's first taste of baseball limbo came shortly after leading the Reds to a second-place finish. The Reds had won back-to-back championships in 1975 and 1976. Sparky had always kept his team in contention. After getting his pink slip in November 1978, he promised himself that he would be back . . . right at the top.

It took six long years for him to complete that promise. But after that final San Diego out to end the fifth game of the 1984 World Series, he released a long-awaited sigh of relief.

"I never wished any bad luck on the Reds," he said. "They gave me my first chance. They're a great organization. They were good people. They were only doin' what they thought was best for the team. I remained friends with everyone. But I have to admit I did feel just a little pinch of vindication after the Tigers won."

Sparky was only 44 years old when he was out of the game for the first time since he signed a contract with the Brooklyn Dodgers just after high school in1953.

He was hurt but never allowed himself to become bitter. He carefully chose his words when speaking to the media. He understood that managerial firings are an inherent element of the game. Even Casey Stengel got the boot.

While Sparky handled his dismissal with class, almost all the people of Cincinnati and the state of Ohio were upset with the firing. Informal polls conducted by various media outlets indicated that 90 percent of the respondents disapproved of the dismissal.

Players on the Reds were outspokenly upset and didn't try to mask their feelings. And mail carriers in Thousand Oaks weren't too excited about the bags full of mail that were sent to Sparky's home in support of the now removed manager.

Eventual Hall of Fame manager Whitey Herzog perhaps summed up Sparky's situation best: "There's a whole lot of managers squirming at home right now with that little white-haired guy sitting by the phone waiting for the calls to start coming in," Herzog quipped.

Sparky was sure he would get another opportunity to manage. But when you're trying to make your way through limbo, it sometimes gets iffy, and confidence can crack like an old brittle bat.

His stay in limbo was, of course, relatively brief. Just two months into the following season he signed with the Tigers, where he remained for the rest of his managerial career.

Sparky chose to put away his spikes at the end of the 1995 season, when his contract expired. His time in Detroit had been a magnificent run that included one World Championship, one American League pennant, two American League East Division titles, and plenty of smiles along the way. Sparky was the face of Tigers baseball.

Speculation was rampant, however, that he wouldn't have been asked back by ownership after having refused to manage replacement players during spring training of 1995.

Sparky made it easy for everyone when he decided to walk away proudly. Only 61 years old, he was in baseball limbo once more. Despite any misgivings he may have felt, Sparky would do nothing to stain the game he cherished.

Would he have accepted another managerial job? Under the right circumstances, no question about it.

Did he think he would get that opportunity? He really didn't know.

All he was certain of at the time was that he had done everything properly. He was at peace with baseball and with himself.

That opportunity to return to the game occurred shortly after he had spent some time at home. And it certainly wasn't the offer he had imagined.

I had received a call from a representative of the Hanshin Tigers of the Japanese major leagues, which featured a rapidly improving brand of baseball, as is evidenced by the growing number of Japanese players now competing in America's major leagues. The Japanese had been successful with signing several American players and a couple of managers.

Landing a marquee name like Sparky would have been bigger than the Rolling Stones kicking off a worldwide tour in Japan.

Sparky was flattered by the unexpected offer. He had toured Japan twice and was enamored with its beauty and the kindness of its people.

But a two-year road trip halfway around the world isn't something one immediately starts packing for. Not even someone as impulsive as Sparky. He and I discussed the matter for three straight days—morning, noon, and night.

"Maybe you can moonlight as a sumo wrestler," I teased him. "You can run around that circle till the big guys get tired. Then all you have to do is fall on them."

For those three days before the evening of decision, Sparky fretted as much as he had before the start of a World Series. Playing golf on all three afternoons at Sunset Hills, Sparky never bothered to keep score.

"Daniel, my boy," he said, "do you realize, when you step on that plane, how long it'll be till you finally get home again?"

I wasn't shocked by the question, but I quickly fired one back to him. "Who said anything about me going?"

He eyed me with that familiar impish look on his face implying I had to be part of the deal. "Well, I ain't gonna be the only one in Japan who can't speak no Japanese," he said. "You gotta go. We gotta be able to talk."

Sparky was considering much more than the magnitude of such a commitment. Without any sense of pretense, he was aware of his stature in baseball. He knew he would be eligible for election into the Hall of Fame shortly after turning 65 in 2000. He wondered about the possible consequences for his reputation a move like this might make.

Perhaps his decision had already been made. Finally, though, midway through the round on the day his response was to be given, he said he had to decline. "You're gonna tell 'em how deeply I appreciate their offer," he said. "You're gonna tell 'em how much of an honor it is. But at this time, I just can't make such a commitment. Tell 'em I'll always be grateful for the consideration they gave me."

Again I stared at him blankly. "Exactly what do you mean *I'm* going to tell them?" I asked.

He gave me another one of his familiar looks. "You gotta tell 'em," he said as if I should have known. "I don't speak no Japanese."

Of course, I didn't either. But I simply smiled and told him I'd handle it, even though I knew it would be one of the toughest calls I ever had to make.

It did look for a while like Sparky might return to the American League as a manager. In midautumn of 1996, the California Angels were searching for a new manager. General manager Bill Bavasi and two of his assistants visited Sparky's home to determine his interest.

When the three-hour meeting finally ended, Bavasi felt he had landed the perfect man to execute his long-range managerial plan. Bavasi wanted coach Joe Maddon to serve and learn as a coach under Sparky for two years before replacing him as manager. All that remained to finalize the deal was for Sparky to be interviewed by Tony Tavares. Tavares was the former head of Disney Sports Enterprises that belonged to the Walt Disney Company which owned the Angels and the Anaheim Ducks of the National Hockey League.

Tavares was looking at a long-range option that consisted of hiring the right man immediately. Recalling the interview, Sparky laughed at how he may have sealed his own fate.

"When he asked me how I would handle a certain player situation, I leaned over and put my arms on his desk," Sparky said. "I told him I couldn't give him an answer to that till I knew who the player was and what the situation was."

Then Sparky took it one step further.

"But let me tell you something," Sparky told Tavares. "I ain't afraid of no players . . . and I ain't afraid of you."

Sparky, of course, meant no disrespect. He was simply being Sparky.

Perhaps it was best that Sparky did not return to managing. He did make it into the Hall of Fame in his first year of eligibility, and he traveled all over the country making speeches, appearances, and commercials and attending a variety of corporate promotional events. He also devoted considerably more time to promoting the charity he had created to help underprivileged children in Detroit.

The end of Sparky's managerial career happened to collide with a wave of changes that flooded the game. Some made Sparky shake his head. A few made Sparky laugh out loud.

A radar gun? That's for police on the highway.

Pitch count? That's for Figure Filberts devising their picks for the fantasy leagues.

Quality start? That's for a player's agent to squeeze out an extra million for his client and maybe 200,000 for himself.

Sparky managed with his head, his eyes, his heart, his gut, and good old-fashioned instinct enhanced over the years.

"I don't need no radar gun to tell me how fast a pitcher is throwin'," he used to tell me when we watched baseball games on TV. "If the ball is flyin' out faster off the bat than when it was comin' in, then my pitcher's got a problem. Do I need a radar gun to tell me that?

"What does it matter how many pitches a guy has thrown as long as he's still gettin' everybody out? As soon as they reach a hundred now, the manager comes runnin' out of the dugout like the sheriff's chasin' him. As strong as those players are today, they oughta be able to throw all night."

Sparky told me about a conversation he'd had with fellow Hall of

Famer Sandy Koufax. Does anyone think someone counted pitches for him? Koufax maintained that a pitcher can't learn to be a real pitcher until he's able to work his way out of trouble in the seventh, eighth, and ninth innings. "You can't learn to pitch without pitchin'," Sparky succinctly summed up his well-qualified friend's theory.

And a quality start?

"Two outs in the ninth inning of a 2–1 game and I strike out the batter for a complete-game victory," Koufax said. "And there's a cold beer waiting for me in the locker."

Behind many of the changes is baseball's transition into the corporate world. Player investments must be protected as any big-time corporate commodities are. Sparky never begrudged a player from making whatever he could.

But with salaries rising as quickly as the national debt, he feared the game might one day price itself beyond the reach of the average working family man.

Despite the changes, Sparky never lost his love for the purity of the game. He wondered, however, if some of the fun inherent in baseball's tradition somehow got lost on its way to the bank.

He never looked back to speculate on what might have been. He was grateful for his time, which no radar gun could measure.

He taught me that loyalty to the principles in which one believes never comes with a price tag.

30

Now Immortal

I never wrote a speech for Sparky. I often gave him a few lines or suggested where to emphasize a certain point he wanted to make. For the most part, though, all of his speeches belonged to him.

It didn't matter that he couldn't spell . . . thought syntax was a pill for headaches . . . believed tense was a mild case of anxiety . . . and was convinced premise was a French ice cream.

He had the heart of a writer, and that's what brought all of his speeches to life.

I was complimented many times by people who mistakenly thought I had written those speeches, especially one they had particularly enjoyed. Even after confessing I could never write anything remotely as humorous as the way Sparky spoke, some just nodded and smiled at what they perceived to be humility.

Sparky may have added a whole new dimension to the English language, but he had a gift for painting pictures with words. They may have been misused, misspelled, mispronounced, or a combination of the three. But they had a certain sparkle that only something straight from the heart is able to create. No grammarian had a chance to match his insight into humanity. No linguist could top the impact of one of his misplaced words that magically captured the moment.

Over the years I wrote thousands of letters for him. He would give me the idea of what he wanted to say and then leave it to me to—as he would say—"make me look good."

I knew the words and phrases he liked to use and the thoughts and feelings he wanted to share. I developed my own Dewey reference system for his figures of speech. I became so proficient at making each letter sound like him, I discovered that some of my personal letters began to mirror his style. Now that was a scary thought.

"I'll do the talkin' and you do the writin'," he used to say. It sounded like a vaudeville routine.

I typed the letter for his signature. Once in a while I had to sign his name. There was a time when I could produce a mirror image of his handwriting. Letters to special friends he almost always wrote himself.

He believed in the power of the written word. He chose letters over phone calls to congratulate or send condolences to current or former big-league managers and players as well as friends. He also sent letters to average people who sought encouragement during a tough time. He insisted that a written note of thanks be sent to the sponsor of each event for which he had been paid to appear.

"Treat 'em right, Daniel, my boy, and they're likely to ask us back," he said. "All it takes is one small U.S. stamp."

Though I never wrote a speech for him, I filled him with ideas. Sparky liked to be fed a plate full of ideas for any speech he was assembling in his mind. He kept those that he liked and discarded those that didn't fit.

He rarely bothered to write anything on paper. He kept it all in his heart. He always sounded better shooting from the hip than reading from a prepared script. On the few occasions I had jotted key words on an index card, he always forgot to pull the card from his pocket. It didn't matter. His heart was his guide.

Even when filming a commercial he disdained the use of cue cards. He grasped what the director wanted him to say and then put it into simpler words that made more sense to him.

He knew the speech he had to deliver in Cooperstown when being inducted into the Hall of Fame would always be the most important one of his life. He knew he had to thank his family, his friends, and all the players and coaches who had helped to get him there. He also had to thank all of the baseball greats that had preceded him into the Hall, as well as baseball fans around the world who had made his Cinderella career so special.

Although induction day—July 23, 2000—was six months away, Sparky started to piece together all of his ideas on the day he got the call from the Hall.

We altered that speech about 1,288 times before he was satisfied with each sentence, phrase, and word. It had to be perfect. No one he wished to thank could accidentally be forgotten.

As many times as he altered that speech, he flipflopped on the hat he would choose to be displayed on the plaque forever. He owed so much to the fans in Cincinnati and Detroit, the only two major-league cities where he had served. He asked what I thought about the decision.

"Follow your gut," I answered. "True fans will understand."

His choice was Cincinnati, where he had been given his start. General manager Bob Howsam had taken a chance on the 35-year-old California Angels coach, still widely unknown to anyone outside of baseball. He knew his good friend the late Jim Campbell, who had brought him to the Tigers, would have understood. The choice of hat wouldn't have mattered to Campbell. He, along with all real Tigers fans, were proud of and satisfied with all that Sparky had done for the franchise and the city.

It was the first year of eligibility for Sparky to be considered by the Veterans Committee, responsible for electing managers. While the media widely speculated that Sparky was a lock for enshrinement, the stakes were too high for Sparky to take the decision for granted.

I had visited Cooperstown about a half dozen times over the years before making an informal exploratory trip the summer before his eligibility. I wanted to familiarize myself with procedures, accommodations for Sparky's family and friends, and a list of other details in the likely event that Sparky would get the call.

I had been fortunate to share in the preparations for a World Series in my hometown of Detroit. I had assisted my professional colleagues with Series in other cities. But this celebration was different. There would be just one chance to get everything right. Induction into the Hall of Fame is the highest individual honor accorded to any player or manager. And this one belonged to Sparky—not only a history-making manager, but my best friend.

I shared everything I had discovered in Cooperstown with Sparky and Carol.

"Now all we have to do is worry about him getting in," Carol said with a smile.

That was quite a concern for Sparky, who still wondered whether his 1995 decision not to manage replacement players might have a lingering negative effect.

"Would you have changed your mind and managed the replacement players if you thought it would have affected your election into the Hall of Fame?" I asked him.

"Never!" he shot back before I got the last word out of my mouth.

"Then get it out of your mind," I told him. "You made the right decision. Just be proud."

Sparky asked for me to be in Thousand Oaks a few days before the results of the voting would be announced. Perhaps I was as nervous as Sparky. I arrived 11 days ahead of judgment day.

For 11 straight days, it never stopped raining. There were lakes on the golf course where we should have been playing. We kept our fingers crossed in the hope that all the inclement weather wasn't a bad omen.

Time crept slowly on the morning of announcement day. Each minute felt like an hour until nine o'clock arrived. With the three-hour time difference between Thousand Oaks and Cooperstown, we estimated a call—one way or the other—would surely come sometime before 10.

As the clock crawled to 15-minutes past 10, I could sense the anxiety running head to toe through Sparky. Before going upstairs to get something from his bedroom, he mumbled: "Maybe next year, Daniel . . . maybe next year."

About five minutes later I answered the telephone. The caller was Joe Brown asking for Sparky. Brown was a longtime friend and a distinguished former executive of the Pittsburgh Pirates. I immediately called Sparky to get downstairs as quickly as he could.

"One way or the other, this is it," I told him, and handed him the phone.

Upon hearing the news, Sparky couldn't fight back the tears. Carol came into the kitchen and Sparky thanked her for the patience and strength she provided throughout 42 years of a game that had now made him immortal.

Earlier in the week I had visited the Sunset Hills Golf Club to secure a room for a press conference if Sparky was elected. The general manager graciously offered us the use of the dining room and provided any assistance necessary to the most celebrated member of the club.

Tables and chairs were placed in front of the area where Sparky would be interviewed by ESPN, all the Los Angeles local television outlets, and as many newspaper writers as could make it to the hastily arranged press conference.

Unbeknownst to Sparky, a package from the Hall of Fame had been mailed to me at Sparky's home earlier in the week. It contained a Hall of Fame jersey and baseball cap. The package was to be opened only in the event that Sparky was elected. After retrieving it from my bedroom, I opened it in the kitchen.

"I think you're going to like this," I said. "Looks like a good fit to me."

In front of all of his golfing buddies at the club, Sparky looked to be self-conscious about putting the apparel on.

"You better put it on," a voice came from the back of the room. "Sunset's in the big time now. Are we going to have to treat you better now?"

We celebrated that evening with take-out burgers and fries from the local In-N-Out Burger franchise, one of Sparky's favorite restaurants. Carol and I figured he had earned the treat of his choice.

However, there was little time for celebration that evening. Early the next morning, Sparky and I were flying to Detroit. Several months before, I had booked him for a speaking engagement in Toledo, Ohio. The host of the event met us at the airport for the quick drive to Toledo, where we spent the night.

His unexpected appearance in the Detroit airport generated a response in the crowded terminal only slightly less than those accorded to a rock star.

"You're the man, Sparky," several shouted.

"Thanks for all the good years," came another.

"We want you back here, Sparky," another said.

Sparky was congenial and shook hands like a campaigning politician. He signed as many autographs as possible before finally getting into the waiting car.

In April, Sparky and Carol were invited to Cooperstown to familiarize themselves with the village and preview the events of Hall of Fame Weekend in July. I drove from Detroit and picked them up at the Syracuse airport for the hour drive to Cooperstown and Carol's first look at the Hall of Fame.

We had played two Hall of Fame exhibition games during Sparky's Detroit tenure. He was familiar with the village, but had never stepped into the Hall itself.

He had promised himself never to walk inside the building until, if fortunate enough, he was elected.

Never had April raced so quickly into July. So many details for the three-day induction weekend had to be settled. It was strikingly reminiscent of preparing for the World Series, which seemed to have happened in another lifetime.

For Sparky's family members, friends, old high school buddies, and colleagues from baseball, I arranged for more than 50 rooms for the weekend. That's quite a squeeze and a sizable population increase for the quaint village of Cooperstown. Guests came from Los Angeles, Cincinnati, Detroit, Denver, New York, and a few other cities. Celebration of induction into the Hall of Fame is not restricted solely to the inductee.

A week before baseball's most prestigious individual event, Sparky was busy hosting his own annual summertime affair in Detroit. It was the weekend of the CATCH golf tournament. The outing supports the charity Sparky created in 1987 to help underprivileged kids in Detroit.

Needless to say, the tournament that year had an entirely different glow. How often is the host of his own tournament inducted into the Hall of Fame the following weekend? Sparky spent extra time posing for pictures and signing autographs for supporters of the charity that meant so much to him.

Instead of returning to Los Angeles on Tuesday only to fly back to New York on Thursday, Sparky spent the rest of the week at my house before driving to Cooperstown early Thursday morning. Carol, the kids, and their families would meet us there.

After an early-morning round of golf on Tuesday, we spent almost all the rest of the time working on Sparky's speech, now only days away. While walking through the neighborhood, Sparky smiled and waved at well-wishers without skipping a word of what he was trying to implant into his mind.

There was no room for failure. There were people to thank for all of their support. There were fans to meet for all they had done for him.

Through the courtesy of Edsel Ford, the Ford Motor Company loaned us a superloaded luxury van for the triumphant trip to Cooperstown. Edsel is the great-grandson of Henry Ford and served 10 years as chairman of the board for Sparky's charity.

The van that Ford provided came with a magnetized banner that read: "Sparky's Ride to the Hall of Fame." Sparky immediately removed it and courteously handed it to one of the men who had delivered the vehicle. As well-meaning as the sign was, ostentation like that definitely did not fit Sparky's taste. Or as he aptly stated: "You don't put a tuxedo on a pig."

He even felt self-conscious when a local television crew showed up in front of my house to film the early-morning departure. "What's the big deal?" Sparky joked. "All we're doin' is goin' for a little ride."

Along for that ride were my son, Dan Jr., and former Tigers trainer Pio DiSalvo. We laughed about the ride, which felt like a baseball road trip from so many years ago.

We traveled through Canada to reach the New York State Thruway in Buffalo. At each stop we made, at least a handful of people took time to congratulate Sparky.

Sparky spent the two days before induction shaking hands and swapping stories with Hall of Fame members he had known for many years. After extending congratulations, each member gave the same warning to Sparky: Your life is about to change in a way you never could have imagined.

At the induction on Sunday, Sparky delivered his acceptance speech as if he had rehearsed it for months . . . which, in his own peculiar way, he had.

Sparky may not have been able to formally define the concept of spontaneity, but he understood its essence. He understood it in his head and his heart and throughout each nerve in his body.

"Please sit down" were Sparky's first words to the thousands of fans who rose for a rousing standing ovation after baseball commissioner Bud Selig introduced him. "I learned a long time ago at ballparks, when they stand up, they're gettin' ready to boo. So please, just sit on down."

A communal, sincere laugh exploded from all of the excited fans. Instantaneously, he held them in his hands. He followed his comedic icebreaker with a more serious request from the already captured crowd that clearly expressed the humility he felt in his awesome moment of baseball history.

"This will be the last time I ever get to speak like this," he said. "When I walk away from here today, I'll never win another game. And I'll never lose another game. I know that. So in that respect, it's a sad moment for me.

"But I want you to take a look at the people [Hall of Fame players] behind me. And put them in your brain. Look at them and those that came before them. That is baseball. Those people made this game and they will protect this game. It makes me think, how could a young man from Bridgewater, South Dakota—600 people and couldn't play—ever be in front of a microphone talking about the third-winningest manager in history."

Those weren't false words of humility from Sparky. I had heard them thousands of times before. I know for a fact they were real.

And then Sparky went on to explain himself.

"Let me tell you this and get it straight," he began. "I hope every manager that follows me will listen very carefully. Players earn this by their skills. Managers come here as I did—on their [players'] backs for what they did for me.

"I never believed different. I will never believe different. That's what made my career so lucky. I was smart enough to know the people that were doing the work. I could never, under any circumstances, thank them enough."

Sparky paused just long enough to accept a round of applause that he believed was directed at his players.

"There's two kinds of managers," he resumed. "One ain't very smart. He gets bad players, loses games, and gets fired. Then there was somebody like me that some called a genius. I got good players, stayed outta the way, let 'em win a lot, and then just hung around for 26 years. It was a lot of fun."

The crowd laughed again. They understood that nobody should underestimate the depth of Sparky's managerial skills and how much he had meant to the game.

As with all such celebrations, there was a litany of people that Sparky thanked from his heart. Players. Coaches. Managers. General managers. Boyhood friends. The media. Family.

In a moment of levity, he extended his gratitude by acknowledging his friends at his beloved Sunset Hills Golf Club in Thousand Oaks. "I thank everybody up at Sunset," he cracked. "They ain't gettin' all of my money this week. I'm the sucker up there and they get all my money. They ain't gettin' nothin' this week."

The laughs felt good. But even for Sparky, there came a time to be serious.

First, there was Carol, the one true love of his life. Sparky had always respected her insistence on anonymity. But such a historic occasion demanded its own set of rules. "She'll kill me 'cause my wife does not ever want anything said about her," Sparky said. "She don't wanna be photographed. She don't wanna be interviewed. She let me have all the freedom in the world.

"And that's the reason I was able to be so lucky. She let me go and let me be free. And for that I can never thank her enough.

"She raised our three children and I cannot take any credit for that. There were some tough times and she had to raise 'em. And what a job she did."

Finally, when he remembered his deceased parents, Sparky's eyes misted with tears.

"My father never got past the third grade," Sparky said. "But there ain't a guy that went to Harvard smart as my daddy. He said, 'I'm gonna give you the greatest gift to take all the way through your life and it will never cost you a dime. If you live with this gift, everything will be perfect. Just be nice to every person you meet. Treat them as a person.'

"I tried as hard as I could and there's no way I could have tried any harder thanks to my daddy."

Sparky's mother was just as wise. Throughout his life, Sparky marveled at her gentle kindness. "Mama was so quiet and so gentle. My mama was a real mama. I know they're here today."

With a character such as Sparky, no one could have written a better speech than the one that came from his heart.

When the ceremony was behind him, the circus began. After about a week at home Sparky and I embarked on a 10-day road trip for speaking engagements, signings, and other promotional purposes. That first year of membership in baseball's most exclusive club is one no member ever forgets.

The trip to Cooperstown became an annual affair. Sparky always returned for induction weekend, even when he really wasn't healthy enough to travel. "I owe it to those men on the stage and the ones up there for the first time," he said.

Most of all he felt obligated to the fans. They're the ones, he believed, that really own the game.

The same midsummer week always resembled the one from the previous year. Following his charity golf tournament we spent a couple of days visiting children in Detroit's Children's and Henry Ford Hospitals. The car trip through Canada became as familiar as a drive to the supermarket. The promise of going to the following year's festivities always was made.

The first trip, of course, will always remain special. I was able to share the moment with my son, Dan, and my daughter, Andrea, who were invited to the ceremonies. Their presence helped to fill the void formed from all the time throughout the years when I was at some ballpark somewhere around the United States.

I came from an era when almost every young boy grew up dreaming he would one day be a member of the Hall of Fame. I was no different. In fact, I was convinced it was a mere matter of time.

Obviously, reality almost always trumps dreams.

But my best friend made it. And along the long road I tried to help him in every conceivable way.

That's good enough for me.

As impulsive as Sparky was in almost everything he did, he did all the right things to make his professional life complete.

It was a living lesson that he unselfishly passed to me.

31

A Good Reunion

The sun was beginning to drop behind the majestic mountains that surround Sparky's home. Even with evening quickly approaching, there were still more stories to tell.

Sparky was apprehensive about returning to Detroit in 2009 to celebrate the 25th anniversary of the 1984 World Champion Detroit Tigers. As we recalled the event 13 months later, Sparky was happy that he had decided to attend.

A handful of players shared Sparky's apprehension. Some felt upset over the treatment they had received from the club after their playing careers ended. Others did not like the way Sparky was treated by the club after he refused to manage replacement players in the spring of 1995.

Some not so subtle persuasion from a few others such as Kirk Gibson and Dave Bergman made the case for returning perfectly clear. Of course, no one could be certain, they argued, but it might be their last chance to share a few precious memories and a couple of laughs with their beloved manager.

In spite of any feeling of angst, Sparky did return. He knew it would be a tough trip. He also knew he had to be there. He was the leader. It was his team. It was the right thing to do.

"I ain't gonna lie, Daniel, my boy," he said during the drive to the park. "I'm a little nervous about this one."

Bellies on some of the players were a little bit bloated. Some of the hair once thick under their caps had thinned in inverse proportion to the thickness of their tummies. But each player left satisfied for having decided to attend.

Thirteen months later, after Sparky's passing, every player who attended the reunion was grateful that Sparky had come. It marked their last chance to thank their leader, who had helped to mold them into better baseball players and stronger men.

Despite still living in the city, I had been in the new ballpark only three times since leaving the club with Sparky after the 1995 season. I, too, had my moment of angst about returning. But seeing the gleam in Sparky's eyes as he swapped stories with each player made the return worth the anxiety.

The reunion occurred at Comerica Park on an oddly scheduled final Monday-night game of the regular season. Despite a steady rain and bone-chilling temperatures, all players and coaches signed autographs at various locations throughout the stadium before being introduced on the field.

The fans cheered loudly in spite of the rain. They waved pennants. Flashes from cameras blinked like a long string of lights hanging from a 20-foot-tall outside Christmas tree. Many chanted "Bless you boys," echoing the title of the book we had written about the magical year and the unofficial slogan of the season that filled the hearts of so many loyal fans.

After the pregame introduction of players was complete, Sparky was asked to deliver a few words over the public-address system. He thanked his players, to whom he gave all the credit. He thanked all of Detroit's incredibly faithful fans, who had made his 17 years in the city feel like a dream.

And, as usual, he made each fan feel especially proud by promising that in spite of all the economic woes plaguing the city, "Detroit will be back . . . and stronger than before."

The crowd began to chant: "Spar-kee . . . Spar-kee" and cheered wildly as the team departed from the field. At that moment, Sparky wished he could have hugged each person in that rain-soaked stadium. As he neared the tunnel leading under the stands behind home plate, Sparky stretched his arms as wide open as possible and spoke as loudly as he could: "I love all of you. . . . I'll never forget you as long as I live."

A few moments later the game was postponed because of the weather. At least the fans had the chance to relive a moment of magic that enraptured the city, what seemed a lifetime ago.

So did Sparky. So did I.

Before leaving the park for his evening flight to Los Angeles, Sparky asked me to arrange two quick meetings with a pair of unsuspecting individuals. He wanted to share a few words with Tigers manager Jim Leyland and Minnesota Twins manager Ron Gardenhire.

After being informed of Sparky's request, longtime Tigers clubhouse manager Jim Schmakel invited his former boss into the manager's office. A Hall of Famer like Sparky would be welcomed into any current manager's office at any park in the country. Courteously though, Sparky declined. He asked, instead, for Leyland to meet him in a hallway under the stands.

Sparky maintained a self-imposed rule of not entering clubhouses after he retired. To him the clubhouse remained sacred. It belonged to the players and the manager in charge.

"I ain't no greenfly who just wants to hang around," Sparky said firmly to Schmakel. "My days are gone. These guys belong to the present. They got more important things to worry about than talking to an old man like me."

Leyland, who managed in Detroit's minor-league system when Sparky was leading the Tigers was of course happy to meet with him. Leyland told him how much Sparky had meant to the franchise, to the city, to the state, and to baseball as a whole. He thanked him for all the wisdom and encouragement Sparky had given so generously along the way.

Once more, Sparky simply wished to express his encouragement and offer best wishes for many seasons to come.

Through a Minnesota Twins media relations representative, I arranged for Gardenhire to meet Sparky in a small room outside the visitors' clubhouse. Again Sparky declined an invitation to enter Gardenhire's office. We waited silently until the manager apprehensively walked into the room.

Gardenhire had never met Sparky. But he's sure to treasure for life those few precious moments he shared with him in that tiny room.

"I just wanna tell you how much I admire the way you manage," Sparky said. "I watch the way you handle things and get the players to do things the right way. You got everything under control. They keep takin' players away from you and you keep findin' new ways to fight back. You never complain. You just get the job done."

Over the years, the Twins have lost several productive players to ridiculously lucrative contracts from other teams. Yet Gardenhire somehow continues to scrap and scrape his teams into the postseason.

"I can't even begin to understand how you do it," Sparky said, becoming slightly emotional. "But you get all you can get out of every player. You make 'em play hard and do the right things with no excuses. You're what managing is all about. And don't you forget it!"

Obviously moved by the unexpected visit and praise, Gardenhire thanked Sparky profusely. He put an arm around Sparky's shoulders and told him how much he admired the way Sparky conducted himself throughout his career. He said he always tried to emulate the respect for the game that Sparky and former Twins manager Tom Kelly always exhibited.

"I watched both of you guys a lot closer than either of you realized," Gardenhire said. "You guys had your share of problems too. But I never heard either one of you complain. I learned so much about the game just by watching you. This is really an honor talking to you. I'll never forget it. I thank you for your kind words and taking time to talk to me."

The two embraced. Sparky cleared his throat and Gardenhire returned to his clubhouse. Shortly thereafter, Sparky signed autographs for several fans who followed us from the stadium to the parking lot.

The following June I called Gardenhire to ask a small favor. I explained that Sparky wasn't feeling well and wondered if he might give him a phone call. No more words were needed. Less than an hour later, he called Sparky to return a special favor that Gardenhire will never forget.

Sparky loved speaking to young managers and was generous with sharing his wisdom. He especially respected Gardenhire and Los Angeles Angels manager Mike Scioscia. As a parishioner of Sparky's church—St. Paschal—Scioscia grew quite close to Sparky.

Sparky was impressed by how both managers enjoyed working with young players. He admired how each stressed the fundamentals of the game.

Sparky cherished the responsibility put into the hands of a major-league manager—responsibility not only for developing the physical talents of his players, but also for shaping the character inside of each one. The opportunity to enrich so many lives was the one factor of managing that Sparky missed the most.

He recognized some of those same qualities in Gardenhire. He was grateful for the opportunity to tell him in person.

Sparky called the day after the reunion just to say he had made it home safely. He also wanted to thank me for arranging those meetings with the two managers at the park.

"I want you to write a thank-you note to each one from me," he said. "You know what I wanna say. Make me look good."

Sparky never did need help when it came to that.

Despite his apprehension over returning to the reunion, Sparky based his decision on more than his personal feelings. This was for his team and all the fans who had supported it.

No individual is ever bigger than the team. And no one deserves the team's best more than the fans who invest much more than money.

That's a lesson for all to savor. Whichever path a person chooses to follow in life, no one is more important than all of those around him. Teams are not restricted only to those who play games on a field.

32

★

Casey and Sparky

Sparky needed a break between stories. He told me it was my turn to "throw a little somethin' good into the pot."

He always loved listening to the stories I told him about growing up in Detroit during the '50s. No other city in the world came close to matching Detroit's manufacturing supremacy. Few cities purred with that unmistakable sense of economic power that permeated the whole state of Michigan simply because of Detroit.

Detroit factories spit out shiny new vehicles around the clock, seven days a week. There was a limitless assortment of models, makes, colors, and options. Almost 2 million people lived right within the city's borders because of the always steady work opportunities at those prosperous auto factories.

Despite my Detroit background, I've never taken a special interest in cars. As long as mine remains reliable enough to deliver me to my intended destination, I ask nothing else of its performance or appearance.

Growing up in Los Angeles, Sparky felt pretty much like I did. Also like me, all he really cared about as a kid was the next baseball game he was going to play.

Sparky was fascinated by the fact that I had lived close enough to the ballpark to walk there. It was called Briggs Stadium then and was regarded by many members of the media, and by most players who had visited all of them, as the finest park in either league.

Walter O. Briggs owned several factories that produced parts for the Big Three auto companies. He purchased the Tigers and put a significant amount of his own fortune into upgrading the old park, turning it into the yardstick by which all others were measured.

Sparky was also fascinated by how I was able to sneak into the park and watch all of those legendary teams of the '50s for free.

After managing in Detroit for several years, he became as familiar with the ballpark—then known as Tiger Stadium—as he was with his supermarket back home. I led him to the service gate where heavy equipment was often moved in and out. It also served as the entry and exit for members of the grounds crew.

A kid from the old neighborhood possessing any kind of street smarts knew how to charm at least a couple of crew members into looking the other way while he made a swift and clean entry into the park.

Over and over again, the way I peppered Sparky with baseball questions, he used to drill me for stories about the teams and players that I was privileged to have seen. More often than not, he wanted to hear what I remembered about those old storybook New York Yankees teams.

I must admit I hated the New York Yankees when I was a kid. Growing up in the '50s, almost every kid living anywhere west of the Hudson River hated the Yankees.

For baseball purists, it was the American thing to do.

It was the only team that could have printed the World Series dates on their season schedule, leaving only the opponent to be added once the season ended. And they would have been right far more often than not.

When they made it to the Series, of course, we all pulled for the

Yankees. As much as we hated them, they were part of the American League. No kid ever rooted against his own league.

The thrill of sneaking into the park to watch the New York Yankees was anticipated for several days in advance. Despite my emotional disdain for them, it was impossible to disrespect the history and talent of sports' most celebrated franchise.

There were more day games than night games at that time. Nothing was more satisfying than a summer afternoon game at the park with the sun beating straight down mercilessly. We could see the sweaty grimaces on the grizzled faces of the Yankees.

Sparky occasionally asked how many times I saw Mickey Mantle hit a ball over the right-field roof and out of the park.

"Twice," I told him. "But I saw him hit a lot out of the park during batting practice, too."

Batting practice was half the fun of going to the park. Over the years I got six balls hit into the stands during batting practice.

Even during batting practice, watching Mantle hit baseballs over the towering right-field roof onto Trumbull Avenue was better than talking one of the vendors into giving up a hot dog for free. The wonder of watching Yogi Berra turn line drives out of pitches into the dirt or over the head of his squat body was mesmerizing. Whitey Ford and Bob Turley were a devastating one-two pitching punch of finesse and raw power.

There were so many others. Roger Maris. Hank Bauer. Gene Woodling. Elston Howard. Bobby Richardson. Gil McDougald. Their bench was full of players that could have started for almost any other team.

We laughed at all the funny things manager Casey Stengel used to say in the newspapers every day. We used to joke that the Yankees had all the best players and a manager funnier than Milton Berle to boot. We also used to think that with the Yankees' roster, Casey could have phoned in his lineup from the hotel and listened to the game on the radio without even leaving his room.

Of course, that was a ridiculous overstatement. Casey was the right man at the right time in the right city to handle the enormity of those legendary teams.

"Don't you ever think Casey just floated along for the ride with his players," Sparky often lectured me. "Hell yeah, he had a lot of talent. But it ain't easy drivin' the car with giants like Mantle and Berra and the rest of 'em sittin' in the backseat. Casey was the one who kept everything under control. There wasn't nobody better than Casey."

It was easy for writers and fans to compare Sparky to Casey.

Both had faces that looked as if they had been chiseled out of granite. Both were small. Both managed legendary teams. Both got a head start on talking even before brushing their teeth in the morning. Both demolished the English language more thoroughly than a wrecking ball did a house made of balsa wood. And both loved people.

"I'm honored by the comparisons, but there was only one Casey," Sparky maintained.

Not until I started covering baseball did I start to appreciate the importance of the clubhouse leadership that only the right manager brings to a team. Not until Sparky came to the Tigers did I realize all of the nuances necessary for a manager to extract full potential from even the most talented collection of young players.

And not until my box seat study sessions with Sparky in his office and the hotel suites with no one else around did I come to appreciate the game's most subtle intricacies.

Not even the coaches were as privileged as I.

His two most poignant lessons were to get to know each player as a person and never to take your eyes off either pitcher throughout the whole game.

Sparky learned that from Hall of Fame manager Al Lopez, who was retired in Tampa when Sparky was a young manager for the Reds. The Reds conducted spring training there.

"He told me my eyes would tell me what move I had to make," Sparky said. "He said to trust your eyes and never let 'em wander."

I never had the privilege of meeting Casey. Like many of the boys of my generation, I felt like he was an uncle I just never had the chance to meet.

I have a hunch, however, that Casey utilized a tactical ploy to protect his players that Sparky lifted to another level to protect his.

The entrance to the home clubhouse in old Tiger Stadium was through the manager's office. After a particularly tough loss, Sparky quickly began to spin a story he knew would captivate the media. He didn't restrain the media from entering the clubhouse. He merely cleverly kept the story going long enough for players to shower and depart—if they so chose—without having to face a sometimes unforgiving press. If players chose to stay, at least they had a few personal moments to collect their thoughts before giving an answer that had the potential to be controversial.

Players appreciated their manager's subtle maneuver . . . and so did Sparky because it gave him more time to talk.

"No one will know how much the players appreciated him for doing that," longtime Tigers first baseman Dave Bergman once told me. "We knew what he was doing. And he never said a word about it."

Sparky was armed with a secret weapon shared by only a few managers throughout the history of the game. Without ever having met Casey, I know this weapon also belonged to him.

They both were blessed with charisma that couldn't be taught in charm school.

Few, if any, managers were blessed with the charisma of Casey and Sparky. Each personality was different. But both were magnetic.

Casey was that grizzled veteran who could disarm any writer with a story that took more turns than a screw being drilled into a hardened two-by-four. Sparky had his own stories decorated with fractured pieces of English that sometimes had no beginning and often had no end. Still, they sounded hilarious at the time.

No one had to wonder who had just entered the room when either Casey or Sparky appeared.

Players felt that charisma. So did umpires. And so did opposing managers. Casey and Sparky had a natural two-step lead even before the first pitch was thrown.

There was a lot of Casey in Sparky. And it transcended all the funny stories each could fire at will.

Anything I know about baseball I owe to Sparky. It would have been fun to watch him manage those old Yankees teams.

33

★

One Love

"Managing in the big leagues can't be that tough," I joked with Sparky. "We put it all together in just one day."

Sparky smiled and nodded his head slowly. Then he rose from his kitchen chair and looked around the room. He had that faraway look in his eyes that said he wasn't quite finished. There was one more story to tell that day. It may have been the most important because without this person, Sparky might have wound up being the house painter his father was. Or maybe a used-car salesman, as he had been for one off-season during his minor-league days.

It's the story about Mrs. Carol Valle Anderson. Only when asked is she Sparky's wife.

Of course, she is proud of the life she shared with one of baseball's true legends. Her preference to be called Mrs. Carol Valle Anderson is a matter of personal choice and character. And Sparky constantly and publicly acknowledged his admiration for her commitment throughout their 57 years of marriage.

"She knows who she is and how much she means to our family," Sparky often said. "She's stronger than anyone I know. A whole lot stronger than me. Without her, nothin' I did in baseball coulda happened. She raised our kids, keeps our house together, pays the bills. She does everything I don't know how to do. I never have to worry about nothin'. All I had to do was go out to the park, put on a uniform, and manage a game. Now that's like stealin'. How can anyone ask for anything more than that?"

Often he confided to me that he hoped he'd be "the first to go."

"I couldn't survive without her," he said. "I know that. And so does she."

That was one thing he never joked about.

It's impossible to appreciate the complete character of Sparky without understanding the role Carol played in his life. In a much more subtle way, in fact, I learned as much from Carol as I did from Sparky. Through her gentle and generous guidance, I learned the true difference between Sparky and George.

Only a fraction of the thousands privileged to have met Sparky ever had the opportunity to meet the only woman in his life. After a brief few moments with him, however, most walked away with an impression of her that would have made Mother Teresa feel proud.

"I don't ever remember having to write a check," he said. "That might be a record, but it's true. That's Carol's job and there ain't no one who does it no better."

Her trickiest job, however, was learning to accept such a double-edged character as Sparky, who reveled during his time at home when he could relax simply as George.

Sparky was the showman. He thrived performing on his personal stage. Once a season ended and back in the security of his home, though, the bubbly Sparky character morphed freely into George. In just a few months, the show resumed once more.

George appreciated the Sparky image that enabled him to become one of baseball's all-time colorful characters. He was a true ambassador for the game pushing baseball and goodwill.

He also appreciated being plain old George, the guy next door who was happy to hibernate in front of his family room TV during each off-season.

He enjoyed playing a few rounds of golf with friends. He wasn't particularly talented with tools, but he did try his hand at some regular household repairs that invariably ended with a call to a handyman. He did all the things a husband and father down the street usually does throughout the year.

He just had to pack everything into a couple of months. That time to be Sparky always came quickly.

Carol had no choice but to accept both characters for who they were. But each could be as trying for her as it was for Sparky or George . . . whichever role he happened to fill at the moment.

"He's all yours for the next six months," I remember Carol teasing me over the phone each year shortly before spring training began.

And once again, the show would go on.

I learned to distinguish one role from the other. It took a little time, but I came to embrace the sincerity of both. Sparky needed George. And George certainly needed Sparky.

Together the polar personalities enjoyed quite a run. Except in public places, I always called him George. Even during a season, it was George who shared so much with me.

George married Carol Valle when he was a 19-year-old minor-league player. At the time, the name "Sparky" wasn't even a figment of anyone's imagination. It sounded like a name befitting a fire station dog. Two years later while playing for Fort Worth, Texas, George was tagged with the name by a radio broadcaster doing the Class AA games.

Sparky was a fiery competitor from the first day he put on a pair of spikes. The number of his encounters with umpires mounted light-years faster than his batting average climbed. During one confrontation with an umpire, the broadcaster commented, "The sparks are really flying tonight." The word "sparks" soon gave birth to "Sparky," and the name stuck tighter than the glove on his left hand.

Carol caught his eye when both were in the fourth grade soon after the Anderson family moved to Southern California from Bridgewater, South Dakota. No one could have dreamed they would spend the next six decades together. Fortunately for him, he made the best decision of his life.

It wasn't, however, because their personalities were a perfect match.

While Sparky was impetuous and made most decisions on gut feelings, Carol is deliberate and patiently examines the options and alternatives of every situation. While Sparky was restless to voice an opinion on matters about which he was already convinced, Carol remains open to all perspectives and usually winds up keeping any opinion to herself.

Both remained remarkably well informed about political matters and news from around the world. And that led to some rather spirited arguments in which they eventually called a truce without a winner.

Sparky expressed his commitment to Carol daily throughout his career. He called her each night after a road game merely to ensure that the family was safe and for her to feel the same about him. On each trip to Detroit during his retirement, his first step into my house was straight toward the telephone. He had to tell Carol he had safely arrived. Each conversation ended with him saying "I love you."

And that's the way it was for 57 years!

Through 17 arduous seasons of playing and managing in the minor leagues, the couple learned to tolerate crisscrossing the country with three kids in the car and a trailer full of household necessities. That also included two separate seasons in Montreal and five in Toronto, along with a handful in Latin America during the winter to earn a few more dollars.

It was all part of the journey that led to the creation of Sparky. And George never forgot the commitment from Carol that allowed him to follow his dream.

Even after enduring the grueling test and finally hitting the big time when Sparky became Cincinnati's manager at just 35, their lifestyle remained modest. They preferred simplicity and the same low profile usually attached to a mailman or a clerk in a hardware store. Unlike many major leaguers with a taste for ostentation, they never moved from the home they built in 1967. It's a normal-looking two-story home in an average middle-class neighborhood. Despite many opportunities to move, it's the home they could never leave.

"At the time, we couldn't afford the prices in the Los Angeles area," Sparky said. "We had to look for property up north. There was hardly anything around here when we first came. Not even a highway. Just a two-lane road."

The home has two bedrooms upstairs and two bedrooms down. The house resembles those of all their neighbors. Only a few, such as the Andersons, are original owners in the subdivision, which looks pretty much the same as when they arrived.

The home is fastidiously maintained and features a colorful front yard rock and flower garden that Sparky planted and maintained himself. Except for the striking garden, it's easy to pass by the house unless specifically looking for it.

That's what happened during one of my visits when Sparky and I were tinkering in the front yard.

A car stopped and a pair of unfamiliar men approached. The driver lived in nearby Newbury Park and happened to know where Sparky's house was located. The passenger was a visitor from Michigan who couldn't resist the opportunity to at least drive past his favorite manager's home.

Sparky answered the usual questions that all fans ask. The excited visitor wanted to know how Sparky had enjoyed his stay in Michigan. Upon reaching the car, the visitor from Michigan offered an innocent observation. "It's a beautiful home," the man said. "I just thought you'd live in something a whole lot nicer."

Sparky was more amused than offended, understanding what the man meant.

"Why should I move to someplace else when Carol and I feel so comfortable right here?" he asked. "Ain't a home the place where you feel good? Since the day we moved here we couldn't feel no better."

Sparky never felt compelled to prove his success through any monetary measure. He had already proved everything he wanted to throughout his record-setting career.

"What we don't got, we don't need," Sparky said. "This is home and we're happy. We ain't goin' nowhere else. Wherever we wound up wouldn't be home."

Everyone in the neighborhood, of course, knew Sparky. He was the guy who drove his 1995 Ford Crown Victoria up and down the streets at various hours of the day.

The car is white and accentuated by an appropriate number of dents, dings, scrapes, and scratches. It's equipped with windshield wipers that choose to work at their own discretion . . . usually when the sun is high and no rain has fallen in the last several weeks. The car is fairly well seasoned with about 180,000 miles on the odometer. On my visits, he often had us work on a minor cosmetic repair job such as smoothing one specific scratch that somehow clashed with the car's overall personality.

It's a beautiful machine that Sparky promised never to let go. He affectionately christened it "the Tank." A later-model silver Crown Victoria is rarely removed from the garage. The Tank meant more to Sparky. It became a legend of its own.

For years Carol drove a compact Ford Probe. She still misses the feel of her small car, about half the size of the Crown Victoria, which nevertheless featured all the extras of a full-size luxury vehicle.

After all the years of traveling through the tiny towns of the minor leagues and spending summers in Cincinnati and Detroit, Carol is content never to leave her beloved mountains, which surround the home they built two years before the first man walked on the moon.

She remains Mrs. Carol Valle Anderson and proud wife of Sparky. It's still impossible to truly appreciate Sparky without knowing the one and only woman in his life.

Even more than from Sparky, being true to yourself is a lesson I learned from Carol.

34

★

And There Was Lefty

Before going that evening to my room, which over the years had become as familiar as the bedroom in my home, I flipped on the light switch for the room next door. A few years earlier, Sparky had converted the bedroom into a personal den. After weeks of planning and moving items from one spot to another, he rarely stepped into the room.

The average-size room houses a wide-screen television set, a handsome leather recliner, and two comfortable armchairs, which make the room feel as invitingly warm as a wood-paneled library. The room radiates a rustic quality, particularly inviting to men. This is the room whose walls bring to life the celebrated career of one of the game's most colorful characters.

Framed full-color photos and paintings of him throughout the years tastefully hang on all four walls. The photos are accompanied by specifically selected magazine and newspaper covers and articles that depict the life of Sparky.

There's also a handsomely framed photo of President Ronald Reagan with a personalized message to Sparky. A long line of autographed baseballs, including those from his three World Series Champions, is featured on a shelf running the length of one wall.

Perhaps the most eye-grabbing mementos are 11 signed Hall of Fame bats. They stand as proudly as a line of Swiss Guards in proper salute to an individual who served baseball so well. At the annual Hall of Fame induction ceremonies, each member receives a bat signed by all returning members.

After his 2000 induction, Sparky returned to Cooperstown for each celebration. "I owe that to all of the newcomers who earned their way into the Hall," he once told me. "I owe it to all of those guys who came before me. Most of all, I owe it to the fans who were so good to me for so many years. Those fans are the most important part of the Hall of Fame."

The room also houses some miscellaneous pictures that demand explanation for their presence among images of such baseball luminaries. A couple of those pictures are of Sparky and me. Just making that Wall of Fame is, by far, the most touching baseball honor I ever received.

Sparky rarely stepped into the history-filled room. He knew everything he had accomplished in his career. He never felt compelled to remind himself of all he had earned.

"I lived all those times," he once told me. "I don't need no reminders. I know one thing for sure, though. I didn't do all that stuff by myself. I had a lot of help along the way. That's what all the stuff in the room does. It reminds me how much so many people helped me along the way."

That was not the voice of false humility. That's what Sparky believed.

I don't know why I decided to visit that room that evening. I had relaxed and read in that recliner countless times before. The feeling that evening, though, was different. It seemed as if I were feeling the magic of that room for the first time.

After rising from the recliner, as I was walking toward the light switch on the way to my own room, out of the corner of my eye I discovered a photo I didn't remember from before.

Perhaps coincidentally, but certainly serendipitously, in that instant everything seemed to make sense. The photo was a snapshot of Harold "Lefty" Phillips.

Phillips was an anonymous pitcher who made just five minor-league appearances in 1939 when a bad arm ended his playing career before it had a chance to start. He became a baseball "lifer," though, serving as a scout, coach, manager, and front-office executive for the California Angels until he died in 1972.

Phillips was more than Sparky's ticket to professional baseball. He taught him how to be a professional in baseball—on and off the field.

Phillips was scouting for the Brooklyn Dodgers when he first spotted Sparky playing on the sandlots of Los Angeles. Although he detected some playing talent in the skinny shortstop, he was more impressed by this prospect's fire for the game and his natural baseball instincts.

Throughout Sparky's four years at Dorsey High School, Phillips became a fixture at the Anderson home. After scouting him in games, Phillips would drive to the Anderson home. He and Sparky spent hours almost every night sitting on the front porch simply talking baseball. Phillips had never encountered a kid so eager to learn the nuances of the game and those unwritten rules of life.

A few days after graduating from Dorsey, Sparky signed the Brooklyn Dodgers minor-league contract offered by Phillips.

"Lefty Phillips is the reason I made it into baseball," Sparky often said. "He taught me how to play. He taught me how to act and represent the game away from the park. He taught me how to be a professional."

Sparky always talked about Phillips whenever asked why he never wore his World Series rings. "'Cause they don't really belong to me," Sparky always answered. "He's the guy who taught me all I know. They belong to Lefty. I'll never be able to thank him for everything he did for me."

After being named as the Angels' manager at the conclusion of the 1969 season, Lefty hired Sparky to serve as one of his coaches. Before spring training began, Sparky was offered a contract to manage the Cincinnati Reds.

"Lefty told me I had to take that job," Sparky said. "Managers' jobs don't just fall out of trees. If it wasn't for Lefty, though, I never would have had that opportunity."

So there it was. Maybe that's why Sparky enjoyed sharing so much of the wisdom and experience that had been passed to him. Perhaps it was his way of simply saying thanks.

He learned and practiced the lessons that Lefty taught him. Then he was generous enough to pass them on to me.

The last of those three days in October was now only hours away. I didn't want the time to pass, yet I was anxious for our Tuesday session. Sparky said we had some "serious stuff" to talk about . . . some "real serious stuff."

I was anxious to savor everything he had taught me. I was even more anxious to learn anything more he had to share.

I knew in my heart that Tuesday was going to be a day I'd never forget.

TUESDAY

★

Some Serious Stuff

It was slightly after midnight when I finally went to bed. I picked up the book I had brought from home to read on the plane to and from California.

For maybe the fifth time I was reading John Irving's *A Prayer for Owen Meany*. Some of the pages were dog-eared for ready reference. I had scribbled notes on others. It's a work I turn to as a calming antidote to anxiety. I appreciate the smile and a little peek into the goodness of humanity that it always provides.

This time it had less effect than reading the Los Angeles Yellow Pages. I placed it back on the nightstand almost as soon as I had picked it up. There was no sense trying to read. I would have forgotten all that I had read before morning arrived.

After a career in baseball, it's almost impossible not to think in the clichés of the game. With Tuesday now officially here, we were down to "our last game of the season." The "last few pitches." Our final opportunity to "hit a home run."

I always hated such clichés. Still do.

But clichés and irreverent humor have been two of baseball's staples throughout the years, unforgettable even after several years away from the game.

How was I to prepare myself for what I knew was going to happen? More important, did I have the wisdom to get myself prepared?

I didn't want that time to come. Yet I didn't want my best friend to suffer.

I tried to convince myself that he had the easy part. I'm a believer, and I had no doubt he was going to a better world. Nobody spreads as much goodwill as Sparky without going to heaven. It was those of us who had to stick around to handle life without Sparky that had the real problem.

I told myself that he had prepared me well. He had taught me so much about baseball and about life. He had taught me even more about how being a good person is far more important than baseball or writing or any of the other things he and I did in life.

I knew he was right. But was I strong enough to live all those lessons he had so generously taught me?

I heard every tick of the clock that night till I finally fell into a restless sleep at about 3 a.m. I forced myself to remain in bed for almost two more hours. Then I arose to shower and sit with the newspaper and a cup of coffee at that familiar kitchen table. If only for a few moments, that table had an uncanny way of making life slow down.

By the time Sparky arose, I had finished reading the newspaper. I had also delivered the newspapers to the neighbors across the street, snipped out a couple of coupons for the supermarket, and watered the flowers in pots hanging from the roof of the patio.

"Daniel, my boy," he began. "How come you're not still in bed?"

The question needed no answer. Some things are better left unsaid.

I asked him about the "serious stuff" he wanted to talk about that day.

"Time, Daniel, my boy," he said. "Just give it a little time."

He finished a half glass of orange juice and looked through the coupons I had clipped. "Now you're gettin' with it," he said with a grin. "I was beginnin' to wonder about you."

Almost imperceptibly, Sparky slipped into a story that I never dreamed he had even remembered.

We had taken a ride to the old neighborhood one sunny spring afternoon. Not Sparky's old neighborhood. The one where I was raised, less than two miles from where old Tiger Stadium used to stand.

We had no special purpose. The excursion was just one of those experiences friends such as us like to share. I had always wanted Sparky to see where I had been raised as a boy. Neighborhoods tell a lot about the person. They answer questions never asked. They confirm what others only surmised.

I wanted him to taste what Detroit once was and how some parts of the city still struggle to survive.

Sparky had already retired before our informal inner-city tour. He had returned to Detroit for the filming of a commercial.

Even with the anal peculiarities of a typical commercial director who feeds his sense of self-importance with the shooting of needless retakes, the project was completed quickly. Sparky was good. He still had the stuff. I had been at many shoots where he needed only a couple of takes. The early-morning session left us with an entire afternoon of nothing to do.

The commercial was staged in one of Detroit's most prestigious suburbs. I thought the clash in cultures from a drive through the old neighborhood might be a healthy shot of reality that both of us could use.

Over the years Sparky had listened to me talk so much about the old neighborhood I loved, he might have thought he had seen it many times before. But eyeing the surroundings as we crept closer to our destination, he looked at me suspiciously and whispered: "This better be good."

The old neighborhood is crammed with all the history upon which Detroit was founded. What was once a vibrantly eclectic mix of ethnicities is now a ghostly portrait of its former self. Abandoned homes. Boarded windows. Windowless frames on the now empty buildings that once bustled with life on frantically busy "factory rows."

There was a time when every factory in the city ran three eight-hour shifts of workers to sate the insatiable appetite of the automobile industry. Now only the hollow shells of those buildings remain. Many serve only as shelters for homeless squatters. Almost all are infested with rodents and an array of stray animals that make them home.

Slightly north of the busy Detroit River and a short streetcar ride to the heart of downtown, the area became a magnet for European immigrants and those from other parts of the world seeking the security of a guaranteed factory job after World War I.

Irish. Polish. Italian. Russian. Hungarian. Maltese. Mexican. African Americans from the southern states. There were pockets of every ethnicity. They all flocked to the city with the promise of a better way of life. Affordable wood-framed houses sprouted like weeds. The auto industry had given birth to the middle class.

The royalty of industry belonged to Detroit. No other future shone brighter than that of the city that made the cars. The Big Three felt invincible. The city felt powerful. The good times, it was believed, would never end.

Still standing in the middle of the old neighborhood is the Holy Redeemer Church and its all-encompassing complex. As the Catholic-dominated immigration wave settled, Holy Redeemer became the nation's largest Roman Catholic parish for a period in the mid-'50s.

The once-filled rectory was home to about a dozen priests. They were Redemptorist missionaries who split time between the parish and missions around the world. A convent housed about 50 nuns. They belonged to the teaching order of the Immaculate Heart of Mary. They were highly educated and painfully thorough, and specialized in discipline.

The square-block complex featured a separate building for the high school and another for the grade school. There were a sufficient number of miscellaneous buildings to stage community functions such as plays, recitals, bingos, and boxing matches.

Of course, there was the church designed in the image of St. Peter's Basilica in Rome. The imposing gothic brick-and-marble structure would be far too costly to replicate today.

Still a picture straight out of the Bing Crosby movie *The Bells of St. Mary's,* the complex has suffered through attrition and disrepair over the years. While the core remains intact, a significant portion of operations has disappeared.

The convent is gone, its remnants now a parking lot. The rectory is home to only a handful of priests. The high school building is leased to another private school. Only the grade school, in its 129th consecutive year of operation, has bravely resisted the radical change.

The area still remains densely populated. But as with many urban centers around the country, inescapable blight and a bleeding economy have leveled the neighborhood to a ghost of its former glory. Because of the dominant Hispanic population of the area, the number of parishioners in the church remains strong.

"This better be *real* good," Sparky said, and again rolled his eyes, after I parked the car and said we were getting out.

He twisted his head in every direction before finally asking: "What's a church and school like that doing in a neighborhood like this?"

I told him to relax. This was the school I had attended. I was giving him the opportunity to meet one of his most loyal fans.

The office secretary dropped her jaw in shock at the first sight of Sparky. She nervously directed us to the class that the principal, Sister Elizabeth, was leading for the day. A longtime friend and a hopelessly loyal Tigers fan, she spotted me through the glass in the door and walked into the hall to inquire about my visit.

"We just happened to be driving around and my friend asked if he might be able to meet you," I said, and asked her to turn around.

It's never a good idea to lie to a nun. But this was a special circumstance. Except for disciplinary purposes, throughout my 12 years of tutelage under the nuns, I had never heard one scream so loudly. This scream, though, consisted of pure delight.

"Easy, Sister," I said. "It's not the pope."

At least for the moment, there could be no other person in the world that she would prefer to have standing in front of her than Sparky. A lifelong Tigers diehard, she knew more about the records of the man who had so successfully managed her team than the record setter himself. The two hugged, and the long, dark hallway was suddenly filled with laughter. A couple of other nuns peeked out at the commotion in their normally placid school.

After one quick glance through the window of the classroom door, Sparky had mapped a plan for the kids. Even more than he needed his usual half cup of coffee after each game, Sparky couldn't resist any opportunity to spend some time with kids.

"Would you mind, Sister, if I said a few words to your kids in there?" he asked.

Still slightly shaken, Sister Elizabeth said only if she could join in the fun.

Sparky started with the usual tales about working hard in school and being unafraid to follow their dreams. Then he made an abrupt left turn and broke into a story I was sure would earn me an old-fashioned crack on the knuckles with a ruler, which had become a daily ritual many years ago.

"My mama taught me a long time ago never to worry about not goin' to church every Sunday," he began. "What you really gotta do is treat everybody right.

"Every person out there is a child of God. Ain't no one person more special than anyone else. God likes to see all of His children happy. If you wanna make God happy, just go out and make His children feel good. Don't be like those phonies that go to church each Sunday and then go home to be a jerk. God knows who you are and what you're doin'. That's the only scorecard He keeps."

I could feel that ruler coming after Sparky told the kids that Sunday Mass had just become optional. Maybe she'd be lenient and at least postpone her wielding of the ruler until my next visit after Sparky had gone home.

Instead, Sister suddenly jumped from her seat to lead a standing ovation. She thanked Sparky for his thoughtful words and told all the children to cherish them for the rest of their lives.

Sparky then signed a picture of himself that hung on the door of Sister's office until her retirement. He was happy with the visit, which provided him with another opportunity to touch the kids.

If Sparky could have batted by talking he would have been a .400 hitter. His performance that day was the first miracle I had witnessed since the time—ages ago—I saw my own principal break into a sincerely beatific smile when John F. Kennedy was sworn in as the first Catholic president of the United States.

How could anyone but Sparky walk into a Catholic school seventh-grade class and resolutely proclaim that "you don't gotta go to church on Sunday to get into heaven?"

And then leave the classroom to a standing ovation led by the head nun herself?

Sparky knew exactly what he was saying. The kids got the message. And so did Sister Elizabeth, who flashed a smile warmer than mittens in the middle of a winter snowstorm as she stood to lead the robust standing ovation.

Sparky always had the words. He may have jackhammered syntax into a million tiny pieces and probably gave a whole new meaning to a few words. But he always had the right words to make his message clear.

In a matter of moments, Sparky could humble a recalcitrant player, then bounce from the dugout before a game to make a grizzled old fan feel like a kid once more. He had a gift for pitching a little bit of baseball with a lot of goodwill.

Sparky was glib—or "glub" as he once phrased it. He had a turbocharged gift for measuring an audience. Anyone venturing into hearing range was pretty much entranced before having the chance to fully appreciate that the speaker was really him.

On the way home, I decided to show Sparky the house and street where I had been raised. On the way we passed the old home of John Gillis, who attended the Holy Redeemer Grade School many years after I had left. Now an internationally acclaimed rock star known as Jack White, he seems to appear on almost every entertainment show on TV.

"I don't know Jack White from Snow White," Sparky said. "But if he survived this old neighborhood I wanna shake his hand."

Weeded, vacant lots have swallowed half the houses that used to stand so proudly behind a line of oak, elm, and chestnut trees. When I pointed to the house that had once been mine, a look of going back to his old home burst upon Sparky's face.

Despite all of the countless days I had spent in Thousand Oaks, we had never visited the Los Angeles home where he lived as a boy after his family moved from Bridgewater, South Dakota, when he was only nine years old. I had seen it, though, many times in my mind from the vividly colorful images he painted so precisely with his typically jumbled words.

That's why I knew he would appreciate this brief visit. It was as much of a trip to the past for him as it was for me.

"I've seen all this before," he said. "It's exactly where I came from. We didn't have all your snow, but I guarantee you, I've been here before."

I showed him the park where we played baseball from sunup to sundown, from the spring through the fall. I showed him the box that we had chiseled into the brick of a factory wall. The space in the box determined a strike in the classic game of "strikeout" we played so often when we didn't have enough kids to play a real game. I showed him the route I walked to sneak into old Briggs Stadium, that jewel of a structure that was renamed Tiger Stadium and that now stands no more.

Then I drove him past the site of the now gone Cadillac Fleetwood Plant, where the grandfather who raised me worked from the day after his discharge from the United States Navy after World War I to his retirement.

Sparky looked and listened as we traveled through time and the neighborhood. While looking at all the sights, I knew, he was seeing a few flashes from his own past. The geography was totally different. At the core, though, it was precisely the same.

"It don't matter where anyone comes from," he finally said. "Home is home and it'll always be home. All that matters is what you learn from being there. And it ain't got nothin' to do with anything you find in the books."

Instead of an ocean about 10 miles to the west, we had a wading pool in a public park a few blocks from home. Instead of mountains rising majestically in the distance, we were surrounded by skyscraping smokestacks sprouting from the ubiquitous automobile factories where round-the-clock work shifts gathered seven days a week.

The obvious physical differences between neighborhoods didn't matter. The neighborhood Sparky kept so proudly in his heart is hauntingly similar to the one I'll forever keep in mine.

It was a good trip.

35

★

Three Legends

A trip to the old neighborhood was a good way to start the "serious stuff." Sparky always had a good sense for drama. I poured him another half cup of coffee and filled mine to the top. We returned to baseball and one of those classic what-if questions.

One of the game's most engaging charms is the what-if questions that all fans love to play.

What if Ted Williams hadn't lost four of his prime baseball years to fight in two different wars?

What if Joe DiMaggio had played his entire career in Boston with Fenway Park's cozy left-field wall?

And what if Red Sox owner Harry Frazee had not sold Babe Ruth to the New York Yankees for the $100,000 he needed to produce the Broadway musical *No, No, Nanette*, which debuted on January 3, 1920?

Is there any doubt that a lot of baseball history would read considerably differently based only on those three classic what-ifs?

So often in baseball, as well as in life, we are left merely to ponder.

Perhaps of somewhat less historic impact, a big what-if is very much alive in the rich history of the Detroit Tigers.

What if the franchise's leadership triumvirate of Jim Campbell, Bo Schembechler, and Sparky Anderson had not been dismantled before the club was sold in August 1992? Would the club have turned into the plankton of the American League and not even sniff post-season participation for 11 more years?

Might Sparky have come dangerously close to John McGraw, who trails only Connie Mack for the most wins by a manager in baseball history? Might Bo have realized his vision of turning the franchise around, as he had with the University of Michigan football program almost four decades prior? Might Campbell justifiably have been voted into baseball's Hall of Fame for compiling one of the longest executive careers in the history of the game?

All we're left for certain are three glaring what-ifs.

In the history of the game, perhaps no other organization had assembled such an auspicious leadership team. The serendipitous coming-together of such a dynamic sports trio might be compared to a totally imaginary union of Warren Buffett, Norman Vincent Peale, and P. T. Barnum.

Campbell had been running the entire Tigers organization since before John F. Kennedy completed his second year in office. From 1962 till August 1992 he served as either general manager, president, chief executive officer, or chairman of the board. Executives from both leagues constantly sought his counsel in the way that brokers and speculators cling to each word uttered by Buffett today.

Through sheer determination, spirit, and the gift for recruiting an inexhaustible pool of football talent to the University of Michigan, Schembechler willed his way into the College Football Hall of Fame as a record-setting coach fans still fondly remember. With his high-octane persuasive powers, he could have provided some penetrating chapters to *The Power of Positive Thinking* that Peale hadn't even considered.

Bo had multiple opportunities to coach in the National Football League. Instead, he chose to leave the field for an executive position as president of the Tigers in 1990.

Sparky, of course, was the Hall of Fame manager who made the game fun even for lukewarm fans. He had an inexplicably inherent feel for running a game and for spreading goodwill each step along the way.

P. T. Barnum was a legendary showman. But certainly no more than was Sparky, who, almost accidentally, could generate just as many smiles for fans in all cities.

For pure leadership qualities, the Wharton School at the University of Pennsylvania couldn't have assembled a more impressive baseball management team than Detroit's second "Big Three."

"I never seen nothin' like it in all my years in baseball," Sparky said. "I think we coulda done somethin' special for the fans."

The distinctive personality of each individual brought strength to the whole.

Campbell was a businessman who demonstrated just as much concern for balls and strikes as he did for dollars and cents. He was a bottom-line guy who fearlessly made bottom-line decisions. Although sometimes chastised by fans for his pecuniary policies, never did he compromise the talent on the field.

Campbell was pragmatic and expected loyalty to his decisions. Rarely did he compromise after coming to a conclusion. No one was more loyal to the club and its employees than he.

Bo's legendary status as a football coach transferred seamlessly to baseball, a game he played, loved, and followed all of his life. His first concern was always for the team and the athletes who played the games. He recognized their strengths as well as their weaknesses. He also understood the resources necessary to produce a consistently winning team.

Bo welcomed all well-prepared opposing viewpoints about any matter. But any such argument had to demonstrate how it would improve the team. In all my years working for the club, Bo was the only one to tackle Campbell with an argument and walk away a winner.

Sparky was that beautiful blend of baseball savvy and theatrical flair. Even when managing overmatched teams, he had a knack for making the game fun. Sparky sometimes conceded arguments, but never his position. Similar to Campbell and Bo, nothing mattered more to him than the team.

While their personalities differed, they shared the required tools of all winners.

All three had a sense of humor they were unashamed to reveal. Campbell's was droll. Bo's was penetrating. Sparky's was outrageous and oozed with good-humored compassion. He could make the pope laugh on Good Friday.

All three were dedicated to the single premise that nothing was more important than the development of the team.

The integrity of each could inspire the sternest judge. There was never a scandal in any of their careers. A promise made was a promise kept. No more than a handshake was needed to complete the most complicated deal.

Few in sports are fortunate to have worked for a true legend. I'm far more fortunate than anything I deserved. I'm privileged to be the only person in Michigan to have worked personally for all three.

"Do you know how lucky I am?" I often said to Sparky.

"Yeah," he would crack. "The big question is how did you manage to stay lucky for so long?"

The term "legend" is sinfully overused. With technology having raced past our collective sense of ethics, the media have diluted the word to a ghost of its former self.

Accuracy has been sacrificed to speed. Taste has surrendered to sensationalism and titillation. Media once governed by honesty and common sense have been displaced by the mad dash for corporate gains.

Each home run now is hit by a legend. Every close game now approaches epical proportions.

True legends aren't created in one at bat, one game, one season, or even one decade. True legends are measured by consistency and longevity. True legends arise slowly from a superior body of work over an extended period of time. True legends withstand all unexpected adversity inherent to the games they play. True legends aren't manufactured by tweets, Facebook, hits, and blogs. True legends transcend the standards of their particular sport with a corresponding contribution to society.

A true legend loses, but never breaks down.

By any measure, Sparky, Bo, and Campbell were legends.

Being close and watching them work together gave me an insight into sports and giants that few are privileged to see.

The wisdom, ethics, direction, sense of responsibility, and humor they imparted are impossible to discover in any volume of books or any profession beyond sports.

Sparky and I were relaxing in his room in the Lakeland Holiday Inn during the last week of spring training in 1985. It's the time of the baseball calendar when all players, managers, coaches, and members of the media are bored with the meaningless games in Florida. In a matter of days, the regular season would begin, and everyone was anxious to get back up north.

We spent most March evenings watching the NCAA Basketball Tournament in his room. With no games scheduled for that particular evening, we talked about what to expect going home as the defending World Series Champion.

I could detect the edge in Sparky's voice that had become habitual at that time of the year. He always grew edgy over the many dangerous little possibilities. In a 162-game season there are so many things that can go wrong. He was concerned about things that the average baseball observer doesn't imagine. Even the players are blind to all the risks.

Sparky was painfully aware that defending champs get no passes. They come into a season wearing a big bull's-eye on their backs. All clubs take aim at bringing the Big Boys down. He had witnessed his great Cincinnati teams handle the pressure. He was unsure if his young Tigers would be as graceful with success.

"You're the man now," I cracked, and poked him in the ribs. "You could run for governor and win without giving a single speech."

Sparky smiled and modestly acknowledged his popularity. He was familiar with the routine. Win and you remain the poster boy. Lose and all the posters turn to doormats.

He had learned long before that popularity is more fickle than a teenager's puppy love. It remains unshakable only till the club's first six-game losing streak.

"Right now, yeah, I'm ridin' pretty high," he said. "But there ain't but one man sittin' at the top of all sports in the state of Michigan. That's Bo Schembechler. He owns the state. Always will."

Over the years, we both had got to know Bo socially. Never did we dream, however, that five years later the celebrated University of Michigan head football coach would become president of the Tigers.

Bo's football records are as impressive as those carved out by Sparky in baseball. He won more games than any coach in the history of the University of Michigan. In 21 seasons, his Wolverines posted 194 victories. His teams won 13 Big Ten championships. They appeared in 17 bowl games, including 10 Rose Bowls. They had 17 top-ten finishes in the final wire-service polls. His epic battles against Woody Hayes and Ohio State are still worth all the replays.

As much as for all of his success on the field, Bo was idolized for his exemplary off-the-field behavior and the principles that he refused to compromise. He took great pride in his passion for turning promising young football players into champions. He felt equally proud for helping them mature into responsible citizens, husbands, and fathers.

Bo became the standard by which all successful college coaches are measured. He was as fearless in running his smashmouth attack as he was in playing by all the rules . . . in football and in life.

Not only was Bo a standout lineman at Miami University of Ohio, he was also a pitcher for the baseball team. He was a student of baseball and rooted for the Cleveland Indians while growing up in Barberton, Ohio.

Bo pitched a game against Ohio State University when Campbell was an outfielder for the Buckeyes. As executive leaders for the Tigers, both claimed victory in that collegiate head-to-head matchup that took place so many years ago.

For health reasons, Bo was advised to step down from coaching after the 1989 season. Only days after finishing his career with a Rose Bowl appearance on New Year's Day 1990, Bo stunned the world of sports by accepting the presidency of the Tigers.

Bo and Campbell had long been friends. Obviously, Campbell was keenly aware of Bo's character and ability to lead. Legends like Bo could lead a football team or the Salvation Army. He understood athletes and the essence of all sports.

So why not the Tigers?

Precisely . . . why not the Tigers? In the two and a half years of his presidency, I witnessed more innovations than I had seen in the previous decade.

When Campbell decided to step away from day-to-day operations of the club to serve in an advisory capacity as chairman of the board, he seized the opportunity to name Bo as his successor.

The sporting world was skeptical about Bo's ability to cross from one high-profile sport to another. But Campbell wasn't fazed. Nor was Sparky, who also had befriended Bo and marveled at his talents.

"If Bo had been given more time, he woulda become one of the best general managers in the game," Sparky told me. "He knew what made any kind of player tick."

Bo demanded a lot from every person working under him. In return, he gave them all the tools necessary to succeed. Bo knew there were no shortcuts to success on any field.

Before the end of his first season, Bo had developed a vision for what the Tigers had to do to stake their claim as an annual title contender. And he wasted no time convincing owner Tom Monaghan that a lot of money had to be spent.

Visions like his don't come cheap. Rewards, however, can be immeasurable.

Bo's vision started at the top and ran clear to the bottom of Detroit's baseball operations. He ordered a reshaping of the Tigers' spring training facilities in Lakeland, Florida. Extra batting cages were constructed. A strength and conditioning coach was hired. A weight room with state-of-the-art equipment was established.

For the minor leagues he authorized the hiring of an additional coach at each level. Bo was a coach at heart. He was convinced that one manager couldn't be expected to provide the proper coaching for untested and impressionable young players. He also added weight facilities to the clubhouse of each minor-league team.

Next on his ambitious agenda was to be a revamping of the scouting system, which had grown stale. Having recruited so successfully his entire football career, Bo appreciated the continual influx of fresh young talent. Under his plan, no team would be allowed to top the Tigers in signing good, young, hungry prospects.

He proposed a study of the most recent major-league drafts to determine which scouts from which organizations enjoyed the most success identifying such prospects. The final step was easy. He planned to lure those scouts to the Tigers with hefty pay raises that rewarded their singular talents.

Through his personal experience and his feel for players and the game, it took less than one full season for Bo's vision to become clear. Once it was realized, the Tigers wouldn't have to worry about losing any player to free agency. A capable replacement would be ready to rise from some rung of the minor-league system to fill the hole.

The organization was being rejuvenated and now only needed time to blossom.

That time, however, was never to come.

A financial crisis in Monaghan's sprawling empire forced the sale of the Tigers in August 1992. Before the sale was complete, Bo and Campbell were unceremoniously fired from their positions.

Their dismissals were unexpected, particularly that of Campbell, who had served the Tigers organization since 1949. Since his discharge from the United States Navy and graduation from Ohio State University, he had served only the Tigers.

His 43-year tenure—the last 32 as either general manager, president, CEO, or chairman of the board—remains legendary to baseball. A reign such as his is not likely to be repeated in today's corporate game. No corporate executive remains in the same place for 43 years. The old days of baseball had come to a stunning end.

Campbell was once termed the consummate "baseball man." He was a throwback to the old days when the general manager was responsible for all aspects pertaining to the club.

Lawyers, marketing madmen, and anyone unwilling to devote 24 hours a day to the team had no place in the world of old baseball lifers. Player trades were made on a handshake, and contracts were written without a conga line of addenda that had to be cleared by agents, attorneys, accountants, and a handful of others with fancy titles after their names.

In 1975 at baseball's annual winter convention, Campbell agreed to a major deal with Philadelphia Phillies general manager Bill Giles. It would have sent longtime Tigers fan favorites Bill Freehan and Mickey Stanley to the Phillies. Because both were 10-year veterans with at least the last five years with the same club, Campbell had to get their approvals.

A few lesser-known players were also included in the deal, but the centerpiece of the package coming to the Tigers was catcher Bob Boone. After some long-distance midnight telephone convincing by Campbell, Freehan and Stanley agreed to the trade. After shaking hands with Giles to solidify the deal, the teams agreed to announce the trade to the well-represented media early the next morning.

A funny thing happened after those few nervous hours of sleep before the next morning. The press conference never happened. An early-morning phone call to Campbell from the Phillies told him the deal had been scratched.

Campbell, of course, was furious. The deal had been done. Hands had been shaken. Two starting players on the Tigers would now have to be told they weren't going anywhere.

Apparently, handshakes and verbal agreements were losing their place in the brave new world of baseball. It would take time for the new world to be firmly established. But in the next 17 years before Campbell was unceremoniously discharged, a broken handshake would become no more than a venial sin.

Campbell remained loyal to the game and its unwritten traditions. He maintained loyalty to all who worked for him as long as loyalty was returned to the club.

Campbell had the reputation for being frugal with the payroll. He believed part of any employee's reward was the opportunity to work for the Detroit Tigers. Former Tigers infielder and longtime Boston Red Sox coach Johnny Pesky nicknamed him "the Clamp" for his tightfisted fiscal policies. A longtime employee aptly observed that Campbell was "cheap . . . but he was loyal cheap."

Only a handful of employees ever left the club before it was time to collect Social Security.

Campbell's loyalty to the Tigers was as strong as Henry Ford's to the car company that bears his name. Campbell was a gutsy leader and unafraid to make any move he believed was in the best interest of the club.

He signed Gates Brown and Ron LeFlore while each was serving time in prison, to give them a fresh start. He traded local folk hero Denny McLain when he discovered a way to improve the club. He hired Billy Martin as manager when the club needed a breath of his fire. He later fired the fan favorite for unacceptable behavior off the field. No individual was allowed to compromise the reputation of the club.

It was Campbell's old-fashioned persistence that landed Sparky with the Tigers. Sparky had suffered his own unceremonious discharge as manager of the Cincinnati Reds after the 1978 season. He was planning to take the entire 1979 season off and return in 1980.

With a legend like Sparky, though, there is no extended period of rest.

In June 1979, Sparky was courted seriously by the Chicago Cubs. Negotiations were ongoing between Sparky and Cubs owner Phil Wrigley himself.

The two longtime baseball men were within a handshake of consummating a deal. Then along came Campbell with a string of long-distance phone calls that eventually convinced Sparky he appreciated Detroit's tradition even more than he did the Cubs'.

Sparky couldn't resist the opportunity to serve under a baseball lifer such as Campbell. He also felt the Tigers were loaded with a talent-rich system of promising young players only searching for the right leader to teach them how to win.

His assessment was shared by Campbell, who realized that the pool of talent was hungry for an experienced winner to lead.

The two shook hands—figuratively over the phone—and the working relationship endured until that fateful day in August 13 years later when Campbell and Bo were discharged.

Bo's vision for the future of the Tigers pegged Sparky as the anchor.

Besides the more than 1,758 victories already in the record books, Bo also was enamored with Sparky's unblemished character.

As much as Sparky admired Bo, the old football coach may have had even more admiration for him.

Sparky had a work ethic similar to Bo's when he was coaching. There were obvious differences between the two sports, but their underlying philosophies were basically the same.

Bo never understood why the leader of a baseball team is called a manager. "Isn't he a coach above everything else?" he always asked. "Isn't he supposed to take the talent given to him and then coach that talent to its highest potential?"

Sparky never bothered with the subtlety of semantics, but he thoroughly enjoyed the challenge of molding raw young talent into a final product that could compete for championships year after year.

All the pieces for Bo's long-term vision were in place. Sparky was only 61 years old when his contract expired and he stepped away from the Tigers after the 1995 season. He was confident he could have managed till he was 70. But speculation swirled strongly in the media and throughout the legion of Tigers fans that the new owners of the team did not want him back.

And so the what-ifs of baseball and life continue.

What if Campbell and Bo had been allowed to remain with the Tigers long enough to enact Bo's long-term plan?

What if Sparky had managed for at least another five years? He finished with 2,194 victories, history's third highest number at the time. Would he have stuck around just a little longer to challenge John McGraw's number two spot at 2,763?

And what if he had? Would Sparky have missed enjoying so many good times for having been elected to Baseball's Hall of Fame in 2000 after he turned 65?

The what-ifs of baseball remain mysteriously intriguing.

Certain, however, was the presence—albeit brief—of perhaps the most auspicious leadership triumvirate in the history of the game. Another "Big Three" in the history of Detroit.

On that there is no what-if. It will never happen again.

36

The Equalizer

After completing our intriguing what-if tale, Sparky simply smiled and silently nodded his head a few times. He never spent much energy worrying about anything that could have been.

Any what-if belonged to yesterday.

On that third day in October, though, there was one slice of the past he felt compelled to mention. We had talked about it many times before, but never with such candor.

He rose from his chair and walked to the sink to draw a glass of water. The expression on his face reflected the heavy weight of what was running though his mind.

"Sometimes bein' Sparky wasn't always as easy as maybe I made it look," he said.

Maybe he had been so consumed he didn't notice that Carol certainly knew. His kids knew. And so did I.

How could it have been easy?

Playing with the media. Teasing the fans. Smiling when tired. Signing autographs till his fingers hurt. Secretly visiting kids at the hospital. Kibitzing with his players. And managing a major-league baseball club for 26 successful seasons.

He did everything everyone had come to expect over the years. He did it all so smoothly. And always with a smile. Of course it wasn't easy. He just made it look that way.

Sparky wasn't perfect. Like all human beings, he had shortcomings, too. At times he could be stubborn. No amount of factual evidence could change his mind once he had made a decision. There were occasions when his impulse to act quickly landed him in a patch of quicksand when just a pinch of patience would have put his feet on solid ground.

His sincerity of purpose made everything look natural. His effervescent personality made everyone feel good.

No act was ever scripted. No speech was ever rehearsed. From his treatment of the fans to his interactions with the media, everything came straight from the heart. Because he believed that he'd been blessed far beyond any imaginable measure, he felt obligated to share his good fortune by being a good guy.

But it wasn't always easy.

"Even the president of the United States sometimes must have to stand naked" is a line from the Bob Dylan classic "It's Alright, Ma (I'm Only Bleeding)." The line refers to a moment of truth that all of us must face at least once in our lives.

I thought about that poignant line when Sparky met his moment of truth in the spring of 1989 when a confluence of complicated on- and off-the-field situations conspired to set a trap even Mandrake the Magician couldn't escape.

Nor could a character as charismatic as Sparky.

The pressures of managing a major-league team are enormous. Coupled with playing the role of Sparky, those pressures once staggered the character in a lonely moment of despair he never imagined could happen to him.

On an early-April morning in 1989 when the Tigers broke spring training camp to head north for the regular season, Sparky was sitting in his usual right-side window seat on the team bus headed for the Tampa airport. He was staring out the window as laughing players trickled from the clubhouse onto the bus. Chances are he never saw a thing. His eyes looked glazed. They appeared never to blink. I thought he might be looking in the direction of Cape Canaveral, searching for a morning space launch.

After shoving my briefcase up onto the overhead rack, I plopped into the seat next to him. He didn't budge an inch.

"Now we get serious," I tried to joke. "Let's start the season with six straight W's."

The look on his face after slowly turning his head toward me gave me the feeling he didn't really see me at all.

"We might be the first team in history to lose 162 games this season," he finally mumbled. At that moment, I'm sure he thought that was true.

Sparky possessed a natural theatrical flair that often led to melodramatic overstatement. I had learned to dismiss many similar statements that even he forgot immediately after speaking.

But all 162 games? Even the hapless 1962 New York Mets dropped "only" 120.

Something was wrong. I had no idea what it was, but somehow I figured it ran deeper than our lackadaisical play throughout the exhibition season.

Except for the family, no one knew that his only daughter, Shirlee, was battling a crisis far worse than any string of poorly played ball games. She was pregnant when her first husband walked away from the family.

There are few problems more gut-ripping for a loving father than a daughter in distress. And home was 2,000 miles away from where Sparky happened to be.

All Sparky shared with me was that there was a "big problem at home." I didn't push him. He knew I was there.

Even the most pessimistic preseason prognosticators picked the Tigers to finish in the middle of the East Division pack. No one dreamed they would lose 103 games. On the bright side, at least they finished with 59 more victories than Sparky had envisioned on that gloomy spring morning in Florida.

We started the season with a two-game series in Texas, and Sparky showed up bouncing around like the same baseball pixie he always was. We were shut out, 4–0, in the first game and dropped the second, 5–4.

Despite the losses, we returned to Detroit for the home opener and Sparky greeted all the fans with the enthusiasm of a five-year-old on Christmas morning racing down the stairs to see what Santa had left for him under the tree.

We hammered Milwaukee, 10–3. Sparky's problems didn't magically disappear. At least for the moment, though, they were anesthetized. We proceeded to lose six of the next seven games, and it was getting tougher for Sparky to hide his quickly sinking sense of despair.

Injuries to players changed the lineup. Regardless who was playing, though, nothing seemed to work. As never before, Sparky started to blame himself for the losses mounting so quickly.

Despite the team's struggles, he fulfilled every charity appearance to which he had committed, along with trying to help resolve the distasteful situation his daughter was enduring 2,000 miles away. The daily, lengthy long-distance phone calls to Carol and his daughter kept chipping away at his endurance.

That moment of truth to which Sparky wasn't immune was closing in quickly. It finally landed with a crash the morning of May 19.

The previous evening Sparky had attended a fund-raising dinner for Children's Hospital. Once more he smiled, schmoozed, and shook more hands than an underdog politician on the night before the election.

When he returned home, he knew something was seriously wrong. He broke into a sweat and fell into an ugly form of unconsciousness. It couldn't be called sleep with the devils and demons that kept dancing through his mind.

In the morning he was awakened by a phone call from general manager Jim Campbell. Sparky's meandering mumbles left no doubt in the boss's mind.

Something was wrong and Campbell responded quickly. He immediately phoned team physician Dr. Clarence Livingood, who diagnosed

Sparky's condition as a severe case of exhaustion. He recommended that Sparky return to Thousand Oaks for rest. Immediately!

Campbell called me to his office for a briefing on the situation. He ordered me to drive to Sparky's house right away to transport Sparky and housemate coach Billy Consolo to the airport.

"Don't pay attention to anything he tells you," Campbell said. "He'll listen to you. Just make sure he gets on that plane. And tell him not to call me till he feels better."

Almost immediately after I pressed the doorbell, Sparky opened the door and apologized for what was happening.

"Daniel, my boy," he said. "I don't know what the hell is goin' on. But I gotta get myself back home to California."

After I helped him pack a suitcase full of clothes, he told me to take whatever I wanted and to give anything left to charity. I told him, of course, that he'd be upset when he returned if the house was empty.

He just shook his head as if uncertain he would be back. "I don't know, Daniel," he mumbled. "I just don't know."

As we drove down the familiar freeway to the airport, his head kept swiveling side to side. I knew he was making mental images of all that had become familiar.

"You're gonna see all this again," I reassured him. "Just get home safely. Get some rest. And take care of whatever you have to do back there. Everybody will be waiting to welcome you back."

For several years, I replayed the whole scene in my mind over and over again. I could never feel the pain and anxiety running through the body of a man who had given baseball so much. But I had a pretty good idea about all the demons running through his mind.

How can a major-league manager leave his team on May 19? he must have thought. How can a manager who has won three World Series now not even lead a team to play at least .500 ball? How can I ever come back and look my team in the eye again? How can I say I'm sorry to the fans for leaving their team when it needs me most? How can I tell my family that I'll never manage again?

It would take time for all those wounds to heal. But the process miraculously started with the first sight of his daughter.

"I can't explain it, but when I hugged her, I knew everything was gonna be all right," he told me over the phone before his return to Detroit.

With each call that he placed to me during his 17-day recovery at home, his voice sounded stronger. The determination was coming back. I could feel his smile through the phone.

He returned on June 5 when the Boston Red Sox visited Detroit. Campbell had suggested a June 9 return when the Tigers were scheduled to play in Toronto, because the pressure might feel lighter away from home.

Sparky insisted that the comeback had to be in Detroit. That's where he had left his team, and that's where he had to make his way back. "I owe that to my team and to the fans," Sparky said as we drove from the airport the evening before his return.

Naturally, Sparky felt apprehensive. He wasn't quite sure what kind of reception he would receive the next evening. From his players. From the media. And most important, from the fans. After leaving the airport he asked if we might drive downtown. He wanted to slip by the ballpark without going inside.

The silence of Sparky as we slowly circled the stadium was louder than anything he could have said. He had been leveled. Now he was back. He would make the next day one of the most memorable of his career.

Emerging from the dugout to take the lineup to the umpires in the ritual pregame meeting, Sparky was treated to a standing ovation. On his return he stopped in front of the dugout to take off his cap and salute all the fans.

Redemption in baseball can be as near as the next time at bat or as far as the beginning of next season. But the opportunity is always waiting for those who are sincere. Baseball asks only humility and the admission that no one is bigger than the game itself.

With its working-class core and blue-collar ethic, Detroit is a forgiving city. The sins and shortcomings of one day are quickly forgiven the next. Sparky had given the fans so much. Now it was their turn to give in return.

Fans can tell if a person is sincere. There's no place to hide in

Detroit. That's one of the reasons Sparky fell in love with the city. It's hardworking, honest, and always ready to forgive the sincere.

What Sparky perhaps didn't realize was that during his unexpected absence, the fans missed Sparky even more than he missed them.

I never saw Sparky lose any intensity for managing. I never saw him not bleed after any loss.

I did see a man humbled by his trials. I did see a man rearrange family and baseball into a more balanced perspective. That wasn't easy for Sparky. But he knew it was the right thing to do.

On that third day in October I realized even more how, at times, he had struggled to give all the fans everything they expected from Sparky.

I also realized how much each of our families meant to us. And our appreciation for them grew even deeper.

37

Ego

The sun now was shining brilliantly through the kitchen window. Autumn was always a special time of year for Sparky.

Of course, he cherished all those crisp October days and evenings when he was managing the Reds and Tigers in postseason games. But he also relished that spectacular change of season when he could step away from the game and once more become George.

Sparky paused slightly after recalling his sabbatical from baseball. It was a significant part of his history that triggered even more serious thought for both of us.

His personal midseason hiatus from the game could have been an ego-busting knockout. Instead, he used the bumps and bruises to finally establish the priorities in his life.

Sparky had an ego just like everyone else. But as much as he was a riveter with the English language, he was a diamond cutter with his ego, which he always kept under control.

As he was inclined to do, he used a story he and I often shared to show how ego can be a blessing instead of a curse.

Except for when I was a kid going to games at old Briggs Stadium,

I never collected autographs. In my position with the ball club, it wasn't the right thing to do.

I do, however, have a collection of five baseballs personally signed to me and dated by Sparky. I keep them in a closet to avoid their fading in the sun. They are baseballs that were used in the following historic games:

- September 27, 1992, when he set the Detroit franchise record for most wins (1,132) by a manager
- April 15, 1993, when he became the seventh manager to reach 2,000 wins
- June 3, 1995, when he became the third-winningest manager in history
- September 1, 1995, when he became the fourth manager to manage at least 4,000 games
- October 1, 1995, when he managed his final game

Sparky knew I would never have asked for these balls. He knew they would be hot items for collectors. He also knew my sense of history and how much they meant both to him and me. After each of those games, he had them signed and waiting in his office for when I came down from the press box.

"You take 'em," he told me. "I want you to have 'em. You were part of the action. Keep 'em for your grandkids."

Sparky was never presumptuous about his personal accomplishments. Only when asked did he discuss the highlights of his career. And he gracefully handled such matters with discretion.

He understood his position in baseball history. No one knew his records better than he. He chose humility over spectacle, however, and let the records speak for themselves.

"If someone don't have an ego then he don't think too much about himself," he reasoned. "Show me a player without an ego and I'll show you one who ain't gonna be in the big leagues too long. It's the same thing for every walk of life. I sure hope my doctor and dentist have an ego or I better find a couple that do. All that matters is what you do with that ego."

Except for some of the excessively intrusive marketing gimmickry that started to pervade the game before his retirement, there was no aspect of managing that Sparky didn't embrace.

He loved getting to the park early and staying long after the fans had already got home. He loved batting practice. He loved making tough decisions in tight spots. He loved sparring with the media. He loved signing autographs. He loved fooling around with the fans.

Big-league managing is a constant ego-feeding lifestyle with a pantry that never runs out of food.

"Where else but in baseball can a grown man dress in a little boy's uniform and have writers and TV and radio reporters scribble down every word he says?" he asked. "On some days I got quoted more than the president of the United States."

Unlike many major-league managers, who are skeptical of the media, Sparky was thoroughly amused by his relationship with writers and broadcasters. He never ducked their questions even after the toughest loss.

"I never wrote a paper in my life that a teacher didn't use a whole bottle of red ink to correct," he joked. "Then all of a sudden I was getting myself quoted every time I opened my mouth. And that was a lot."

Sparky managed as much with charisma as he did with all the baseball wisdom he had accumulated from 42 years in the professional game. No manager could have done that without having his ego in check. He not only accepted his responsibility as a role model, he was proud of the influence entrusted in him pertaining to kids and community.

"Don't tell me these players don't have an influence on youngsters," he used to preach. "They better know. It comes with the territory. A player or anyone in a position of influence oughta get nailed double for usin' drugs or committin' any other crime."

Throughout his entire life there was never a hint of scandal with Sparky. He played the game hard. And he played strictly by the rules.

Despite managing his entire career in a pair of blue-collar, mid-market midwestern cities such as Cincinnati and Detroit, Sparky soared his way into becoming a national figure. It's staggering to speculate on the stature of his celebrity had he managed in a media capital such as New York or Los Angeles.

He once confided that he would have liked to have a shot at managing his hometown Los Angeles Dodgers. But that was just a daydream he knew would never happen.

Primarily because of the work ethic that Sparky discovered in both of his managerial stops, he came to appreciate the people of the Midwest and their passion for baseball.

He liked the way people came out to the park early enough to watch batting practice. He liked the way hardly anyone left the park before the end of the game regardless of the score. He liked the way the fans would cheer a good play even when made by the visiting team. He liked the way the autograph seekers were always polite. He never liked—but came to appreciate—the round of boos he would receive when the team was playing poorly.

"They know the game," he used to say. "How can anyone get upset with that? If I was payin' good money to see some of the things we pulled at different times, I'd be booin', too."

Fans in both cities came to love the little man with the white hair and the funny way he talked. They loved him for what he did on the field and for how well he represented the community away from the park.

When I once asked for his definition of success, he told me of an incident he had with longtime Dodgers radio voice Vin Scully. "Success is for the moment," Scully said to Sparky. "Accept it. Appreciate it. And remember it will soon be gone."

It seemed that way once when Sparky got an ego check on a visit back to Detroit. He had just finished an autograph session in a shopping mall. He and I were speaking to Jim and Lynn, the dynamite executive director and his assistant for Sparky's charity for kids.

An attractive lady burst through the door of a store and was racing toward Sparky. Sparky gave a sly smile and joked: "The old man's still got it, folks."

The lady handed him a pen and a piece of paper and said: "Would you please sign this for me? I love the way you say 'That ball is long gone.'"

Jim, Lynn, and I had to hold our breath trying not to burst into a belly laugh. The "long gone" phrase referring to a home run was popularized throughout the state of Michigan by longtime Tigers broadcaster Ernie Harwell. Obviously, the lady had mistaken Sparky for Harwell.

"Yeah, the old man's still got it all right," we teased him.

Sparky was always good at controlling his ego. But a check once in a while never hurt anyone.

38

★

"Nothin' to Do with It"

From all the tales of those three days in October, those kitchen walls were now magnificently filled with a story of a friendship that happens just once in a lifetime. Fortuitously, we had saved some of the best stories for last. Even more than as a baseball immortal, they define Sparky as a man.

It had been 15 years since Sparky made the gutsiest career-defining decision of his entire life.

And as we sat at his kitchen table late that afternoon he quickly snapped: "I wouldn't change a thing."

Of course, there are no records to measure such matters. But his refusal to manage replacement players in spring training 1995 has to be among the bravest personal decisions made in the history of the game.

"After making the decision, I never thought about it again," he said proudly. "In fact, it never entered my mind."

No defining moment is free of paralyzing risk.

And certainly the stakes were high for Sparky when he unflinchingly made the decision that forever helps to define not only his career, but also his character.

His $2 million salary. His job. His legacy to the game. His opportunity to be elected into the Hall of Fame. All were on the table when he chose not to compromise principle in the face of such staggering consequences.

I had never witnessed a braver career decision during my years in the game. And never was I more proud of a man—for his character rather than for his managerial records.

For Sparky, there simply was no risk too steep for remaining true to the lifelong baseball principles he had held sacred since he was a boy. "If you don't stand up for everything you believe in, you got no place to stand," he eloquently told me when he made the decision final. "If principle has a price tag, then it ain't worth nothin' in the first place."

That's an unforgettable lesson to be cherished forever by kids and adults alike.

Principle must remain a sacred trust. Its purity must be preserved from the pollution of money, no matter the amount.

Sparky was no hero and shook his head when he was called one. He believed there are plenty of genuinely good guys in the celebrated world of sports, but rarely any heroes.

Heroes, he believed, are the protectors of freedom. Some work silently searching for miraculous medical cures. Others sweat and bleed in a classroom teaching our youth to stretch beyond their potential to make a better life for themselves, their families, their communities, and mankind.

Most real heroes remain anonymous. They seek no public acclaim.

The closest thing to heroes I had the privilege of meeting in baseball were Ted Williams and Bob Feller. Each spent a large chunk of the prime of his Hall of Fame career protecting our freedom in World War II and the Korean War.

So when Sparky put his career on the line, he knew it wasn't heroic. It just took a lot of guts and the commitment to do something almost all baseball fans knew was the right thing to do.

Sparky understood that the norms and mores of baseball had changed since he broke into the game. At times, labor relations between owners and players made contract negotiations between Teamsters and management look like a birthday party. Work stoppages forced gaps in seasons that sometimes went unfilled. Unwelcome as they were, though, they never compromised the integrity of the game.

This particular situation, however, trespassed the boundaries of common sense.

"I got my regrets from some of the things I did in my career," Sparky told me after stepping away from the game after the 1995 season. "But that ain't one of 'em. If I had to do it again, I wouldn't blink an eye. I'd do it a thousand times if I had to."

The fiasco that led to Sparky's career-changing decision began on August 10, 1994, when commissioner Bud Selig aborted the rest of the season because of the labor impasse between the players and the owners. The war between the millionaires and the billionaires eliminated any season-ending dramatics. No playoffs. No World Series. Not even the promise of a new season.

Just a stain on baseball's soul. Baseball's shameful plan for spring training of 1995, in fact, was uglier than a mortal sin.

As always there would be about a week of workouts before the exhibition schedule began. Most games would be played during the day in Florida and Arizona sunshine. Fans from the North were expected, as usual, to visit all the camps to escape the winter snow and get an early shot of their favorite team.

Everything would be the same except for one missing element. Major-league players would not be playing the games. And baseball's scheme to compensate for that probably would have made P. T. Barnum snicker.

Replacement players would fill the uniforms and play the games till, hopefully, the real major leaguers returned.

The "Hiring Now" sign was hastily hung at every major-league camp. Baseball would plod along even if the real guys weren't in town to do the plodding.

These replacements included a mismatched collection of former high school, college, sandlot, and minor-league players. A few Walter Mitty wannabes—some old enough to have grandchildren—showed up daily just for the opportunity to wear a big-league uniform if even for one day. Any major leaguer willing to break the union line was also invited to join the free-for-all.

"If this is what baseball has come to, I guess the game don't need me," Sparky said.

What it came to was a genuine Wes Craven nightmare . . . filmed in 3-D. It was the perfect Stephen King horror story. Rumblings began in the winter and triggered unanswered prayers for the return of common sense.

During each off-season, Sparky and I talked at least every other day. Most conversations were no more than rehashes of football games we had watched on TV or discussions about some of the prospects we were anxious to see in spring training.

Sometime late in January, however, I detected a hint of disillusionment in his voice. The bounce was there, but noticeably softer. I could see in my mind that the impish grin normally shining on his face looked a little dimmer.

I knew about the tug of war going on in his soul. He respected my knowing that this time he preferred to work things out on his own.

As in all previous spring trainings, I picked him up at the Tampa airport a couple of days before the official opening of camp. He followed his unwritten rule of reporting a little ahead of time, with the futile hope that both warring sides might come to their senses with a last-tick-of-the-clock compromise.

Words, for once in his life, were scarce and softly spoken. He waved at fans who recognized him in the airport. He merely smiled and shook his head in disbelief when asked if baseball was really serious about using replacement players.

A flush of embarrassment covered his face.

He must have been thinking that these fans had more concern for the integrity of the game than any of the people responsible for the impending circus of horrors.

There was silence in the car as we wound our way from the parking lot onto Interstate 4, which cuts east–west across Florida's belly.

Once on the highway, he spoke softly. His eyes stayed fixed straight ahead into the night.

"I just can't do it, Daniel," he said. "I just can't do it. There's just no way I can be part of this whole thing."

He didn't have to say any more. I had been confident all along that he would make the right decision.

The following evening he was scheduled to have dinner with newly appointed Tigers president and general manager John McHale Jr. I drove Sparky to the hotel restaurant in Orlando and walked the lobby until their meeting was finished.

Sparky explained his reasons for refusing to manage replacement players. Nothing McHale offered could persuade him to compromise.

On the drive back to Lakeland, Sparky began to think out loud. "I might have worn that uniform for the last time, Daniel," he said. "And I don't think any of the other owners are gonna be knockin' down my door to give me a job."

If that's the way it was going to be, then Sparky was prepared for the consequences.

Upon reaching the hotel, Sparky immediately called Carol to tell her he had cleared the first hurdle. Carol, of course, was supportive of Sparky. She's always been a lady of extraordinarily good common sense.

He later called Selig. They had known each other for many years, and Sparky, of course, respected the office.

"I wanted you to hear this directly from me," Sparky told the commissioner. "I want you to know exactly how I feel."

Sparky emphatically stated that he was not choosing sides in the labor dispute. His decision supported neither the owners nor the players. It was, instead, a simple statement of principle about everything he held sacred about the game.

The game, he believed, was bigger than all the players and owners, present and past. The idea of putting major-league uniforms on players who hadn't earned them undermined the very foundation upon which the game was built.

During the conversation, Selig asked Sparky what he would do to settle the situation. Sparky said he would put locks on all the spring training camps. Then he would hide the keys till an agreement was reached.

In a hastily prepared press conference the following morning in his Marchant Stadium office, he addressed all the reasons for his decision to a collection of writers from the various spring training sites of Florida.

The story had the wallop of a Mike Tyson knockout punch. It was probably larger than Sparky had imagined. This was not a young manager still striving to make his mark. This was Sparky Anderson, who had three World Series Championships in his back pocket. He was on a straightaway path to induction into the Hall of Fame.

The press conference was unlike any of the thousands he had conducted before. No jokes. No small talk. No bold predictions about what the outcome to this bizarre nightmare might be.

In his opening remarks, he emphasized that he was not taking sides between owners and players. He held no ill feelings toward the replacements, who were only seizing an opportunity they had never dreamed was possible.

His decision, he said, was based purely on principle. There was no price tag on the game he loved so dearly.

His press conference turned into a call for common sense.

Common sense for Sparky included respect for tradition and all the players, managers, coaches, and owners that had come before him.

Sparky always made his ideas clear through the use of concrete examples rather than through ambiguous terms such as "tradition" and "history."

What if replacement players were used for an entire season? he asked the spellbound writers. What if some young slugger hit more home runs than Roger Maris or Babe Ruth? What if some flamethrower fired five perfect games? What if a sprinter, used only as a pinch runner in each game, stole the absurd total of 162 bases?

And what if one franchise was able to assemble such a collection of misfits that it won an unthinkable 150 games, and made a mockery of history's greatest teams?

All were exaggerated hypotheses beyond the reasonable realm of possibility, no doubt.

But just what if?

Anything was possible with such an unlikely assortment of players, almost all of whom had never played a day of professional ball in their lives.

"How would you explain that to the legends of the game who were the greatest of their generations?" Sparky asked. "The record books wouldn't mean a damn thing."

And what about the fans? Even if ticket prices were to be cut in half, how could anyone tell them they were watching major-league baseball?

"I don't want somewhere down the line for one of my grandchildren to see a film from this year and have to say that their grandpa had anything to do with it," Sparky concluded. "Well, they don't have to worry, 'cause they ain't gonna see Grandpa in it. Grandpa ain't gonna have nothin' to do with it."

That was a thought Sparky simply couldn't digest. So he packed his gear and headed back to Thousand Oaks, unsure if he would have to buy a ticket to see the next baseball game he ever attended.

I felt as proud of Sparky for that press conference as I did for his acceptance speech into baseball's Hall of Fame five years later.

Even before the coming of replacement players, I had become disillusioned with the game. It was becoming as corporate as General Motors up the street from Tiger Stadium. Marketing began to dilute much of the game's purity. There was no gimmick too big, no gimmick too small. It all got down to money.

I certainly realized that with the cancellation of the World Series, every effort to resuscitate interest in the game for disappointed fans was critical. But this compromise of principle, for me, stretched far beyond reason and common sense.

The game had become a tentacle of big-time corporate interests. That didn't make it bad. It just made it different. The game had become just too impersonal since the time I received my opportunity of a lifetime.

I wondered how the mom and pop with a couple of kids would be able to put together the $200 it would soon take for a night out at the park.

Not that it would have made a speck of infield dirt of difference, but I asked Sparky if he wanted me to join his boycott.

"When this is over they'd hire Humpty Dumpty before bringing you back," he answered swiftly and emphatically. "You stay where you are. You can help me while I'm gone."

I called Sparky daily to report on the circus he was missing. Among the hodgepodge of players that changed almost every day, there were only a handful that could perhaps make the roster of a low-rung minor-league team.

That was it. Not a single Roy Hobbs.

Sparky asked me to deliver a message to the manager of each opposing team. He wanted all to understand that he respected their decision to manage during this blotch on baseball history. He particularly wanted the younger ones to know he could appreciate their concern for being bounced from the game without a good chance of returning.

Nevertheless, Sparky did wonder, at times, why he was left to be the "Lone Ranger" and carry the whole load.

Speculation throughout the media covering spring training grew stronger each day that Sparky might not be asked to return. A few suggested that ownership had wanted him fired immediately, but for a variety of reasons had been dissuaded by the general manager.

After common sense finally prevailed and a tentative agreement between owners and players was reached the day before the regular season was scheduled to start, teams were ordered back to Florida and Arizona for an abbreviated spring training.

Upon returning to Lakeland, Sparky was greeted by players and fans as their favorite uncle who had come home for Thanksgiving dinner. Not only did his own Tigers players express appreciation for his bold commitment, but so did opposing players, who approached him on the field before and after games.

Sparky accepted this graciously, but reminded them that he had not chosen sides. Sometimes commitment to principle is more important than either side of a dispute.

He told them that he followed his heart for the tradition of the game. He asked them never to forget how important that tradition would always remain.

Throughout his absence, Sparky received bagfuls of mail from people around the country who saluted his resolve. In the labor-intensive and sports-tradition-rich city of Detroit, Sparky was treated to a standing ovation upon his return to Tiger Stadium on Opening Day. Handmade signs showing fan support for Sparky's decision hung over the rails of the upper and lower decks.

Obviously unable to respond personally to all who supported his stance and shared his commitment, he publicly thanked all and was humbled by the outpouring of their support.

Although no mention of Sparky's defining moment appears on his plaque in the Hall of Fame, his commitment to the game perhaps best reflects the real spirit of baseball. More than any of the memorable accomplishments he notched on the field, this was Sparky . . . Sparky at his best.

There were many proud moments during Sparky's 26-year career in Cincinnati and Detroit.

In Cincinnati there were the 1975 and 1976 World Championships. There were four National League pennants. There was the careful guidance of one of history's most powerful batting orders.

In Detroit there were the 1984 World Championship and the 1987 American League East Division title. So many talented young players whom Sparky helped to mold into men. The election to the Hall of Fame. And, of course, the charity he created for underprivileged children.

He had done so much for each franchise, each community, and the game. It's ironic that the one memory he left by choosing not to do something may reverberate loudest of all.

Not heroic, just compassionate common sense. A defining moment during which he never wavered.

"I never considered myself no martyr," Sparky said. "I never made the decision for nobody but me. It was the right thing to do. I don't need any medal for what I did. But I do know one thing. It was the proudest decision of my career."

I wasn't surprised. I never expected anything less.

39

Lesson Learned

Before leaving the kitchen early that evening I had one more story to tell. It was about a lesson Sparky had taught that inspired the most significant professional decision of my life. Sparky smiled appreciatively the first time I told him about it 15 years before. He smiled proudly when I brought it up again.

Compared to Sparky's defining moment with baseball history, my career-changing decision was only a hiccup. Still, it fills me with pride that surpasses any monetary measure.

As with Sparky, it began early in 1995 with the replacement-players folly. Like any baseball purist, I felt betrayed: not by the game but by those who ran it.

Many of those dream chasers posing as players looked as if they hadn't played a game in more than 10 years. Some looked like they hadn't even worked out. At tryouts each day, I felt I was watching Lee Marvin doing a baseball version of selecting his Dirty Dozen.

And that was just a movie. This was the real thing!

It wasn't the replacements' fault that the circus had come to baseball's front porch. Baseball was open for business and had pitched a tent in each big-league camp.

Players, managers, coaches, and above all the fans were appalled by the impending stain on baseball history. The distasteful decision to use imposters for the games was ridiculed by all but the owners.

Among all major-league managers troubled by such a potentially unimaginable charade, only Sparky chose to rise in support of his convictions. The rest reported to their teams while Sparky returned home to wait until the tragicomedy ended. That move cost him about $150,000 that he would have earned in spring training.

The situation made me feel dirty. I felt like a barker at a Friday night opening of a carnival. I knew I was easier to replace than the torn canvas on first base. Still I felt inherently complicit.

When I shared that with Sparky, he told me he could use me there. He wanted to be kept apprised of what was happening at all the camps. "None of this is your fault," he reasoned. "Just use your head and hope sanity comes back to the game."

Although the opening of the regular season was slightly delayed, no replacement player appeared in a regular-season game. However, speculation in the media was strong that the line between ownership and Sparky had been drawn.

With his contract expiring at the end of the year, Sparky chose not to seek an extension. He wanted to avoid a potentially sticky situation for ownership and himself. He told the press it was just time "to move on."

One month after the end of the season, I submitted my resignation to pursue other opportunities. I chose to continue working for Sparky, which turned out to be the best decision of my professional career.

I wish I could take credit for that decision myself. But at least I was wise enough to embrace a lesson from Sparky, who regretted a move he had failed to make three years earlier.

In August of 1992, lifetime Tigers chief executive Jim Campbell and president Bo Schembechler were fired before the official announcement that the club had been sold.

Campbell was the man who had brought Sparky to the Tigers in

1979. Bo was a longtime friend and charismatic Michigan sports icon whose plan for rebuilding the franchise was just beginning to take root.

Campbell and Bo emphatically urged Sparky to honor his contract and stay with the team. Walking away, they convinced him, was not going to bring either of them back.

"I shoulda left right then," Sparky told me. "Jim was the guy who brought me here. Bo was a friend and a giant in sports who everybody trusted. I shoulda walked out the door with them."

Nevertheless, he listened to their logic even though his decision haunted him for the rest of his life.

No life is lived without regrets. Not even one as colorful and full as Sparky's.

He regretted time lost with Carol and his children due to the demands of his storybook career. He regretted his impatience with certain players while still finding his own direction as a major-league manager.

But that one move he failed to make was particularly painful.

Loyalty is one of those precious pieces of friendship defined far more emphatically through actions than with words. A spoken expression of loyalty remains hollow until it is supported by a risky action.

Baseball is a breeding ground for multiple levels of loyalty: to owners, to managers, to coaches, to teammates, to fans.

Rewards from loyalty aren't measured by money. They're personal and subtle, felt only by the heart.

The inherent risks of loyalty are correspondingly more costly. Sparky learned the steep cost of his commitment to loyalty when he lost his job as manager of the Cincinnati Reds in the fall of 1978.

Despite a second-place finish in the National League West Division, the Reds were determined to make a few changes. Although some of the pieces to the Big Red Machine were missing, a second-place finish was one notch below their annual expectations.

One of the changes the Reds were determined to make was the replacement of a couple of coaches on Sparky's staff. Sparky was open to almost any suggestion to make the team stronger. Replacing any of the coaches who had been loyal to him, however, was not one of those options. "I'm the guy who put that staff together," he said. "I'm the one responsible for the way they did their jobs."

He told the Reds that they would have to let him go before any change of staff would occur.

And so they did. On November 27, 1978, the Reds stunned the baseball world by firing the popular character. Sparky paid the price for his conviction despite the overwhelming outrage of Cincinnati fans, who couldn't believe their favorite manager was gone.

Just that quickly, Sparky found himself out of professional baseball for the first time since he signed a contract the day after graduating from high school.

Later Sparky conceded that he could have handled the matter leading to his dismissal better. He admitted that perhaps he let his ego get too much in the way.

He still would not have released any of the coaches, who had been loyal to him. But both sides could have been creative while searching for a mutually acceptable solution. Perhaps it could have prevented a revision to baseball history that affected so many teams and so many fans across the country.

Sparky wound up putting a face on the Tigers for the next 17 years. He was sincere and effective convincing fans about the importance of the franchise for the good of the community. His relationship with Campbell clicked from the start. For the decade of the '80s, only the New York Yankees' 854 victories exceeded the Tigers' 839 in the American League.

Sparky finished his Tigers career with a franchise record of 1,331 victories by a manager. He already held the Cincinnati franchise record with 863.

In 1988, Sparky got another loyalty check. It came from a phone call that lasted only long enough for Sparky to say no.

Sparky had just returned from an all-star tour in Japan. While he was out of the country, California Angels owner Gene Autry called Campbell to ask permission to speak to Sparky about managing the Angels.

In accordance with baseball protocol, Campbell called Sparky to inform him of Autry's interest. The conversation lasted only about as long as it took Sparky to decide on a pitching change.

Campbell: "The Cowboy asked for permission to talk to you."

Sparky: "About what? Does he wanna put me in a movie?"

Campbell: "He wants to know if you'd consider managing the Angels."

Sparky: "I'm sleepin', Jim. Go to bed."

Campbell: "What do you want me to tell him?"

Sparky: "I promised you when I came here I wouldn't leave till you sent me packin' back to Thousand Oaks."

Campbell: "Thanks, Sparky. That's all I wanted to hear."

Sparky: "Just don't tell me how much he offered to pay me. I don't wanna feel bad over the lousy check you give me."

The two friends laughed. Sparky went back to sleep, and Campbell probably lit up a victory cigar.

It would have been easy for Sparky to accept a job where he could live at home and drive to work when he wasn't on the road. But he had grown to love Detroit. He felt comfortable living in the middle of a blue-collar community. And the charity he had created for under-privileged kids was only one year old.

Even more important was the promise he had made to Campbell 10 years prior. He had even shaken Campbell's hand.

For a pair of old-fashioned baseball buddies, that was enough.

Sparky taught me so much about loyalty, more with his actions than with the words he spoke. They obviously helped me to make the most significant professional decision of my life.

I know that made Sparky feel proud.

40

The Stories Live

Even before I arrived in Thousand Oaks, I wondered how that third day in October would end.

It had to be spontaneous. Nothing rehearsed. Something natural. Something both of us would have chosen on any day between 32 years ago and that very moment of good-bye.

Now the stories had been told. And even though we had shared them so many times before, we both had that feeling of hearing them for the first time.

That's the heart of a good baseball story. That's the soul of a story made by best friends. Some of those memories were made decades before. Yet every time we told those stories there was something new to learn about baseball, about life, and, most important, about friends.

Some stories would be told again to other friends looking to learn about Sparky Anderson as a baseball manager and George Anderson as a man.

For the first time in 32 years, though, any more telling of those stories would be left only to me.

It was good we spent those three days in October alone in the kitchen. Like so many tiny pieces to an intricate jigsaw puzzle, those memories we recounted helped to paint the portrait of a priceless friendship: a friendship born of—though not bound by—the innocently simple game of baseball.

From our memories to our tongues to the words we chose to express our feelings those recollections took form, shape, and color right before our eyes. We enjoyed a kaleidoscopic performance of the most precious moments from a friendship unencumbered by any conditions.

I was amazed at the ease with which Sparky snatched such details from so many years ago. He recalled minute details about people, places, and events we had experienced. I felt a sense of urgency that such treasures must not be forgotten.

They offered so many lessons. So much kindness. So much love. So much direction. I'm certain he was making sure that I would always treat them with care. Perhaps there would be others looking for a little of those stories' magic to rub off on them.

More than a certifiable master at managing a baseball game, Sparky was an inspirational teacher—not just of the game, but of life's unwritten rules. He knew them. He lived them. And he taught them more by example than by words.

I couldn't help wondering if he was ensuring that I would do the same.

Shortly after the evening network news, Sparky crawled into the hospital bed that had recently become part of the family room. Carol rented it so that he would not have to maneuver his way up and down the staircase so many times day and night.

My flight out of Los Angeles to Detroit was scheduled to leave at 6:30 a.m. the next day. Coach Sliwak volunteered to drive me to the airport at 4:15. I was planning to return to Thousand Oaks in about two weeks.

Obviously fate makes plans of its own.

I didn't want to wake Sparky in the middle of the night. So on that tender evening, I quietly approached his bed. I said a prayer to God as I gently clasped his right hand with both of mine. Then I bent to brush his white hair back and kiss him on the forehead.

"Thank you, George, for everything," I whispered in his ear. "I'll love you for the rest of my life."

He stared at me silently and squeezed my hand as tears filled our eyes.

When I reached my room I knelt to pray. Before I finished, tears trickled down my cheeks.

A reel of random images streaked through my mind at lightning speed. Strolling the aisles of the supermarket. Watching my best friend humbly marvel at the hug of a child. Hearing the victorious tone of his voice after finding another golf ball.

The baseball memories would have to wait. These seemingly mundane moments were far too precious and impossible to ignore.

Three days in October. Now they were gone too.

Although I couldn't wrestle myself to sleep that night, I stayed awake on the plane all the way to Detroit. For the entire five-hour trip I silently stared straight ahead. If I had any thoughts, I simply don't remember.

All I recall telling myself was that I would be back to see my friend in two weeks.

I didn't get that chance.

NINE DAYS LATER

★

41

"He's Gone"

During my next week at home, I spoke to Carol a handful of times for a brief update on Sparky's condition. On the morning of the ninth day and only three days before my scheduled return to Thousand Oaks, I got the call.

"He's gone."

The voice on the other end of the phone was solemn and typically stable. I didn't have to ask who was calling and certainly not what those chilling words meant.

Carol was an immovable rock throughout the inevitable ordeal. Strong. Loyal. Patient. Wise. Protective. Full of love and unwavering commitment.

The call came at 11 a.m. eastern time. It had been about an hour since Sparky had passed away. She had called to summon her three children and notify the fire department before calling me.

Ironically, only 10 minutes before her call, I had purchased an on-line airline ticket to Los Angeles for the upcoming Sunday. I canceled it later. For the moment, my hands were full.

Only two days before, Carol and I had unknowingly rehearsed the procedure that we needed to follow now.

A couple of days after my departure from Los Angeles, Sparky was admitted to Los Robles Hospital. On Tuesday, Carol was notified that he would be released to hospice care at home. Throughout Tuesday afternoon and evening, I called a significant number of Anderson family friends and a select number of Sparky's former players and coaches to alert them to what they would see in the media on Wednesday.

Some cried. Some were speechless. All were numbed by the news about their seemingly invincible friend.

I arranged to use the CATCH office on Wednesday to notify media outlets around the country about Sparky's condition. Executive director Jim Hughes, his assistant Lynn Hubenschmidt, and I were either on the phone or handling interviews throughout the day and up to midnight.

"Remember to be professional," Carol reminded me. "Keep your control. Look straight ahead, the way he would have done it."

I promised. The tears would have to wait.

Sparky was under hospice care for only one day. That's the way he would have wanted it. I could just hear him saying: "Let's just get on with the action."

On Thursday afternoon and into the night, I was back at the CATCH office, following the same routine we had carried out the day before.

Before addressing the media, I called my son, Dan Jr., and my daughter, Andrea. Since the time they were in grade school, Sparky had played an instrumental role in their lives. I called Kathy, whom Sparky and Carol had so fondly befriended and who had remained faithfully steady throughout this final struggle.

I shared with them the same message Carol had shared with me: Be professional. Look straight ahead. That's the way Sparky would want it.

On my drive downtown I thought about all the times Sparky and I had talked about death. Over the last couple of years, the subject had been raised quite often, as many of his friends and former baseball colleagues had died.

Again we would turn to good old-fashioned irreverent baseball humor. When driving past a cemetery, Sparky looked the other way and joked: "See ya soon, Charlie. Keep my spot warm."

I would glare at him and tease by asking: "Who would want you anyway? God's still making His mind up and even the devil wants no part of you."

I offered to keep my Sunday airline reservation, but Carol insisted there was nothing anyone could do now.

On Saturday I decided to remove myself from any means of communication by getting lost in the middle of 113,000 people. The University of Michigan football team was hosting Big Ten rival Illinois at Ann Arbor. I decided to attend the game alone.

I left early from home so as to visit with Jon Falk, the longtime Michigan equipment manager, who had known Sparky for many years. I answered all his questions and assured him that Sparky had always regarded him as a friend.

Following our discussion, I walked slowly across the field toward the elevator to the press box perched high atop the renovated stadium large enough to seat an entire city of people.

Despite the overwhelming mass of humanity, I felt so very much alone. Exactly what I wanted.

Upon reaching the lobby housing a bank of elevators, I encountered several media colleagues whom I had known for years. Each expressed sorrow over the loss of Sparky. I patiently answered all questions and assured each how much respect Sparky had felt for him.

After I took one step toward the elevator, one of the older volunteer attendants stopped me to say he had seen a lot of me on television over the last two days.

"For all the wrong reasons, sir," I courteously answered. "For all the wrong reasons."

"He was a good man," the attendant offered. "He did so much for the people. Nobody else in sports did as much for people as Sparky did."

I thanked him—and stopped short of boarding the elevator. Instead, I suddenly turned and quickly walked out the door that led to the street. I walked briskly to my car for my hour-and-a-half drive home. In this particular situation, I decided, it was easier to get lost in front of the TV in my living room than somewhere in the middle of 113,000 people.

I don't remember many details, but after three overtimes, Michigan rallied to a 67–65 victory. ESPN had enough highlights to fill a whole week of programming.

My first impulse after the game was to call Sparky. For years, that's what he and I did at least a half dozen times on each football Saturday.

Suddenly I remembered. There would be no more calls. The games didn't matter. Nothing much did.

Baseball would go on. Sparky always reminded people that the passing of Babe Ruth in 1948 proved that. So would CATCH. So would Carol and the kids. And so would I.

That's what he would have wanted. That's what he taught me.

But he didn't know how hard that would be.

42

A Promise Kept

A few years ago during one of our rounds at the kitchen table, out of nowhere came one of Sparky's classic declarations.

"I don't want no damn funeral when I go," he stated firmly. "I don't want no kind of fuss."

The year had been emotionally tough on him. He had lost his childhood friend and baseball confidant Billy Consolo. He had also lost some other close baseball colleagues and a couple from his immediate circle of friends at home.

"If someone tries to throw me a memorial, I'll sneak back and lock all the doors so tight nobody can get in," he said. "That's the way I want it and that's the way it's gonna be."

Unsure how to respond, I again relied on the irreverent baseball humor that only a pair of inseparable friends truly appreciate.

"What makes you think anyone would show up at a memorial for you anyway?" I asked.

Carol smiled, and we quickly bounced back to an even more serious matter—newspaper coupons for the day's best bargains at Albertsons supermarket.

Again in March 2010, Sparky mysteriously raised the issue of a funeral. And this time there was no joking.

"No funeral . . . no memorial . . . no nothin'," he pronounced with conviction.

Sparky died almost 40 years to the day after having made that promise to himself. The resolution resulted from an unexpected encounter at baseball's winter convention in December 1970. It happened at the private meeting of all the major-league managers.

Sparky was a 36-year-old rookie manager when he guided the fabled Cincinnati Reds to the National League pennant that year. The Big Red Machine crushed everything fool enough to get in its way.

The room was packed and filled with cigar smoke when he arrived at his first private managerial meeting. The clinking of beer bottles could be heard all the way down the hall. After banging heads against each other all summer long, this was a time for complete off-the-record camaraderie. Each manager was free to relax and tell tall tales about the past season, confident that none of those stories would leave the room.

In a corner at the back of the room Sparky spotted the celebrated 59-year-old Los Angeles Dodgers manager Walter Alston sitting quietly by himself. The stately-looking Alston was already regarded as one of baseball's all-time greats. He was well on his way toward enshrinement in the Hall of Fame. He signaled Sparky to join him so that the two could speak privately.

In his first managerial season Sparky's Reds had posted an impressive 13-5 record against Alston's Dodgers. Still the rookie in the room, Sparky was well aware of Alston's stature and felt proud to be summoned to a private discussion with a man he so admired.

"You see all those guys carrying on?" the quiet veteran asked. "Some of 'em just like to hear themselves talk. That's okay. Let 'em talk. It's all part of the show.

"There's one thing, though, I'd like for you to remember. Never forget who you are and where you came from. Don't ever give yourself the opportunity to change. If you can do that, you'll leave the game with no regrets. If you can leave this game the same person you were when you came in, you'll walk with the giants."

Sparky never forgot those words. I remember the first time he told them to me. He was proud that Alston had taken the time to share them with him. Right to the end, he kept those words close to his heart. He would have made Alston proud.

Sparky enjoyed all the good times that baseball brought to him. He was grateful for the good living it provided for him and his family. And though, at times, it became cumbersome, he appreciated the fame that he was careful never to abuse. He also recognized his impact on baseball history.

At the core, however, he felt proud of the person he always considered himself to be—a blue-collar worker who happened to wear a baseball uniform to work. No better. No worse. He made his mother and father proud. He made his wife and children happy that the person they loved never changed from the person he had always been.

So in the end, he brought it all back to the beginning. He didn't want his passing to become a spectacle for his family. As he joked so many times, he was "gonna leave the dance the way I came in."

After all the awards and honors . . . after all the accolades . . . and after all the fame and glory naturally attached to his Hall of Fame career, Sparky kept his promise to leave the same way he had entered. More than for himself, he wanted that for Carol, for sons Lee and Albert, for daughter Shirlee, and for all of his grandchildren.

"They don't need no fuss and all that commotion," he said.

Surprising as his choice was to most people, the arrangements that he chose perfectly reflected the person Sparky perceived himself to be.

Of course, there was a public outpouring of grief, loss, love, and salutation after Sparky's passing. No one magnificently molds the impressive baseball numbers he did without becoming a national sports celebrity.

Stories of his passing filled the nation's sports pages from coast to coast. Television and radio sports shows ran specials on his career and life. Billboards saluting his life popped up like spring tulips along the freeways of Detroit. Throughout the 2011 season, players on the Tigers and Reds wore Sparky patches on their uniform sleeves. Before the first pitch of the home opener, the Tigers raised a flag bearing Sparky's name that flew above Comerica Park for the entire season. The Reds held a moment of silence on their home Opening Day.

Finally, 15 years after his departure, the Tigers rightfully retired the number 11 uniform Sparky had worn so proudly during his 17 years as the Detroit manager. On June 26, Sparky's name and number joined other Tigers Hall of Famers as a permanent part of the outfield's brick wall. The Reds had already retired the number 10 he had worn during his nine-year Cincinnati career during the 2005 season.

If he had been around, he would have appreciated the hoopla. Then he would have scrunched that beautifully creased face and said something like: "What's all the fuss about? I was only doin' somethin' I loved."

It was the way he did it, though, that made him so beloved.

Even after death, Sparky still shared a valuable lesson. Pride in what you've accomplished is a good thing. Humility in its acceptance is demanded.

TWO WEEKS LATER

★

43

★

Special Tributes

About two weeks after Sparky died, I received an e-mail from Gerry Swanson, the Lutheran pastor who was one of the regular daily walkers with Sparky. Sparky kept them in a special part of his heart, as they did with him.

Having known Sparky as a neighbor and friend before discovering his celebrated background provided them with a fresh perspective on his character.

And they loved him!

I was fortunate to have been welcomed into their circle after they came to feel the special friendship shared between Sparky and me.

Gerry's e-mail was brief and tenderly potent, as might be expected from a pastor who served as counselor to a countless number of parishioners. It read:

Dan:

Many memories from a collage of two men walking to the rhythm of a long friendship. Jan and I always looked forward to your visits. George's spirits would begin to arise as the date of your arrival approached.

With you attached at his hip we could sense the depth and the energy of all that you shared together in what has to have been a storied life. I was always one to try and imagine what it must have been like and so enjoyed the stories that came during the periods of time when you were here. We also treasured the talks we had with you about books and life in general. We were grateful for the gracious way you and George would welcome any and all into the group. May you share in the same peace that George now shares with The Lord.

Gerry

While flattered by Gerry's tender sincerity, the message befitted Sparky more than me. Sparky was never impressed by anyone's station in life. His lone measure of evaluation was how any person treated those around him. His treatment of others remained unchanged regardless of the audience of the moment.

I'm not a keeper of letters or any form of memorabilia that seems to be so important today. I will, however, keep this e-mail from Gerry as a symbol of how those seemingly meaningless times are now invaluable treasures.

A similar tribute was given before a public panel discussion about Sparky in which I was asked to participate. The event was staged in a high school auditorium in Grosse Pointe, an upscale suburb of Detroit. All proceeds were designated to be given to amateur baseball and CATCH.

Joining me on the panel were former Tigers first baseman Dave Bergman and former Tigers pitcher Dan Petry. Both players were integral parts of the 1984 World Championship team. Also on the panel was Father Don Worthy, a Catholic priest and longtime friend of Sparky.

I was hesitant, at first, to accept the invitation. I was still sorting out the pieces to how much life had changed. Then I remembered a lesson Sparky had taught me about not getting buried in the past and dealing with the present.

Or as Sparky more elegantly stated: "There ain't no future livin' in the past."

Standing in the hallway before entering the auditorium, Father

Worthy asked to speak to me privately. I immediately wondered if I had done something wrong. Twelve years of Catholic education don't disappear regardless of one's age.

"I just want to thank you, Dan, for how much you meant to our friend," he said. "I don't think even you know how much you meant to him. He relied on you for everything. You never let him down. It's gratifying to witness such trust shared by two men for so many years. It's so rare now. I know God noticed."

I was speechless, of course, and finally managed to spit out a "Thank you."

"It wasn't a job, Father," I said. "It was an honor. He did so much for so many. Somebody had to watch over him once in a while. All the credit belongs to him."

Like most people, the audience was interested in the secret to Sparky's managerial success.

Petry, the number two starter behind ace Jack Morris in the pitching rotation, posted an 18-8 record and 3.24 ERA in the 1984 championship season. Quiet by nature and a dedicated Tiger for life, Petry drew the loudest laugh of the evening when he addressed his relationship with Sparky. "I was terrified by the man," he said. "He was always a gentleman and conducted himself professionally all the time. But he was Sparky Anderson. When he came to the Tigers I think all the players were in awe."

Often overlooked by some in the media and some of the fans, that feeling of awe referred to by Petry was one of Sparky's most powerful managerial weapons.

There was an aura about Sparky. It couldn't be seen. It couldn't be touched. But it was all around him. He managed as much by charisma as he did by the book.

"I never really talked to him that much," Petry added. "His door was always open, but I just figured if I did my job that was all he wanted me to do."

Bergman was an incredibly gifted defensive first baseman. He was also a clutch pinch hitter and a valuable reserve who wound up playing in 120 games in 1984.

"The thing about Sparky that so many players appreciated was that he got everyone involved with the games," Bergman said. "When you showed up at the park, you better have been ready to play. Even if you weren't a starter there was a good chance you'd get into the game at some point.

"He made all the players want to play for him. Every one of us could see how much he personally was putting into the game. None of us wanted to let him down."

As many questions as there were about baseball, there were about the character of Sparky.

"He taught everyone the importance of being a professional," Bergman said. "On the field and away from the park Sparky expected each player to act as a man.

"He made it clear. It was his way or the highway. Simple as it sounds, that's how it was. He would not tolerate nonconformity. Those that didn't conform were gone before they knew it. And that made the rest of the boys pay a little closer attention."

Father Don talked about Sparky's incurable pursuit to help needy children.

"If a child was wanting, all he had to do was to ask Sparky," he said. "He was so generous with his time when it came to kids. He asked nothing in return. I believe he thought this was what God wanted him to do."

Before the evening ended, I was asked if there would be another Sparky.

"That one's up to God," I answered. "But I can guarantee you we won't see him."

Characters like Sparky come around only once in a lifetime. That's why he left us so many memories to savor and share. That's why his lessons will continue to live.

44

★

"I'm Sparky Anderson"

I usually waited until early evening before calling Sparky on Thanksgiving Day. Up until the last couple of years, he had Thanksgiving breakfast with a collection of high school buddies, then played in the annual "Turkey Bowl" touch football game at a Los Angeles playground.

This year was so different. There was a hole in Thanksgiving dinner that never will be filled. I called Carol for a brief conversation that found us both still trying to put all the pieces together. Later that evening, I spent time recalling the events of the year.

The only two trips Sparky made that year were to Detroit to host his annual charity golf tournament, and to Cooperstown, New York, for the annual induction ceremonies at baseball's Hall of Fame.

My first 2010 trip to Thousand Oaks came in early March. Carol and I tried to dissuade him from participating in both events for at least one year, or maybe to alternate between the two each year. But these two events had become the centerpiece of his summers. His presence at both made them much more meaningful to the fans who supported them.

Sparky refused to skip either one. "Please don't take this from me," he pleaded.

He knew what was happening to him. He knew this would be his last opportunity to touch the two things that, besides his family, were the most important in his life. His commitment would not be compromised.

The golf tournament raised about $175,000 for CATCH. Sparky never missed an induction weekend after he was welcomed into the Hall of Fame in 2000.

For Sparky, each event defined all he had accomplished in life.

Getting into my car after his cross-country flight from Los Angeles, Sparky exhaled a lung full of air that made his entire body shrink as he slumped into his seat.

It was early Saturday evening in mid-July. The flight had stolen all of Sparky's strength and he needed something cold to sip before the 45-minute drive to my home across town.

Sparky rarely drank any alcoholic beverage, but he said he'd like to have a couple of sips of the coldest beer in Detroit. Just outside of the airport, we stopped at a bar that neither of us had even known existed.

Two men sitting at the bar were busy bouncing between arguments on sports and politics. From baseball to Obama. Football to the Middle East.

A pair of waitresses were busy preparing for another Saturday night. The bartender had just switched on the television to a New York Yankees game that was close to ending. Except for Sparky and me, everyone in the room was African American.

As Sparky and I walked to a table, the two customers flashed bewildered expressions on their faces. It looked as if each was asking the other if he had seen the same person he thought he had just walk by. After traveling the country for more than three decades with Sparky, I was well familiar with that disbelieving look of recognition.

"I only look like the guy you think I am," Sparky said quickly before either of them could get anything out of their mouths.

For once I thought Sparky would defer to the fatigue that was swallowing all his strength. I should have known better. As one of the men approached our table for closer inspection, Sparky ended the suspense.

"Hi," he said. "I'm Sparky Anderson."

The stranger didn't have the chance to say a word. He merely stared and extended his arm to shake Sparky's hand. In spite of total exhaustion and his battle with an insidious foe, Sparky obliged. He always had to oblige.

Suddenly the solitude of the subdued establishment disappeared just as I had witnessed so many times before.

"Sparky Anderson sittin' right here with us in this ol' place," one of the men marveled. "Do y'all believe this? This man here is a member of the Hall of Fame. Greatest manager the Dee-troit Tigers ever had. Why don't you come back and manage our team again, Sparky? We need you. Can I shake your hand, Mr. Anderson? I gotta tell everybody my raggedy old hand shook the hand of a legend."

Sparky smiled and began to sign autographs on a stack of napkins for uncles, nephews, neighbors, and friends of each person. Group and individual photos were taken with a camera that had been hidden under the bar. The men peppered Sparky with baseball questions about old-time great players that they believed had far more talent than most of the contemporary stars. Sparky gave them the answers he knew they wanted to hear.

Sparky took exactly two sips from his cold bottle of beer. That was all he needed.

He felt good about the memories he had just made for a handful of working-class people in what he believed to be the toughest blue-collar city in the country. They were memories the group would share with family and friends, grandparents and grandchildren.

Sparky was struggling. But that spontaneous visit with strangers alone made him feel satisfied he had endured the long trip.

No trip was easy on Sparky anymore. This one promised to be painfully tough. Though only the family and I knew, Sparky was suffering from dementia, which was now causing various physical problems.

We tried to make his exhausting trip as pleasant as possible. A wheelchair was waiting at the ticket counter in Los Angeles to take him to the gate. Through a friend at the Detroit Metropolitan Airport

Police Department, I arranged for a police escort to allow me to wait at the gate for the flight's arrival. We also had another wheelchair waiting, and my car was parked in a police zone right in front of the terminal.

We shared a quiet dinner that evening at Sparky's favorite Italian restaurant before the real schedule started the next day. A signing appearance the next afternoon was followed by a large pre–golf tournament party in the evening.

As he did each year, Sparky arrived early at the party. He smiled, joked, and shook hands with all the people who approached him. He chose not to address the crowd from the stage. Rather, he merely stood and waved at the standing ovation given to him by the charity's loyal supporters when formally introduced.

"You always make sure things go right with CATCH," he told me that evening after arriving at my house. "Those kids deserve everything we can give 'em."

For the tournament the next day, we left at the usual time in order to greet the participants finishing the early-morning round and have lunch with the players preparing for the afternoon round.

Shortly after all the golfers had teed off, we left for the day. It was the first time we didn't stay for the evening awards dinner.

Following three days of rest at my house that included only brief walks through the neighborhood, Sparky, my son Dan Jr., and I drove to Cooperstown. Our nine-hour drive had become an annual affair beginning with Sparky's induction 10 years prior.

We alternated routes between one running through Canada to the New York State Thruway and another, completely stateside, that went through Ohio and Pennsylvania and finally onto the Thruway. Regardless of our choice, Sparky was always approached for autographs during rest stops or sandwich breaks along the way. Even the Canadian guards at both ends of the international bridges always smiled at the sight of Sparky.

The drive had become a relaxing ritual for us. We resolved a whole lot of world problems during those nine-hour trips.

Once in Cooperstown, Sparky rallied to greet all of his Hall of

Fame brothers, along with various old baseball friends from his long career in the game.

As usual on Induction Day when all returning members were introduced from the stage, Sparky received one of the most robust ovations from the fans. In spite of having managed in only two major-league cities, Sparky's popularity had spread throughout both leagues.

Sparky took great pride in being accessible to the fans. He loved to talk and listen to them. He loved to touch and be touched by them. No one can be considered a true legend without the ability to be touched, he believed.

Soon after waving to the crowd when introduced on the platform where all the Hall of Famers were gathered, Sparky came backstage, where I was waiting. He simply decided it was time for him to go. Instead of waiting to make the drive home the next morning, he wanted to leave immediately, so we drove through the night.

I was still torn over Sparky's decision to have made the trip. But I was filled with pride about the commitment we knew he would never break.

No one knows for sure if Sparky felt that would be his last trip. For certain, though, I knew he would finish by doing the right thing.

Less than three months later, I made another trip to Thousand Oaks. I had been advised by Carol of Sparky's worsening condition, but refused to even consider that this would be my last visit.

He had one last gift to give me—those three days in October that time can never steal.

45

★

For the Kids

Sparky created a lifetime's worth of memories for a couple of generations in Cincinnati and Detroit, and for baseball fans everywhere.

But for countless underprivileged children in Detroit, he performed a miracle with the creation of CATCH. In fact, the story of his self-made charity captures the essence of Sparky as much as all the records he set during his fabulous baseball career.

CATCH is an acronym for Caring Athletes Team for Children's and Henry Ford Hospitals. In Detroit it's simply called "Sparky's charity." It's the one Sparky created in the middle of a division championship run in 1987. And it's one of the most efficiently run, dollar-worthy charities in the state for one simple reason—it works.

No figure in the tradition-rich history of Detroit sports ever left a legacy as meaningful to the city as did Sparky. Even Sparky was amazed at how his middle-of-the-night "vision" zipped light-years ahead of his wildest dreams.

Sparky was a softie when it came to anything to do with kids.

He could talk tough to his players. He often created new ways to implement some of those spicy clubhouse adjectives that have been part of the normal baseball lexicon since Abner Doubleday came up with the game.

Beneath the tough talk, however, he was a softie.

He cried, for instance, every time he told one particular story about CATCH. It's a story that captures the essence of Sparky's dream.

A seven-year-old boy from Michigan's Upper Peninsula was being treated for cancer at Children's Hospital and the prognosis was not good. As best as a seven-year-old can be made to understand, the boy was aware he was seriously sick. Treatment had stripped the savings of the boy's family, who, of course, did everything they could to restore the boy's health while helping him to maintain a normal life style.

The boy was brave, with an engaging personality. He wanted only a puppy for when he was able to go home. Touched by the determination of the boy, the attending nurses discussed the matter with the boy's family and social workers.

Upon his discharge from the hospital, when the parents brought the boy to the car, a puppy was waiting in the rear seat with a sign hung around his neck: "From the people at CATCH."

No cure. No promises. Just a modest gesture toward making life a little better. Quality of life is what CATCH is all about.

As much as Sparky spoke in superlatives, he was a realist when it came to kids and their well-being. He understood he was in no position to create a foundation large enough to fund meaningful research of cancer, diabetes, or any other life-threatening disease. He certainly wasn't interested in building another hospital wing. Mortar and bricks were for donors looking to attach a name to a building.

Sparky's dream was far simpler. He believed that the ailing underprivileged kids of Detroit deserved help enhancing their quality of life. Maybe that help would not come in major ways, but taking a few small steps toward making their everyday lives just a little bit brighter would be worthwhile.

For years Sparky had been a regular visitor at children's hospitals in both Cincinnati and Detroit. His visits were unannounced and sometimes spontaneous. He made certain they occurred with no chance of any media presence. He wanted the opportunity to talk to the kids alone. He wanted those with no chance to see a big-league game to at least have the opportunity of seeing a big-league manager.

His vision for the creation of CATCH came after an early-morning hospital visit in April 1987. The team flew to Seattle later that day. During a troubled sleep resulting from that hospital visit he did, indeed, experience a vision that continues to serve the needy children today.

"I don't remember exactly what happened in my dream, but somehow I knew I had to do something to help some of the kids who can't help themselves," he explained to me. "I wasn't sure how it would happen, but I promised myself we were gonna get something done."

He started that morning by frantically scribbling a tablet full of notes about the uniforms and equipment he wanted to collect from players in all of the professional sports. He wanted them for auction items to raise money for his yet nebulous dream.

Upon returning to Detroit, Sparky and I met with team physician Dr. Clarence Livingood to discuss the possibility of making Sparky's vision come to life.

After several meetings with representatives from Children's and Henry Ford Hospitals, and through the generous help of numerous volunteers, an auction date of August 29, 1987, was established.

Sparky became consumed by the project. He was on a mission. He had me writing letters to every professional team requesting a signed item from the top couple of players on each team. He didn't want just pictures or balls. He sought bigger-ticket items such as bats, gloves, shoes, and jerseys.

While we were busy collecting auction items, the Tigers, after a sluggish first half of the season, got busy on the field. Through sheer determination, somehow they scrapped their way back into the pennant race and eventually captured the East Division crown. Correspondingly, activities at the park were becoming frantic as we began preparations for postseason play.

One afternoon before a home night game, Sparky came charging into my office as if being chased by the devil. He was going to make me "an offer I couldn't refuse."

"Ya gotta get hold of the Chicago Bulls," he said excitedly. "You gotta get us a pair of signed Michael Jordan shoes."

At the time, Jordan was bigger than Chicago's Sears Tower. It would have been easier getting an item signed by the president of the United States than shoes from arguably the nation's finest athlete. I put down the pen I was holding and told myself to maintain a determined look on my face.

"Do you happen to realize that we're in a legitimate pennant race?" I asked while fighting back a smile.

"It's for the kids," he said with his own sheepish smile.

And then we both laughed.

Not only did we get a signed pair of Jordan sneakers; we also got a jersey signed by President Ronald Reagan with a number 7 on the back representing his seventh year in office.

For the auction we had racks of jerseys and jackets. We had rows of bats, baseballs, and basketballs. We had tables full of miscellaneous celebrity items. All were signed, and all would appeal to even the lukewarm collector.

For the one-day inaugural event, CATCH realized a total of $175,000, and each penny went to the kids.

For Sparky, that was just a start.

We again met with Dr. Livingood, who was awed by Sparky's charisma. He called Sparky the Pied Piper. He was the one guy in town who could easily persuade a stable of willing, concerned community leaders to follow his lead in improving the quality of life of the underprivileged kids who needed it most.

How could anyone refuse the charm and commitment of Sparky? Especially when everything was going to the kids.

Sparky assembled a collection of local captains of industry, media celebrities, athletes, and renowned medical leaders to join together in a permanent organization dedicated to giving a little something back to the community for the good fortune they were so blessed to enjoy.

Through the generously donated time of a handful of legal, business, medical, and social-services experts, a set of bylaws was written and a board of trustees was established.

In a few short years, Sparky's modest vision—to lend a helping hand to needy kids—blossomed into a self-perpetuating permanent charity like few others.

Primarily driven by revenues derived from the annual summer celebrity golf tournament and the annual autumn Night of Champions Dinner, which recognizes committed community leaders from all fields, CATCH now holds an endowment of more than $5 million. In accordance with the bylaws, CATCH annually donates $160,000 each to Children's and Henry Ford Hospitals.

Sparky did more than generously pledge money every year; He also devoted his time to the charity and the kids. Until his retirement and his move back to Thousand Oaks, he attended almost every board meeting. His visits to the hospitalized kids were too numerous to count and were always done without fanfare . . . or as quietly as Sparky could do anything in Detroit.

"That was the most beautiful part about Sparky," said executive director Jim Hughes. "It takes someone special to give something more valuable than money. He was so generous with the time he spent with kids and his participation in all the events."

Hughes has honorably served in his position since 1990. His assistant, Lynn Hubenschmidt, has done the same since 1999. They are the only paid professionals employed by the charity.

And as Sparky was so fond of saying: "All they do is get the job done."

CATCH remains loyal to the spirit of Sparky, who demanded that all funds be used for quality-of-life items. These are the little things that mean so much but often slip through the cracks of medical protocol.

"We don't want no red tape!" Sparky insisted from the beginning. And no red tape has ever been allowed.

Here are examples of the help CATCH funds have provided:

- A teenage boy with multiple disabilities including cerebral palsy, an uncontrollable seizure disorder, and impaired lower extremities benefited from a chairlift, which eased his transportation to and from his second-story bedroom. The need for the lift was intensified when the boy's father, who had been carrying him up and down the stairs, was murdered in a random act of violence. CATCH's funding of the lift provided tremendous assistance for his mother, who also cared for her disabled mother, and allowed her to keep her son out of a foster home.

- While a child was suffering through a fatal illness, his father wished to spend as much time as possible with his son. To do so, he was forced to take an unpaid leave of absence from his work. CATCH funds were used to pay for one month's rent during his father's leave. He missed work and some pay, but thanks to CATCH he didn't miss out on the last days of his child's life.

- A boy diagnosed with cancer fell far behind in his schoolwork as a result of his lengthy hospitalizations. The youngster's dream was to graduate on time with the classmates he grew up with. The only way he could catch up and realize that dream was to enroll in a summer school program that he and his family could not afford. CATCH dollars were used to enroll the child. He made up the work and wore a cap and gown while receiving his diploma with his classmates. It meant the world to the child, but more important, it made the last 18 months of his life rewarding.

- CATCH helped a quadriplegic and wheelchair-bound patient with a seizure disorder who was totally dependent on his single mother for all areas of care. The mother also was wheelchair-bound since age 21. CATCH funds were used to build a residential wheelchair lift.

- CATCH dollars were used to replace Christmas toys for a youngster with a brain tumor who was in the hospital when his home was burglarized.

- An eight-year-old girl with paraplegia and numerous other physical disabilities demonstrated great social skills, but was limited in her interaction with peers due to her disabilities. CATCH helped to pay for a bike with a special back support that allowed the child to play and socialize with her friends.

- Taxi fares for patients needing dialysis are often paid from CATCH funds for families who have no money for transportation.

In the months after November 4, 2010, a wave of contributions totaling more than $50,000 was received by CATCH in respect of Sparky's passing. Donations came from former players, colleagues, friends, corporations, and anonymous donors touched by Sparky's life.

A pair of $25 donations, accompanied by handwritten letters, especially capture the spirit engendered by Sparky and CATCH.

The first reads:

Although I have never been to a Tigers game and I really didn't have a clue as to all the good that Sparky Anderson has done in life, with his passing it all comes to light. What a warm, caring person he must have been. Please accept this small donation for CATCH—Sparky Anderson's charity for children, as helping the special and unique needs of sick and needy children seems to me a very worthy cause.

Virginia Rowe

The second reads:

Enclosed find a check for $25.00 for Sparky's charity "CATCH." I wish it could be more but at 91 and wheelchair-bound I'm not doing any prancing.

Muriel Shepard

An anonymous donor sent a $100 bill with the following handwritten note:

Thank you and God bless you Sparky Anderson.

Many years before Sparky's passing, Dr. Livingood often predicted he would find his rightful place in baseball's Hall of Fame. He also assured Sparky he would be remembered more for what he meant to the underprivileged children of Detroit than for all the honors baseball could bestow upon him.

Often in his later years, Sparky proudly told me, "The doctor was right."

I proudly remain part of the organization as a founding trustee. It's a fancy title for doing nothing much more than to continue to be amazed by all of the loyal support from so many people still generated by Sparky's spirit.

And that will never end.

46

★

Number 11 Forever Sparky's

In a singularly peculiar way, I can't recall a more emotional day at the ballpark than June 26, 2011. That was the day the Detroit Tigers finally retired Sparky's uniform number forever.

Certainly there was unbridled emotion when the Tigers clinched the 1984 World Series in Game 5 against the San Diego Padres in old Tiger Stadium. Although the Tigers won Game 7 at St. Louis in 1968, the emotions on Detroit's celebrating streets that evening were electrifying and contagious.

But the day Sparky's number 11 was hung on the outfield wall evoked a totally different kind of emotion than the one induced by victory on the field.

For every person in the packed ballpark, this emotion came more from the soul than from the heart. This emotion was as much for the essence and character of the man being honored as for his managerial excellence.

That's how much Sparky meant to baseball. That's how much he affected the whole city.

Not only did the ceremony resurrect proud memories of victory for a whole generation; it also generated sincere tears of gratitude for Sparky's making the community a little better place in which to live.

The uniform retirement should have been done several years earlier. All of Sparky's former players felt it was wrong for the Tigers to wait until almost eight months after Sparky's death to retire his number 11 jersey. So did most of the media, who frequently stated their opinions.

And so did countless fans.

The delay, as speculated by many members of the media, was the result of Sparky's choice to live by his principles and not manage replacement players in the spring of 1995.

Former Tigers slugger Kirk Gibson succinctly summed up how many felt: "The man who should have been there [at the number retirement ceremony] couldn't be."

Nonetheless, on June 26, 2011, baseball justice was finally served. In a tearfully moving ceremony witnessed by his three children, a grandson, several of his former players, and a sellout crowd at Comerica Park, Sparky's number 11 became only the seventh number to be retired in the Tigers' 111-year history.

I was honored to speak to the crowd and summed up my remarks as I know Sparky would have wanted.

"I was blessed to have worked with Sparky for 32 years," I said. "That's why I can confidently tell you that number 11 belongs as much to all of you people as it does to him."

Only, he would have said the same thing with a little more color. Something like: "I don't own this honor no more than any of you guys. You all did your part."

Sparky was a baseball traditionalist, a purist in the true sense of the word. Of course, he wanted his uniform retired. But he never muttered a word to help make it happen.

The 16-year wait, in fact, helped to make the lessons he taught all those he touched come full circle.

The Arizona Diamondbacks were in town to play the Tigers that day. The Diamondbacks are led by two of Sparky's prized pupils— manager Kirk Gibson and bench coach Alan Trammell.

The pair are moved by the lessons Sparky taught them every time they put on a uniform.

"It's sorta come full circle," Trammell said. "Everything he taught us about the game, how to conduct ourselves, everything we do . . . it all goes back to Sparky. I know this sounds kinda strange, but I can honestly say I loved the man."

Gibson credits Sparky not only for teaching him the game, but for making him a better person. "Sparky was a giver, not a taker," he said. "He taught us that it's okay to make a mistake . . . but make it giving everything you've got in you."

Gibson said he's proud to preach Sparky's message to his team every day.

"They all know where I'm coming from," Gibson said. "Everything I am in baseball today I owe to Sparky."

Perhaps the most compelling tribute from one of Sparky's players came from relief pitcher Mike Henneman. As a rookie in 1987, Henneman pitched poorly in the last game of a road trip. Still upset when the team arrived at the Detroit airport, he walked straight past his waiting wife.

Sparky's keen eye never missed an incident like that.

The next day, Sparky called his pitcher and invited him to lunch. As a rookie, Henneman didn't know what to expect.

There was no lunch. Instead, Sparky took his young pitcher to Children's Hospital. He told Henneman that what he had gone through the previous evening was not adversity.

"Take a look around you," Sparky told him. "This is the face of adversity."

Henneman treasured the lesson for the rest of his career.

More than 150 numbers have been retired by major-league teams since Lou Gehrig's number 4 was the first to be honored by the New York Yankees in 1940. This total includes players, managers, and coaches. Sparky became only the ninth in history to have his number retired by more than one team.

The others include Hank Aaron (Atlanta Braves and Milwaukee Brewers), Rod Carew (Minnesota Twins and Los Angeles Angels), Rollie Fingers (Oakland Athletics and Milwaukee Brewers), Carlton Fisk (Boston Red Sox and Chicago White Sox), Reggie Jackson (New York Yankees and Oakland Athletics), Greg Maddux (Chicago Cubs and

Atlanta Braves), Frank Robinson (Cincinnnati Reds and Baltimore Orioles), Nolan Ryan (Texas Rangers, Houston Astros, and Los Angeles Angels) and Casey Stengel (New York Yankees and New York Mets).

Had he been at the ceremony, Sparky would have blushed and flashed one of his disbelieving smiles knowing he had joined Casey as the only other manager to have earned such distinction.

Indeed, it was a magically emotional day.

TODAY

★

It was one of those standstill moments that defies any erosion by time.

Free of staged TV lights and flashes from newspaper cameras, only a snapshot by one of the nurses captured the impact of the moment.

While visiting a few of the kids' rooms during one of his unannounced visits to Children's Hospital, Sparky happened to encounter a nurse carrying a tiny girl. The child was probably three years old. Maybe only two.

The nurse's nose and mouth were covered by a mask. She stopped to say hello to Sparky and tell him the young patient's name.

Sparky asked the nature of the precious girl's illness. He was startled to hear she was suffering from AIDS.

Just the name of the horrifying disease was chilling enough for Sparky to fall into one of his rare moments of silence. It was still a time when so much about the disease had yet to be discovered.

All Sparky knew was that something so hideously evil should never touch an innocent child.

Sparky asked the nurse to hand the child to him. He wanted to hold her, if only for a few seconds. The nurse was hesitant and hurriedly tried to explain that it was wiser for him not to make physical contact with the child. That's why the nurse had been wearing a mask.

"Please hand me the child," Sparky insisted.

As the child snuggled into the cradle of his arms, Sparky resumed talking with the hospital personnel who were quickly gathering. By the time Sparky was ready to move to another room, the child was sleeping, and he carefully handed her back to the nurse without disturbing her rest.

Just an innocent, somewhat insignificant moment, easily overlooked by anyone blessed more richly by fate. No words were needed. No witnesses were wanted.

A memory forever. A slice of Sparky's soul.

Even in death, Sparky's spirit survives. His impossible dream of CATCH lives through all those underprivileged kids that were touched during his presence and all of those in the future who may need a helping hand.

Sparky's spirit also survives through the legacies passed to all the players he touched.

Players still feel his presence with each step they take into any ballpark in the country. It was at those parks that he taught them to be professionals. It was at those parks that he shaped them into men.

Sparky's spirit survives in the Hall of Fame. His immortality in baseball's most sacred sanctuary ensures his influence on the game forever.

Sparky's spirit survives at his beloved Sunset Hills Golf Club, where, in his honor, locker number 10 shall be his and forever remain vacant. A few stray balls found on the course are sometimes dropped inside the locker in memory of his passion for hunting lost balls.

Sparky's spirit survives in the stories we tell. The only stories better than the ones he told are those about him.

I can still hear the cackle of Sparky's gravelly voice. I can still feel the gleam that always danced in his eyes. There was always playful mischief hiding just behind his smile.

"Well, Daniel, my boy, how are we gonna shake things up a little today?" I still hear him saying. Usually his question was accompanied by a light slap to the cheek or a punch to the shoulder. Sparky spoke as much with his hands as he did with his tongue.

Though he always looked older than his actual age, Sparky maintained the enthusiasm of a 20-year-old rookie. He had the energy of a teenager. He had the curiosity of a toddler and the street smarts of a gambler.

He was as predictable as a grasshopper bouncing around in a field of weeds. Just when you thought you could scoop him up with your right hand, he was already far off to the left and probably thinking—however a grasshopper thinks—"You weren't even close."

That unpredictability is one of the things that kept Sparky so vibrant. It's also one of the little things I still miss so much.

It's now heading on two years since his passing, which left a hole in my life far bigger than I ever could have imagined. I don't expect it ever to be completely filled.

Of course, I miss some of the more "glamorous" amenities that are automatically attached to being Sparky's best friend: traveling to large and small cities around the country, sharing time with fans and strangers from all walks of life.

But it's the more subtle recollections that make more sense out of life that I miss most.

I miss the walks with him around his neighborhood and those around mine. Some of our most serious decisions were made on those sidewalks and streets.

I miss the banter in the supermarket when Sparky was busy performing for anyone looking for a little lift to his or her day. He could have charged admission for the performance he always gave.

I miss seeing him roam those pesky hillsides searching for lost balls that were more valuable to him than a birdie or even an eagle.

I miss hearing the proud jubilance in his raspy voice when charging down a hill shouting: "I got 12 more, boys . . . it's gonna be a record day."

I miss the half dozen phone calls on Saturdays during the college football season.

I miss him barking "Daniel" to the sound of my voice when I answered each call.

I miss the twinkle in his eye and the warmth of his gaze when visiting kids lying in hospital beds.

I miss, most of all, the assurance of his presence. Whenever either of us needed a lift, the other was always ready.

Memories of all these more mundane moments are irreplaceable treasures. They mean so much more than all the games.

There was no better maker of memories than Sparky. And there was no one more generous in sharing them with all the people he met.

Somewhere within all of those memories he created and the stories he spun are lessons in life far greater than all of the records he set on the field.

Although I rarely visit the ballpark anymore, I still watch parts of some games on TV. When a manager argues with an umpire, I sometimes smile and see Sparky out there pointing his finger and maybe kicking a little dirt. With a pitching change, I sometimes see him reaching silently for the ball.

The games go on as they should. No one person is bigger than the game.

I still call Carol about once a week. I keep her informed about what's happening with CATCH and any activity pertaining to Sparky's name. She remains a comforting link to all good things from the past. She was so integral to the success he enjoyed and so generous with the time she allowed him to spend with me.

A friendship born out of baseball though not bound by the game refuses to end by the loss of one.

The friendship is forever . . . Sparky and me.

"Daniel, my boy." I still hear his voice. "No one will have what we had for so many years."

The lessons he taught and the memories he made belong as much to the fans as they do to me. They are part of the present as much as of the past. For Sparky, the fans were always the essence of the game.

I know Sparky would say, "Thanks."

INDEX